A Garland Series

ROMANTIC CONTEXT: POETRY

Significant Minor Poetry 1789-1830

Printed in photo-facsimile
in 128 volumes

selected and arranged by

Donald H. Reiman

The Carl H. Pforzheimer Library

James Montgomery

The Chimney-Sweeper's Friend

with an introduction
for the Garland edition by
Donald H. Reiman

Garland Publishing, Inc., New York & London

1978

Bibliographical note:

this facsimile has been made from a copy in the Beinecke Library of Yale University (Nvc60.G6.824m)

Library of Congress Cataloging in Publication Data

Montgomery, James, 1771-1854, ed.
The chimney-sweeper's friend.

(Romantic context : Poetry)
Reprint of the 1824 ed. printed for Longman, Hurst, Rees, Orme, Brown, and Green, London.
1. Chimney-sweeps--Great Britain. 2. Child welfare--Great Britain. I. Title. II. Series.
HD6247.C49G75 1978 331.3'81'6485 75-31241
ISBN 0-8240-2190-8

Printed in the United States of America

Introduction

In "A Tale, Too True," the last piece in *Prison Amusements* by "Paul Positive" (1797), young Paul is shown to be enamored of a beautiful girl whose ugly, harsh mother teaches him by beating him. The poem—which at earlier moments reverberates almost in the manner of Blake's "The Mental Traveller"—ends with a flat-footed revelation:

—Behold, in a fable, the Poet's own life;
From whence this lean moral we draw:
The MUSE is PAUL POSITIVE'S twenty-tongued Wife!
MISFORTUNE his Mother-in-Law!

Certainly, by that date, misfortune had seemed to follow James Montgomery and his muse. But by the end of his long life (1771-1854), Montgomery's character, introduced to many by his muse, had made him the best loved and most respected by his fellow poets of all the major or minor writers who flourished during the period.

Montgomery was born on November 4, 1771, at Irvine in Ayrshire, Scotland. His father, John Montgomery, who had begun as a common laborer in County Antrim, Ireland, converted to the faith of the Moravian Church, married a girl of that congregation named Mary, became a minister, and went to Irvine to serve the only Moravian Church then in Scotland. In 1775 John Montgomery and his family returned to Ireland, from which young James was sent to study at a Moravian school at Fulneck near Leeds (1777). In 1783 James's parents went as missionaries to the West Indies. Mary Montgomery died at Tobago in 1790; John died of yellow fever at Barbados in 1791.

At Fulneck, James neglected the curriculum to compose two epic poems, one on Alfred the Great and the other a Miltonic epic called "The World," in which the Archangel Michael takes Satan by surprise and lops off one of his wings. In 1787 Montgomery ran away from the boarding school with only three shillings six pence "and a bundle of verses, which proved more valuable than might have been expected, for a poem, written out fairly and presented to Earl Fitzwilliam, brought him a guinea." (This and most of the biographical details come straight from Richard Garnett's excellent *DNB* account, based in turn primarily on *Memoirs of the Life and Writings of James Montgomery* by John Holland and James Everett [7 vols., London; 1854-1856], *James Montgomery, A Memoir* by J.W. King [1858], and two papers—one a bibliography—by G.W. Tallent-Bateman in *Papers of the Manchester Literary Club* [1889], pp. 385-392, 435-440. See also Samuel Ellis, *The Life, Times and Character of James Montgomery* [1864] and Samuel Carter Hall, *A Book of Memories* . . . [1871].)

After working in a general store at Wath, Yorkshire (with one more literary flight to London), until April 1792, the orphaned young man answered an ad in the *Sheffield Register*, becoming clerk and bookkeeper to that newspaper. From this position, Montgomery became a contributor to the liberal weekly, and when Joseph Gales, the paper's owner/editor, fled to America because he was in danger of arrest before the infamous treason trials of 1794, Montgomery moved into the editorship of the paper with the financial aid of the Rev. Benjamin Naylor. In order to relieve the pressure by government agents, Montgomery changed the paper's name from the *Register* to the *Sheffield Iris*, and in 1795 bought out Naylor, possibly with the aid of Joseph Gales's three sisters, Anne, Elizabeth, and Sarah Gales, with whom Montgomery (who remained a bachelor) maintained his home for the rest of his life.

Though Montgomery had muted the radical tone of the paper, he was imprisoned in 1795 and in 1796 under the stringent libel laws of the day that made criticism of any official or of government policy very risky. While imprisoned,

Montgomery wrote the poems in *Prison Amusements*, as well as the manuscript of a four-volume novel (which he destroyed) and a volume of essays published in 1798 as *The Whisperer* by "Gabriel Silvertongue" (of which he later destroyed all the copies that he could recover).

Having thus been launched into *belles lettres*, his first love, Montgomery persisted. His first long poem, *The Ocean* (1805; of which no copy has been found—see *NCBEL*), was not reviewed and—so far as I can determine—was not influential in any way. But *The Wanderer of Switzerland and Other Poems* (1806) had great success, even by the standards of poetic popularity set by Scott, Byron, and Moore. Three editions of the work had appeared in England and two in America by 1807, the thirteenth British edition appearing in 1841. There were at least eighteen British reviews of the volume, most dated 1806, but some—appearing in annuals that fell behind in their publication schedule—dated 1805, a review in *The Quarterly Review* in 1811, and one in *The Northern Star* in 1817. These figures compare with fourteen reviews of Southey's *Madoc* (1805), fifteen of Scott's *Lay of the Last Minstrel* (1805), thirteen of Moore's *Epistles, Odes, and Other Poems* (1806), and seventeen reviews for all editions of Byron's *English Bards and Scotch Reviewers* (1809)—all volumes by poets who had been widely noticed for earlier works. Garnett finds *The Wanderer* "as a whole very feeble" (*DNB*), but it was not so reckoned at the time. Byron repeatedly expressed his admiration of it, and he and Shelley (particularly in *Laon and Cythna* and "Ode to Liberty") paid it the compliment of close imitation in several striking details. Garnett adds that the volume contains several shorter poems of merit, "especially the really fine and still popular lyric, 'The Grave'" (*DNB*). Besides "The Grave," with its haunting short-line rhythms, the volume includes "The Common Lot," one of two poems that Lamb late in life said he envied their authors, "The Vigil of St. Mark," which exactly parallels the apparent plan of Keats's unfinished "The Eve of St. Mark" (one wonders if a discovery of it may have induced Keats to abandon his own effort), and an "Ode to the Volunteers of Britain," which parallels Wordsworth's many poems of patriotism in defense of the homeland.

And here we approach the central fact of Montgomery's universal appeal: he and his writings reflect—perhaps more than those of any other poet of the period—all the central concerns of the Romantic movement as it grew out of the intellectual and moral fervor generated by the American and French Revolutions. He was, almost literally, all things to all men. A Christian poet who was undogmatic, humane, and liberal; an outsider and protester imprisoned for his attacks on an unjust establishment, yet a patriot springing to the defense of his country (and Switzerland) in the face of French tyranny; a working journalist and provincial of the middle class who neither supplicated the nobility and gentry nor dedicated his poems to them (as Leigh Hunt did), yet who did not call for their overthrow or dwell on the special evils of any class, but saw sin or virtue as the choices of all men equally. Coleridge, Southey, Lamb, Byron, Shelley, Hazlitt, and John Clare all praise his character, as do lesser writers such as Bernard Barton (q.v.) and others whose work he either published in the *Sheffield Iris* or praised judiciously in the monthly *Eclectic Review* (1805 et seq.) for which he, Daniel Parken, and John Foster were the chief early reviewers and for which Montgomery reviewed most of the major and well known minor poets before Josiah Conder (q.v.) purchased the periodical in 1814.

Montgomery, who, in addition to all the elements mentioned heretofore, numbered among his fortes imaginative natural descriptions (as at the opening of *Greenland*) and depth of historical perspective (as in his historical accounts of the Moravian Church in *Greenland* and of the slave trade and slave conditions in *The West Indies*), may be one candidate for the most *representative* (not the *best*) poet of his age. But perhaps an anonymous contemporary observer quoted by

William Howitt may have been nearer to the truth of Montgomery's place by comparing him with William Cowper. "The same benevolence of heart, the same modesty of deportment, the same purity of life, the same attachment to literary pursuits, the same fondness for solitude and retirement from the public haunts of men; and to complete the picture, the same ardent feeling in the cause of religion, and the same disposition to gloom and melancholy" (quoted in W. Clark Russell, *The Book of Authors* [London, n.d. but ca. 1880], p. 388). The same quotation begins, moreover, with a strong statement of the area in which Montgomery was more than merely representative, but truly outstanding: "nature never infused into a human composition a greater portion of kindness and general philanthropy. A heart more sensibly alive to every better, as well as every finer feeling, never beat in a human breast." Thus it is in Montgomery's writings on behalf of great humanitarian causes—the abolition of the slave trade and the amelioration of the condition of black slaves and blackened chimney-climbing boys—that his poetry rises to impassioned excellence. Shelley's *Queen Mab* certainly owes something to the rhetoric and structure of Montgomery's celebration of the abolition of the slave trade, and Montgomery's inclusion in his miscellany of Blake's poem on chimney sweeps from *Songs of Innocence* appropriately intensifies a volume highlighted by his own brilliant poems that open and close it—particularly the second of "The Climbing-Boy's Soliloquies."

In other poems Montgomery shows flashes of excellence, but he too often extends a poem on a good subject or a pointed theme beyond the most effective length. He obviously wrote too hastily amid his journalistic labors, leaving half-effective ideas and partly executed characters for other poets to fill out. *The World Before the Flood* was freely plundered by Byron in *Cain* (who took his character Zillah, among other things, from it) and in *Heaven and Earth* and by Moore in *The Loves of the Angels*. Javan in Milman's *The Fall of Jerusalem* certainly owes much to Montgomery's Javan in *The World Before the Flood.* Southey, a steady correspondent of Montgomery's, puts his finger on one weakness of the longer poems by criticizing Montgomery's choice of the couplet: "of all measures the heroic couplet seems to me the most unsuitable for narration. . . . it continually seduces the writer to commit sins against good sense and good English. He aims at pointing his meaning instead of bringing it distinctly out, gets into all the tricks of antithesis and when he should be thinking and feeling, passes off a sort of way-jolt of words both upon himself and the reader" (Southey to Montgomery, November 29, 1811; *New Southey Letters*, ed. Kenneth Curry [1965], II, 13). Southey goes on, at this early date, to recommend Dante's *terza rima*, as it was later to be used by Byron in "The Prophecy of Dante" and Shelley in "The Triumph of Life." Southey's awareness of the need for new forms to hold the new wine of post-revolutionary literature explains why, with less moral sensitivity and, perhaps, less natural poetic talent than Montgomery, Southey achieved a greater poetic influence on his major contemporaries, and why Montgomery remained a much-beloved man, most of whose inchoate poetic ideas awaited the creative talents of his younger contemporaries.

Montgomery relinquished control of the *Sheffield Iris* in 1825, after which he lived by contributing papers to periodicals and giving and publishing lectures on literature. He died in 1854, an honored relic of the Romantic Age.

Donald H. Reiman

To face the Title.

THE CHIMNEY-SWEEPER'S FRIEND, AND CLIMBING-BOY'S ALBUM.

DEDICATED,

BY THE MOST GRACIOUS PERMISSION, TO

His Majesty.

The child of misery baptized with tears. LANGHORNE.

ARRANGED BY

JAMES MONTGOMERY.

WITH ILLUSTRATIVE DESIGNS BY CRUICKSHANK.

LONDON:

PRINTED FOR

LONGMAN, HURST, REES, ORME, BROWN, AND GREEN,

PATERNOSTER-ROW.

1824.

London:
Printed by A. & R. Spottiswoode,
New-Street-Square.

BY

HIS MAJESTY'S MOST GRACIOUS PERMISSION,

(ON BEHALF OF A SOCIETY IN SHEFFIELD,
FOR BETTERING THE CONDITION OF CHIMNEY-SWEEPERS' APPRENTICES,)

THIS LITTLE VOLUME,

SETTING FORTH THE WRONGS OF MANY THOUSANDS OF UNFORTUNATE CHILDREN,

IS MOST RESPECTFULLY AND GRATEFULLY DEDICATED TO

THE FATHER OF ALL HIS PEOPLE,

KING GEORGE THE FOURTH,

IN HONOUR OF

HIS MAJESTY'S CONDESCENDING AND EXEMPLARY CONCERN

FOR THE EFFECTUAL DELIVERANCE OF

THE MEANEST, THE POOREST, AND WEAKEST OF

BRITISH-BORN SUBJECTS,

FROM UNNATURAL, UNNECESSARY, AND UNJUSTIFIABLE

PERSONAL SLAVERY, AND MORAL DEGRADATION,

BY

HIS MAJESTY'S

MOST DUTIFUL, OBLIGED AND DEVOTED
SERVANT AND SUBJECT,

JAMES MONTGOMERY.

Sheffield, April 24, 1824.

PREFACE.

The annexed letter will explain the origin of the present publication. The person whose name appears on the title-page, was not the projector; but, being urged by a public-spirited friend to join in the plan, he had no heart to refuse. There was, indeed, little prospect of securing the co-operation of such powerful auxiliaries as he was commissioned to solicit; nor, if he had obtained it, of much further effect being produced by their appearance in the field, than to attract more prompt and particular attention to the plain matters of fact, wherein consists the strength of the case. He resolved, however, at any sacrifice of private feeling in asking favours, and any hazard of mortification in being neglected or refused, to make the experiment, rather than incur the responsibility of having foregone one forlorn hope of serving a generation of outcast children, and advancing their cause with the public, even by another failure; for, in a righteous cause, every miscarriage of persevering philanthropy is a step towards final and inevitable success. The scorn with which former proposals to abolish the atrocious practice of training up infants as chimney-climbers have been received and rejected in the senate, will never deter those who are duly convinced of its iniquity, from availing themselves of every occasion to press it upon the understandings and the consciences of their countrymen.

This book will exhibit such testimonies concerning the subject, in all its bearings, as ought to satisfy the most supercilious, obdurate, and prejudiced, that such an employment is inhuman, unnecessary, and altogether unjustifiable. The barbarity of the practice cannot be denied: — nor can it be mitigated, for it is next to impossible to teach a child this trade at all, without the infliction of such cruelties upon his person, as would subject a master in any *other* business to the discipline of Bridewell, were he to exercise the like on *his* apprentice. Nor can any necessity, except that which is the tyrant's plea, be proved in support of it. There are *machines in use*, with which ninety-nine chimneys out of a hundred might be swept; and the danger to the boys in ascending those which machines cannot thoroughly cleanse, — namely, angular, tortuous, dilapidated, and *ignited* flues, — is so imminent, that when death ensues, (which, in these cases, is not unfrequent,) the master, who puts a child to such a task, should be punished for *feloniously slaying* at least; and in few instances would it be too severe to implicate those who suffer such outrages to be committed in their dwellings, as *accessaries* before the fact.

The remedy for this evil is simple, obvious, and certain; — let the legislature prohibit the masters from taking any more children as climbers, and, before the present race have outgrown their detestable occupation, there will be improved machines to sweep any chimney, or not a chimney in use, which cannot be swept by the present machines.

This volume is divided into two parts; the first, comprising miscellaneous tracts and documents, (principally republications,) presents the uncoloured and unexaggerated realities of the case in the various forms of argument, authentic narrative, and parliamentary evidence. By these alone would the chimney-sweepers' friends be content to have the issue of the question determined. The second portion of the work, intituled "*The Climbing-Boy's Album*," (with two brief exceptions,) consists of pieces in prose and verse, written expressly for this occasion, in compliance with the suggestion of the friend already mentioned. To enrich this department, copies of the circular letter below were addressed to upwards of twenty of the favourite poets of the day. From most of these, very gratifying answers were received, but eight only contained contributions, which will be found either under the names, or assumed signatures of the respective authors. The rest of the miscellanies under this head have been furnished by friends of the editor resident in this neighbourhood. Of the merits of any of the original articles now submitted to the public, it becomes not him to say more than, that he himself is sincerely thankful for every free-will offering which has been received, either from the illustrious or the obscure. Among the former, who have not directly acceded to his request, he acknowledges with especial gratitude the kind communications of Sir WALTER SCOTT, Mrs. JOANNA BAILLIE, Mr. WORDSWORTH, Mr. SAMUEL ROGERS, Mr. THOMAS MOORE, Mr. WM. SMYTHE, *Professor of History at Cambridge*, Mr. JOHN WILSON, *Professor of Moral Philosophy at Edinburgh*, the Rev. GEORGE CROLY, and Mr. CHARLES LAMB.

All these distinguished characters declared themselves as friendly to the emancipation of the poor Climbing-Boys as their correspondent himself could be; but several doubted whether poetry would interest the public so far in their sufferings as to procure earlier redress by such appeals as were desired. That question need not be discussed here. The origin of the volume has been already stated, and the Editor regards himself as no further answerable for success than to endeavour to deserve it, by making the attempt on the plan prescribed to him, at any peril of present mishap. In consequence of this publication, feeble as it may be, the subject itself *will* be brought before the eye, and, it is hoped, struck home to the hearts of our countrymen, a thousandfold beyond the limited circulation of this petty volume, through the *Periodical works of the day, those mightiest engines of modern literature.* In these, though the Editor may be arraigned for bad taste, he will not regret any humiliation of himself,—having sought neither honour nor emolument by this enterprise,— should he be even the unfortunate instrument of awakening the sympathy and calling forth in behalf of "a poor and afflicted people," the talents of that "*fierce democratie*" of genuine British writers, of every party, who have raised the reviews, magazines and newspapers of this age to a decided ascendancy in the republic of letters. Before the indefatigable energies of these champions, united in a patriotic cause, neither this nor any other factitious evil could exist twelve months.

Sir WALTER SCOTT, however, has contributed something towards this work, which will tell better in the end than even a poem from his own inimitable pen might have done. In a very obliging letter to the Editor, he says, "I assure you I am a sincere friend to the cause which you have so effectually patronised; and in building my house at this place (Abbotsford) *I have taken particular care*, by the construction of the vents, *that no such cruelty shall be practised within its precincts.* I have made them circular, about fourteen inches in diameter, and lined them with a succession of earthen pots, about one and a half inch thick, (like the common chimney-tops,) which are built round by the masonry, and form the tunnel for the passage of the smoke. The advantage is, that the interior being entirely smooth, and presenting no inequality or angle where soot could be deposited, there is, in fact, very little formed; and that which may adhere is removed by the use of a simple machine."

Mrs. Joanna Baillie also, in her letters, after expressing sentiments equally worthy of her enlightened mind and benevolent heart, described the "old Scottish mode of sweeping chimneys" by means of a rope and a bunch of heather, or bushes, worked up and down the flue, between a man at the top and another at the bottom. As this method is elsewhere alluded to, and not likely to be adopted in England, in substitution of Climbing-Boys, it becomes irrelevant to particularize the process here.

There is one great auxiliary, not yet named, whose aid was sought and magnanimously conceded on this occasion. His present Majesty, first as Prince Regent, and afterwards as King, had condescended to be the patron of the "*London Society for abolishing the use of Climbing-Boys in sweeping chimneys.*" Permission was therefore asked, and granted, to dedicate this volume to "the Father of all his people." The Editor, on behalf of those whom he represents, is assured that the most acceptable return which he can make for the high honour and obligation will be this simple acknowledgment.

Should the sale of the present work produce more than the cost of publication, the surplus will be added to the small fund of the *Society*, in this town, *for bettering the condition of Climbing Boys.*

J. M.

Sheffield, April 24, 1824.

(*Circular.*)

FOR nearly twenty years past, a few persons have been associated here, to improve the condition of Climbing Boys, — and eventually obviate the necessity of employing such to sweep chimneys. This evil is so familiarized, that few people are aware of its horrible atrocity. We who have watched all its details during so long a period, are convinced, that the practice ought not to be tolerated at all in a Christian country; and that if the cruelty, which is unavoidable in seasoning tender infants for this most repulsive of occupations, were inflicted on brute animals to qualify *them* for this same office, the legislature would promptly forbid it:

One of my friends, in this small company, conceives that a publication, consisting of poetical contributions by some of the most distinguished writers of the day, appealing to the compassion of all classes of people in behalf of these poor creatures, would fix that attention to the subject, which our feeble efforts have repeatedly obtained, but were unable to keep; though we have twice, by our almost unaided exertions, roused the legislature so effectually as to carry measures through the House of Commons for the immediate relief of the sufferers, and the gradual abolition of this home slave trade in little children.— Why we failed in the House of Lords, it is for those to answer who foiled us there.

May I then, in the name of my friends, intreat your aid to this humble cause? Were you to see all the climbing-boys in the kingdom (and *climbing-girls too*, for we have known parents who have employed their own daughters in this hideous way,) assembled in one place, you would meet a spectacle of deformed, degraded, and depraved humanity, in its very age of innocence, (pardon the phrase,) which would so affect your heart, that we should be sure of your hand.

But I will not believe that the visible representation of the actual misery can be necessary to interest you;—think what that *would* be, and do what you please for us. Any composition of the kind alluded to, long or short, narrative or otherwise, from your pen, will be most acceptable to my friends, and I will thankfully accept it as a personal obligation, though I should not of myself have presumed to solicit such a favour.

(Signed)

J. MONTGOMERY.

Sheffield, January 1, 1824.

CONTENTS.

CLIMBING-BOY'S ALBUM.

COPY OF A LETTER

FROM

THE RIGHT HON. VISCOUNT SIDMOUTH

TO

MR. TOOKE.

SIR, *Whitehall, 3d July*, 1821.

I HAVE had the honor of submitting to his Majesty the request of the Society for Ameliorating the Condition of Infant Chimney Sweepers, that his Majesty would be pleased to grant to the Society the privilege of naming his Majesty as their Patron; and I have the satisfaction of acquainting you, that his Majesty has been graciously pleased to approve of and sanction the use of his name, as Patron of that benevolent Institution.

I am, SIR,
Your most obedient,
Humble Servant,
SIDMOUTH.

To
WILLIAM TOOKE, ESQ.
&c. &c. &c.

TO

THE KING.*

THE torrent, with impetuous shock,
Leaps boiling down from rock to rock,
Triumphant o'er the granite block,
  But glides along the dell;
There, wandering in a thousand rills,
Its waters cheer the little hills,
  And feed the nectar'd bell.

---

* With singular propriety, as well as confidence, may these little oppressed ENGLISH SLAVES call upon *George the Fourth* to break their fetters, and free them from slavery and destruction.

Never, perhaps, existed the man who in his station possessed a heart more feelingly alive to the sufferings and the welfare of others.

No monarch who ever lived (I will not except even that of his venerable parent) hath evinced so strong a regard for the rights of his people, or so great an indifference to his own, as he hath hitherto done. When Prince of Wales, amidst the splendour of courts, the allurements of pleasure, and the hilarity of youth, he

The clouds, with thunder fraught and war,
Launch lightnings (their artillery) far
To rend the giant oak, and mar
  The mountain's craggy brow;
Yet they descend in dews and showers
On herbs and plants, on leaves and flowers,
  And make the violets blow.

O'er ocean's breast the halcyon glides,
The little nautilus too rides,
Delighted, as his bark he guides;
  Or, when wild storms molest,
Dives down, and sleeps in tranquil grot,
Where pensile fibres tremble not,
  Secure in ocean's breast.

---

unostentatiously became the friend and protector of these helpless, oppressed little ones. His name, *now that he is KING*, still stands at the head of the committee, as *patron* of a society whose object is the welfare of *chimney sweepers' climbing boys*. This is indeed conduct worthy of a *Prince!* — worthy of a *King!* — worthy of the King of *Great Britain!* With truth may he exclaim, in the beautiful language of Job, "When the ear heard me, then it blessed me; and when the eye saw me, it gave witness to me; because I delivered the poor that cried, and the fatherless, and him that had none to help him. The blessings of him that was ready to perish came upon me; and I caused the widow's heart to sing for joy."

The *Lord*—the *Lord* our *God*, is great,
Upon his beck the whirlwinds wait,
Clouds are the chariots of his state,
His will the thunders know;
At his command the tempests sleep,
His power controls the foaming deep,
Before him mountains bow.

He comes—earth trembles to its base,
While veil'd is every angel's face,
The darkness is his secret place,
His garment is the light:
The glorious rainbow, arch'd on high,
He set, his witness in the sky;
He rules the day and night.

And, as he guides the rolling ball,
On him the eagle's nestlings call;
He hears their cry,—He feeds them all;
He opens wide his hand,
The earth is fill'd with plenteousness,
All living things his goodness bless,
With joy their hearts expand.

The Lord, O King! hath given to *thee*
Dominion, power, and majesty,

From shore to shore, from sea to sea ;
  Where'er the waters flow,
So far thy keels victorious ride,
And, as the east from west is wide,
  So far the nations bow.

From *thee* the friendless and the weak
With feeble cry protection seek ;
Now let the voice of mercy speak
  For infants in despair ;
Oh ! stretch thy mighty arm to save,
From bonds and death, *the only slave*
  That breathes Old England's air.

M. R.

ON THE

EMPLOYMENT OF CLIMBING BOYS.

The observation of that Englishman who is not at this time, February 1824, astonished at the situation of his country, must be either very weak or very dull; and the heart of him who does consider it, and is not moved by that consideration to wonder, gratitude and praise, must be very hard, and very contracted.

Great Britain is now, like one of the most magnificent of her stupendous and almost invincible floating bulwarks, resting with all her canvass furled and her port-holes closed, upon the peaceful and transparent bosom of the mighty deep. She has survived, almost uninjured, the raging of a tempest, in which the vessels of nearly every other nation have been wrecked or greatly endangered: many of them now are lying around soliciting and receiving her assistance. She has been compelled to part with some of her lumber, and she has been strained a little, but her stores are in abundance, her timbers are sound, and her crew are healthy and in spirits. The heavens above her, and beneath her, are almost without a cloud, and the sun, in all his glory, darts his cheering and invigorating rays upon her from on high, while his image is reflected in the ocean, with softened yet undiminished beauty. Never was there a nation so blessed as Great Britain, never was Great Britain so prosperous as at this moment. " Blessed is the nation whose God is the Lord; and the people whom he hath chosen for his own inheritance!" The voice of faction itself is silenced. Abundance, and the means of obtaining it, were never before so general. The season of winter has smiled throughout like the months of the spring. The resources of the state are flourishing beyond any former example. The prospect of a perfect and long-continued peace is cheering and unobscured. Liberality of sentiment, Christian charity and brotherly kindness have made, and are making, great and rapid strides among all classes of her people; while the very poorest of her paupers are in possession of an inheritance as fully secured to them as the titles and the possessions of her nobles. Her monarch reigns with mercy and justice, firmly enthroned in the hearts of an affectionate people, who feel and acknowledge that their welfare is his object, and that he is alive to the sufferings of the very weakest, the lowest, and the most oppressed of his subjects.

The rulers of the state possess the confidence of the people, so that the voice of complaint, or dissatisfaction, is scarcely heard in the land. The agitated or suffering nations around her look to, and call upon her for protection and aid, and rely upon her promises and her generosity with a degree of confidence and consolation, which nothing less than well-known and long-established integrity, honour, and humanity could inspire.

Such is the situation, at this time, of Great Britain! Prosperity, it has been for thousands of years observed, is ever a state of danger. Kingdoms have never yet been long stationary. When they have ceased to advance, their fall has never been far distant. Britain has advanced far beyond the progression of any former period, or of any other state: it becomes her then, at any rate, to rejoice with trembling: but there is a rock on which even a *kingdom* may rest in safety; there is a foundation even for *states* which cannot be shaken. If, then, Britain be seated upon that rock, — if the superstructure of her building has been reared day by day, stone afte stone, on *that* foundation, she may yet endure. She may stand,—she may stand unmoved,—she may stand increased, and increasing in goodness, in glory, and in usefulness, till time shall be no longer. She may be the land destined to send out her messengers through every region of the world, to call in the fulness of the Gentiles, and to assemble and lead back the long-blinded and dispersed children of Israel to the God whom they have offended, and to the country from whence they were driven. Britain, then, may yet be destined to even greater usefulness and to greater glory. If, however, she long or look for this, she must purge herself from all iniquity. She must put from her all those sins which most easily, and most adheringly beset her. Nothing weaker than the arm of her God can either exalt her farther, or sustain her in the station to which she has been already raised. Let her then put away from her speedily all that she is convinced is offensive in the sight of God. It must be acknowledged, and acknowledged with gladness and gratitude, that she has done more, and gone farther in this way, than ever was done by any other state; and hence hath arisen, more than from the wisdom of her counsels, the bravery of her defenders, or the firmness of her people, that unprecedented degree of exaltation which she now enjoys. She is, at this time, (thank God!) parting with one of the foulest abominations which ever disgraced and degraded a Christian government, the State Lottery. Let her then proceed fearlessly, and with alacrity, in pleasing God, by publicly discarding and discouraging every practice which is either immoral, oppressive, or unjust, and she will find that her power, her glory, and her stability will be increased. Let her cast her bread with unlimited confidence upon the waters, and she will undoubtedly find it return to her, when most needed, after many days.

In the cause of the long cruelly oppressed African race, thousands of abler pens than the one here exercised (and that has not been idle) have been and will be exerted, till their rights are acknowledged, and their wrongs are redressed. But there is a people whose cause almost all but the MONARCH *of his people*, are *ashamed* to espouse, — a people, compared with whom even the enslaved African is in some respects less to be pitied.

Here then is room—here then is a call for tongues and pens, though feeble and hitherto unnoticed, to step forth and join the little fearless band, who dare to rally round their beloved *king*, and setting at nought the derision of the scorner, defend the fatherless and the poor, and him that hath none to help him. So dreadful, generally speaking, is the state of the poor little *British-born Children*, employed by Chimney Sweepers in climbing and cleansing chimneys, that there is not in this wide world of misery one class of human beings, whose cry to us " to come and help them," is so loud, so constant, so near at hand, and so disregarded, as that of these little beings, naturally the most lovely, and rendered by oppression and sufferings the most shockingly disgusting of all others. The poor African negro is kidnapped and sold, but it is by strangers, or by foes. These children are kidnapped and sold, and that by their own countrymen, and by their own parents. The negroes are selected for their strength, and consequent power of bearing hardship; these poor children are chosen for their youth, small stature, and consequent inability to sustain labour. The negro slaves are for the greater part arrived at years of man or womanhood, and therefore able to bear considerable fatigue without injury to their natural constitutions and frames; but these *British Slaves* are *invariably children*, both male and FEMALE, and are totally unable to bear the common degree of employment of adults, without falling sacrifices to it. The labour of the negroes, however severe, rarely impairs their health, deforms their frames, or distorts their limbs; that of these weak little children almost invariably produces some, if not all, of these lamentable effects; it moreover subjects them to peculiar diseases of the most shocking and painful kinds, which rarely fail, if not stopped in an early stage, to terminate in a premature death. The initiating of these tender infants in their horrid, difficult, and laborious calling, is *invariably* accompanied with more or less of laceration; their backs, their knees, their elbows, their shoulders, and their toes, are always rendered sore; and very often they are, when in this state of suffering, compelled, in the severest weather, to wander at the most unseasonable hours through frost and snow, and climb the rough and rugged flues till their wounds frequently ulcerate and become incurable. Their eyes are generally rendered inflamed, and their heads swoln. They are scantily clothed, poorly fed, ill lodged, and exposed to the unrestrained capricious cruelty of one of the most ignorant, violent, and depraved classes of human beings in this or perhaps any other civilised kingdom. It is useless to exclaim that there are laws to restrain any improper conduct in the masters! What better are the children for laws which do not, *cannot* protect them? The sufferings of these poor infants are generally too secret to be noticed — too disgusting to be willingly sought for, and are regarded with too much levity by those who are themselves never likely to be exposed to the same. Nay, painful experience has shown that magistrates can discourage all interference in their cause; and that some of the highest rulers of the state can turn their indefensible oppression into a subject of banter and laughter. What better, then, are these little sufferers for laws which *cannot* protect them. The enactments of such laws are invariably disregarded, or set at defiance; the sufferers themselves have no power; others have no inclination, at least no determination, to redress their wrongs. All then that they can do, is to bear their irremediable sufferings in silence to the end.

But these sufferings are not all—nay, they are not half of those resulting from their miserable lot. The very nature of their employment is such as to be totally unfit for human beings, at any period of life, to pursue. They are deprived of that natural rest which is so essential to the health and strength of children. They are continually exposed to the most dreadful and fatal accidents. They have their flesh torn by the sharp points of projecting stones or lime; they are frequently wedged, unable to move, and almost suffocated with soot, in narrow and crooked flues; they are often falling down those which are too wide for them.

They have been sent up chimnies while the fire was in the grate, to force their way through the heated soot. They have been scalded by steam arising from water thoughtlessly thrown into the fire below; nay they have not unfrequently been compelled to ascend and descend chimnies when on fire, sometimes perishing in the attempt. They have been precipitated from the tops of high chimnies in the loosened pots, and dashed upon the pavement below. They have been slowly roasted to death in the flue of an oven. They have been dug dead out of the sides of chimnies, in which they have been stuck fast, suffocating for hours. They have been extricated from places in which they were fastened, by means of ropes and iron crows, life itself having been the price of the rude operation. These are neither imaginary nor uncommon cases; instances of all of them will be adduced. Is then this a situation in which children, under any circumstances, or from any inducements, ought to be placed? Is not this the most shocking, the most revolting of all slavery? Surely some effects fatal to the prosperity, if not to the existence of the state, must be seriously apprehended from its abolition, or the evil would never be suffered for a single day longer to disgrace a country and a people such as ours! Astonishing as it may appear, it is true that the utmost mischief that could possibly arise from its immediate banishment, would be the alteration of a few, a very few chimneys, and those the chimneys of the opulent only, who would not be plagued with one that incommoded them by smoking, though it should cost them ten times as much to remedy the inconvenience. This really is inconceivable — *incredible!* It is not that the subject has escaped the vigilant eye of the legislature; it has been pressed—it has been forced upon it — it has undergone the strictest investigation that could be bestowed upon it, and the worst consequences have been stated; viz. that perhaps one or two chimneys in a hundred must be altered a little, which, after that investigation, has been declared to be all the loss and evil that could be apprehended from the total abolition of this most inhuman of all practices. Nay, so convinced were the legislators of the fact, that the bill for the abolition passed, almost without opposition, through one house, and would, in all probability, have passed through the other, had it not been turned into ridicule by one of the noble lords, who loved his *jest* better than he seemed to love little children. So children perished that senators might laugh! It is probable that the noble and venerable individual has since learned more clearly and more fully to appreciate the agonizing sufferings which many poor climbing boys have undergone; for it is a fact which will scarcely be doubted, that plebeian flesh is as sensible of pain as that which is noble. Let us not forget, then, when disposed to joke with misery, that that which is sport to us may be death to them; nor that the joke which we sport to-day upon others, may to morrow be returned upon ourselves. *

We have been accustomed so long to have this species of slavery and suffering continually before our eyes, that we not only disregard it, but can scarcely be persuaded that it is such. Had we been strangers to it here, and had learned that some such cruel practice was followed in some of our distant settlements, the horror, the indignation, and voices of the people would have been raised against it from one end of the kingdom to the other. So repugnant

* By the reports in the newspapers of the year 1817, it appears that at the conclusion of the debates in the House of Lords on the *third reading* of the act for abolishing the use of climbing boys in sweeping chimneys, Lord Lauderdale, in opposing it, compared the little climbing boy, with his cleansing brush, to that active, penetrating, and purifying medical agent, calomel. The oddity, not the justness of the comparison, diverted the House. His Lordship then proceeded to relate a story, which proved irresistible, and the bill was negatived. One Irishman was boasting to another of the great facility with which he cleansed his chimney, (a great man no doubt, or he would not have had a chimney in Ireland,) that he only took a goose, and tying a cord round its neck, let it down the flue, when, by the fluttering of its wings, and the scratching of its feet, it effectually swept the chimney. Pat acknowledged that this was a very ready method, but contended that it was a very *cruel* one, as a *couple* of *ducks* might have answered the purpose as well!

How this was meant to apply is not quite evident. The *effect*, however, was quite so; and his Lordship had the satisfaction of carrying his point.

indeed are the feelings of Englishmen to any thing like cruelty, that the legislature have not thought it any degradation of their dignity to protect the dumb and brute creation from abuse. Yet, strange as it may appear, the act for rescuing infant children from inhuman oppression and premature death was thrown out. Who ever heard of any class of brute creatures being generally so abused and maimed, while young, as to be rendered deformed cripples and useless beings ever after, even if they survived; but most generally destroyed by the severity of their treatment before they had arrived at their full strength or stature? Who ever heard of such young cattle being suffocated, dashed to pieces, or burnt to death? Were DOGS to be used in the same employment and in the same manner as these poor climbing boys, it has been observed, that an outcry would be raised by themselves within the chimney, and by their masters without, that would soon cause a stop to be put to the barbarous practice; yet it has been suffered to continue for centuries with these friendless infants, because they cannot so loudly plead their own cause, and are too poor and despised to obtain the effectual assistance of others.

It is scarcely possible to imagine a stronger occurrence to establish the truth of the foregoing observation than one in which the writer was called upon to interfere. A respectable medical man sent to him, as a member of the committee of the society established at Sheffield for the purpose of mitigating the sufferings of climbing boys, or abolishing the practice of employing them, to request that he would call upon one of them whom he described. Accordingly, with another member of the committee, he went to the boy's uncle, with whom he then was, and who had taken him to his own house. They found the child in bed, in an exceedingly weak and emaciated state: he had sores upon his shoulders, hips, elbows, and knees: and the nails of one or more of his toes were torn off. He was then incapable of turning himself in bed. In that condition, however, he had been many times compelled to climb up chimneys, as usual: and the master was then threatening the uncle with a warrant for not giving him up to him again. When the boy was able to leave his bed, the two members of the committtee met the parties before a magistrate. The sores were then in a great measure healed; but it was the nature of the defence, and the success of the plea, which were the most remarkable. The master, instead of denying or palliating the sufferings of the boy, brought forward another chimney-sweeper to prove — what? Why, that such sufferings were inseparable from the nature of the trade, and that *every child* who learnt it must, in the beginning, be lacerated in the same manner. This was one of those half brutes in human shape, to whose uncontrolled tyranny these poor infants are often delivered up. He brought a *son of his own* whose scars and healed sores he exhibited with a kind of exulting triumph, as a proof that he (the defendant) had been guilty of nothing more than what was generally and lawfully practised. This man was one in a very low way. He had generally worked with borrowed climbers; he had never had but one other apprentice, who had died in the workhouse, the governor of which attended to attest that his death was the consequence of the cruel treatment which he had experienced.

Now, after this, we may surely challenge the history of slavery and cruelty throughout the world, to produce an instance of systematic oppression equal to this, or of effrontery carried to the same length. Children who had committed no crime, of the tenderest age, and most delicate frames, nay, some of them *female* children, exposed, by the connivance of the law of that land in which they were born free, to an employment by which they *must* be so torn and lacerated as frequently to render them deformed and crippled during life, and sometimes to cause their deaths. What would have been said if the children of slaves in the West Indies had been so abused? And what would have been our astonishment and horror had the planters dared to defend it by saying that it was unavoidable? Indignation would have been felt and expressed too loudly throughout the country to have been resisted. Yet such instances of unprecedented cruelty are constantly practised before our eyes, not only unregarded, but, sometimes, defended. The defence in the above mentioned case was allowed, and the terrified child would have been ordered to return to his master and employment had not his agonizing cries, on this being intimated, excited the commiseration of the whole court. The boy was allowed to return to his uncle on his paying back the purchase-money to the master.

To talk of regulating a trade like this is absurd. It must be *prohibited.* Justice, mercy, and sound policy all alike demand it! There is not — there cannot be — any sound plea urged for its continuance. This has been tried, and not one *argument* could be brought to defend it. It, however, was preserved! What reason could not accomplish, ridicule effected. Oh! could the noble senator have been made sensible of the horror, which his, perhaps, unpremeditated pleasantry on such a subject caused throughout the land, he would have deeply regretted having indulged in it. Could he possibly know the dreadful sufferings, — perhaps the horrid deaths — which have been the consequence of this perpetuated outrage on human nature, he would never again laugh at the calamities of others, however poor, helpless, young and unoffending the sufferers might be. His Lordship may yet be afforded an opportunity of quitting himself of some degree of the blame which must attach to this unseasonable levity. It is earnestly to be hoped, that in such an event his Lordship may be induced to act a part more worthy of his dignity, high rank, and talents.

The estimation in which this trade is held by the poor, is evident from the circumstance that no child of decent parents was ever put to it; and it is the only trade in which masters *purchase* children for apprentices. In this few, if any, are obtained without being either purchased, given away by parish-officers, or stolen. In all other trades a premium is generally given. Is it to be endured, in a civilised Christian country, that parents should be allowed to *sell* their infant children for money,—though they sell them to almost certain misery and depravity, if not to death? Is not this tempting the most depraved to be guilty of something like sacrificing their own offspring to Mammon? When a man has spent all his money, and made a beast of himself, is it surprising that, in a fit of insensibility, he should barter away his child to a chimney-sweeper for a few pounds to enable him to plunge farther in debauchery? How many hundreds of such drunken fathers are there who, though they may have some natural affection for their offspring, cannot resist the temptation of such a sum? Is it right, then, — is it to be tolerated that parents, under any circumstances, should have the power of disposing of their children for money? As well might they have the privilege of selling their daughters to prostitution. In the former case the children cannot be consenting, because they are only infants.

Unfortunately the man who attempts to plead a cause like this, subjects himself to the ridicule and contempt of the gay, the proud, and the thoughtless. This consideration has deterred many friends of humanity from advocating the cause in that assembly to which the victims must appeal. The world seems as much afraid of being thought too humane, as of being religious over much. But he who lets the fear of ridicule deter him from his duty, is as unworthy of the name of man as of that of Christian. True dignity, as well as true courage, consists in fearlessly doing that which is right in the right way. Whatever the disparity may be between a poor little climbing boy and a nobleman, it is far from being so great as between the nobleman and his God. If, then, the nobleman expects to be regarded by his Maker, he ought not, surely, to turn a deaf ear to the cries for help of the meanest or least of his fellow-creatures.

If, as we are assured, mercy will be shown to us in proportion as we exercise it on others, it becomes our interest, as much as our duty, to extend it to all. If the monarch on the throne does not think these poor children beneath his active exertions to serve them, the highest of his subjects surely need not be ashamed of following his example.

S. R.

INSTANCES

OF

OPPRESSION AND CRUELTY.

THE following are a few cases of cruelty and oppression, collected from former publications, to the time (1817) when the Act for the Suppression of Climbing Boys was proposed. Since then, the master-sweeps, knowing that the eyes of the public were directed to them, have been more upon their guard, and fewer instances of death to the boys from accidents have occurred. Many examples of dreadful sufferings have since then been brought before the public. These are, indeed, under any regulations, inseparable from the employment.

CASE I.—A few years ago, a chimney belonging to the house of Messrs. Coutts and Co. bankers, Strand, being on fire, a boy was sent up to extinguish it. He climbed up part of the way, but was not able to proceed farther, on account of the fire. This was in a sloping part of the flue, where, having thrust some of the burning soot behind him, he might literally be said to be between two fires; in order to save his life, it became necessary to make a hole in the wall from the inside, and he was fortunately taken out alive.

CASE II.—About the beginning of the year 1806, a boy was sent up a chimney in the house of Mr. Creed, Navy Agent, No. 23. Hans Place, Knightsbridge. Being unable to extricate himself, he remained there for about half an hour, while a person went to fetch assistance. A hole was made through the brick-work, and the boy at length released. It appeared that, in consequence of the unusual construction of the flue in one part, a vast quantity of soot had accumulated there, into which the boy had plunged, and was not able, probably from partial suffocation, to get back again. So dangerous was the sweeping of this chimney considered, that James Dunn, chimney-sweeper, No. 46. Hans Town, refused to let his apprentice ascend the flue.

CASE III.—Extract from the Public Ledger, Thursday, Aug. 24. 1809.—An information was on Tuesday heard before the sitting magistrate at Bow Street, against a master-sweep, named Henry Doe, residing in the parish of Mary-le-bone, for having in his service as an apprentice, a child under the age of eight years, contrary to the act of parliament for regulating the ages of children apprenticed to that trade. The circumstances of this case were truly distressing, and exhibited an instance of human depravity scarcely to be equalled. It appeared that the mother of the child went some distance from London, and left her little son, a fine boy, five years of age, under the care of his father, who is a working plumber, named Miller. She remained out of town about a twelvemonth, and on her return, ran with anxious hopes to the lodgings of her husband; but how great was her disappointment and misery, when she was informed by the unnatural parent that, during her absence, he had had the inhumanity to place his infant offspring in the service of a sweep, and thus early to expose his tender frame to all those melancholy vicissitudes, so often experienced by the unfortunate children who are doomed to that employment. Her sensations may be more easily imagined than described. She rushed from the presence of her husband almost frantic, and with some difficulty found the den, (for it could not be called a human habitation,) where her infant, initiated into the horrid mysteries of chimney-sweeping, was doomed to pass its existence without the fostering care of a parent, and subject to all the barbarity of an inexorable master. The measure of her distress, however, was not yet full, for now she heard the horrid account, that the father had absolutely sold the child for three guineas: without the reproduction of which its equally unnatural master refused to restore it to the embraces of its distracted mother. The only recourse now left her was to apply to a solicitor for advice, who humanely took the cause in hand, and summoned this master before the magistrates, who, without the least hesitation, ordered the child to be restored to its mother, and imposed a fine of £5. on the master.

CASE IV.—A boy, named Sharpless, in the employ of Mrs. Whitfield, Little Shire Lane, Temple Bar, fell from the upper part of a chimney in July, or August, 1804, in Devereux Court. The chimney-pot falling, or upper part of the chimney giving way, occasioned this accident. The boy had several bones fractured, and being carried to St. Bartholomew's Hospital, died there in a short time.

CASE V.—In the improvement made some years since by the Bank of England, in Lothbury, a chimney belonging to a Mr. Mildrum, a baker, was taken down; but before he began to bake, in order to see that the rest of the flue was clear, a boy was sent up; and, after remaining some time, he not answering to the call of his master, another boy was ordered to descend from the top of the flue, and to meet him half way. But this being found impracticable, they

To face page 28.

opened the brick-work in the lower part of the flue, and found the first-mentioned boy dead. In the mean time, the boy in the upper part of the flue called out for relief, saying he was completely jammed in the rubbish, and was unable to extricate himself. Upon this a bricklayer was employed with the utmost expedition, but he succeeded only in obtaining a lifeless body. The bodies were sent to St. Margaret's Church, Lothbury, and a coroner's inquest which sat upon them returned the verdict, Accidental Death.*

CASE VI.—In the beginning of the year 1808, a chimney-sweeper's boy being employed to sweep a chimney in Marsh Street, Walthamstow, in the house of Mr. Jeffery, carpenter, unfortunately in his attempt to get down, stuck in the flue, and was unable to extricate himself. Mrs. Jeffery, being within hearing of the boy, immediately procured assistance. As the chimney was low, and the top of it easily accessible from without, the boy was taken out in about ten minutes, the chimney-pot and several rows of bricks having been previously removed. If he had remained in that dreadful situation many minutes longer, he must have died. His master was sent for, and he arrived soon after the boy had been released. He abused him for the accident, and after striking him, sent him

* See Plate, illustrative of this case.

with a bag of soot to sweep another chimney. The child appeared so very weak when taken out that he could scarcely stand, and yet this wretched being, who had been up ever since three o'clock, had before been sent by his master to Wanstead, which, with his walk to Marsh Street, made about five miles.

CASE VII.—On Friday morning, February 16. 1808, a climbing apprentice to Holland, in East Street, Lambeth, was sent at three in the morning to sweep some chimneys at Norwood. The snow was so deep, and the cold so extreme, that a watchman used this remarkable expression, "that he would not have sent even a dog out." The boy having swept two chimneys, was returning home in company with another boy, but at length found the cold so excessive, that he could go no further. After some little time, he was taken to the Half Moon public-house, at Dulwich, and died in the course of an hour. It was supposed that by proper care his life might have been preserved. The master-sweep was brought to Union Hall, Southwark, by Mr. Bowles, the magistrate. Upon examining him, his principal fault appeared to be, sending the boy out so early, and he was dismissed. A coroner's inquest was held upon the body, and a verdict was returned, Died from the inclemency of the weather.

Case VIII.

City and Liberty of Westminster, County of Middlesex. } *Information of Witnesses taken this 15th of January, 1811, at the house of John Lloyd, the White Horse, Orchard Street, in the Parish of St. Margaret, on Joseph Holt, a chimney-sweeper, aged eleven years.*

Thomas Bonnet, a servant to Mr. Hope, chimney-sweeper, in Perkin's Rents, being sworn, saith, " The deceased was apprentice to Mr. Hope. I have lived with Mr. Hope about one year; the deceased was with Mr. Hope all this year, but I cannot say how long before. Yesterday, after dinner, about half-past two, the deceased went to sweep the chimney, in the front two pair of stairs room, in a house in Orchard Street. I attended him all the time; having finished this, he went up the chimney in the back two pair of stairs room; he did not say anything till he got up to the top of it; then he hallooed out, as is usual; I hallooed up the chimney to him, and desired him to do it clean down. He said, " Yes, Thomas." In about five minutes, as he did not come down, I hallooed up to him, to know why he did not, and he did not answer. I hallooed twice again, and then he cried out, " he had stuck." I looked up the chimney, and saw it was quite clear, so that I had no doubt, he had by accident got into another chimney. On this I ran immediately to my master, to get another boy, and my master and the other boy came directly. My master immediately put this boy up the same two pair of stairs chimney; he went up a little way, and returned in a minute, and he said Holt answered him, and was in a chimney down below. We instantly tried the one pair of stairs chimney, and found it was not that. We then tried the back parlour chimney, by hallooing, but he did not answer. We then put the boy up this chimney, and he told us that Holt answered him. My master and I then went into the back yard, and directed the second boy to remain in the chimney, in order to know. A bricklayer was procured without any delay, and he, with our assistance, broke a hole in the chimney, in the part where the second boy knocked at, who was inside. He then told us that Holt must be up higher. We immediately broke another hole about a yard and a half higher, and my master, who was on the ladder, looked in, and immediately exclaimed, "Oh, dear! the boy is dead." The deceased was immediately got out by sending the second boy up higher, which he was enabled to ascend in consequence of our having broke away the narrow part of the chimney. He was taken into a room, and I got a doctor directly, and another doctor came, who endeavoured to restore him to life, but in vain. There were no fires in any chimneys he went up, and I am certain he lost his life by unfortunately (in descending the second chimney) getting into a wrong flue.

Samuel Reim, No. 20. Dartmouth Street, apothecary, being sworn, saith, " Yesterday, near four o'clock in the afternoon, I was sent for to the deceased, who appeared to me to be dead. I opened a vein, but not more than a tea-spoonful of blood issued, and he had no pulse. Another medical gentleman and myself then made a puncture in the throat, to restore life, if possible, by the injection of air. We also tried the usual method of rubbing the stomach with vinegar and salt; but he was too far gone to restore him. He died through suffocation occasioned by the quantity of soot in the nostrils, throat, and stomach.

The verdict, Accidentally suffocated.

ANTHONY GELL, Coroner for the City and Liberty of Westminster.

West Riding of Yorkshire.

CASE IX.—Extract from an inquisition taken at Wakefield, in the county of York, 21st of May, 1811, before Edward Brook, one of the coroners of the said county, on the view of the body of Joseph Fisher, an infant of the age of about twelve years, who, having gone up to sweep a chimney belonging to one John Grace, of Wakefield aforesaid, tailor, on Saturday morning early, the 20th day of April last, adjoining to and communicating with a chimney belonging to one Benjamin Byron, a neighbour to the said John Grace, the fire in the fire-place of which had been raked the evening before, and a quantity of soot falling down therein, the flames communicated by a flue from Benjamin Byron's chimney, to the chimney wherein the said Joseph Fisher was sweeping; so that he was so dreadfully burnt, that after languishing until Wednesday evening, the 24th of April last, of the burns aforesaid, he then and there died. And so the jurors upon their oath, say, that the said Joseph Fisher, in manner, and by the means aforesaid, to wit, by being dreadfully burnt in a chimney from the fire in the fire-place of the said Benjamin Byron communicating with the chimney of the said John Grace, came to his death.

N. B. The said Byron and his wife were capitally indicted, and tried at the York assizes for the alleged murder, but were acquitted.

Case X.—On Monday morning, the 29th of March, 1813, a chimney-sweeper, of the name of Griggs, attended to sweep a small chimney in the brewhouse of Messrs. Calvert and Co., in Upper Thames Street; he was accompanied by one of his boys, a lad of about eight years of age, of the name of Thomas Pitt. The fire had been lighted as early as two o'clock the same morning, and was burning on the arrival of Griggs and his little boy at eight; the fire-place was small, and an iron pipe projected from the grate some little distance into the flue; this the master was acquainted with (having swept the chimneys in the brewhouse for some years,) and therefore had a tile or two taken from the roof, in order that the boy might *descend* the chimney. He had no sooner extinguished the fire than he suffered the lad to go down, and the consequence, as might be expected, was his almost immediate death, in a state, no doubt, of inexpressible agony. The flue was of the narrowest description, and must have retained heat sufficient to have prevented the child's return to the top, even supposing he had not approached the pipe belonging to the grate, which must have been nearly red-hot; this, however, was not clearly ascertained on the inquest, though the appearance of the body would have induced an opinion that he had been unavoidably pressed against the pipe. Soon after his descent, the master, who remained on the top, was apprehensive that something had happened, and therefore desired him to come up: the answer of the boy was, "I cannot come up, master, I must die here." An alarm was given in the brewhouse immediately, that he had *stuck* in the chimney; and a bricklayer, who was at work near the spot, attended; and after knocking down part of the brick-work of the chimney, just above the fire-place, made a hole sufficiently large to draw him through. A surgeon attended, but all attempts to restore life were ineffectual.

On inspecting the body, various burns appeared; the fleshy part of the legs, and a great part of the feet, more particularly, were injured; those parts, too, by which climbing-boys most effectually ascend or descend chimneys, viz. the elbows and knees, seemed burnt to the bone, from which it must be evident that the unhappy sufferer made some attempts to return as soon as the horrors of his situation became apparent. The Jury, upon the view of the body, and after hearing evidence to the effect above stated, which engaged their serious deliberation for two days, returned the following special verdict, viz.

That the master was employed to clean a certain chimney at the brewhouse of Messrs. Calvert and Co. situate, &c., and that he set the deceased, an infant of about eight years, to clean the said chimney for him. That deceased accordingly got into and descended the said chimney for the purpose of cleaning the same, and that by the straightness and narrowness of the chimney, and by the heat thereof, a fire having just been in the grate thereof the deceased was burned and hurt in divers parts of his body ; and also by the foulness and unwholesomeness of the air in the said chimney, the deceased was suffocated: of which said burning, hurts, and suffocation, the deceased then and there died ; and so the jurors, upon their oath, say, that he died in the manner aforesaid, and by misfortune came to his death.

Case XI.—On Friday, the 31st of May, 1816, William Moles, and Sarah his wife, were tried at the Old Bailey, for the wilful murder of John Hewley *alias* Hasely, a boy about six years of age, in the month of April last, by cruelly beating him. Under the direction of the learned judge, they were acquitted of the crime of murder, but the husband was detained to take his trial as for a misdemeanor; of which he was convicted upon the fullest evidence, and sentenced to two years' imprisonment.

N. B. Several other cases have occurred, particularly one of death at Newport, in the Isle of Wight, of all which an account will be given in the next Report of the Society.

Case XII.—June, 1816. A boy ascended a chimney in Albany Barracks, while a fire was in the grate, and was so dreadfully burnt, that he survived only a few hours.

Case XIII.—A boy stuck fast in a chimney at Stamford, uttering the most piercing cries at the attempts to drag him down by the legs. After being two hours in this horrible situation, a part of the chimney was pulled down, and he was taken out.

Case XIV. — August. A sweep and his wife, brought to Hatton Garden Office for cruelty to an apprentice not eight years old. About a fortnight before he had been taken in a most emaciated state to St. Thomas's Hospital, for some very bad wounds, occasioned by ill-treatment, and being forced up a chimney *on fire*.

Case XV. — October. A sweep brought to Bow Street for cruelty to a climbing-boy, whom he had beaten till he bled at different parts of the body for not ascending a flue too small for him. The child was saved from further cruelties by some neighbours whom his cries had attracted.

Case XVI. — December. A boy, nine years old, sent up a chimney *on fire*: the upper part being stopped, he was so completely suffocated as to be taken out apparently dead; but, by the persevering exertions of two medical men, animation was restored.

Case XVII. — March, 1817. A boy was sent up a chimney in Cumberland Street, and, in a slanting part, smothered by the falling soot; when dug out he was quite dead.

Case XVIII. — May. A boy stuck fast in the flue

of a chimney in Sheffield; by pulling down a part of it he was, at the end of two hours, extricated from his shocking situation.

Case XIX. — A sweep taken before the magistrates at Liverpool, for cruel treatment of a child five years old, and committed to prison.

Case XX. — June. A boy was sent up a chimney in a house where a woman in a lower room was cooking; she accidentally set her chimney on fire, and the flames reaching the unfortunate sweep, he was dreadfully burnt, and after lingering two days expired.

Case XXI. — A boy sent up a chimney in Edinburgh, stuck in a turn of the flue. The most barbarous means were used to drag him down, but it was found impracticable. After seven hours he was dug out, but quite dead.

Case XXII. — A boy went up a flue in a gentleman's house in Bryanstone Street, and was smothered by the falling soot; he was also taken out dead.

Case XXIII. — November 3. A boy got wedged in a narrow flue in the Penitentiary, Milbank; and, after uttering the most piteous groans for two hours, was at length, by breaking into the flue in different parts, taken out almost dead. In a short time he must have died through exhaustion.

Case XXIV. — A boy went, a few weeks since, to

sweep a chimney in Somers' Town; he stuck fast, and his groans, after some time, led to his being dug out; but, alas! too late. He appeared to have been partly smothered, and, by the heat of the flue, partly burnt alive.

Case XXV. — At the Dublin Sessions, T. Young, a master-sweep, was indicted at the instance of the Lord Mayor, for extreme cruelty to his apprentice. The boy was examined on oath, in the arms of a nurse; he appeared, from excessive torture, hardly able to speak; he said, that he lived with the prisoner as an apprentice; that the prisoner used to burn straw and powder under him, to make him go up the chimneys quick; and used to pull him down by a cord tied to his leg; it was this cruelty that caused the sores, which prevented him from going up the chimneys when ordered. The prisoner has often thrown him into a tub of water, in order to make his sores pain him. The evidence of the poor lad was corroborated by that of other witnesses; and the Court sentenced the wretch to be whipped twice, at an interval of two months, from the gaol to the Exchange; to be imprisoned two years, and also to be detained in custody till he gave two sureties of £25 each, and bound himself in £50. This sentence was received with evident satisfaction by the whole Court.

High Court of Justiciary, Edinburgh, 22d July, 1817.

CASE XXVI. — Joseph Rae and Robert Reid, chimney-sweepers, were charged with the murder of John Fraser *alias* Thomson, a boy of eleven years of age, an apprentice of the said Joseph Rae: the indictment also contained a charge that the said Joseph Rae did previously evince a deadly malice and ill-will against the said John Fraser *alias* Thomson, by maltreating him and using him harshly on different occasions. The Lord Advocate deserted the diet against Reid, *pro loco et tempore*, and he was committed upon a new warrant.

The counsel for Rae objected to the manner in which the charge of malice was introduced, and also of the want of specification in that charge. The Court repelled the objection. The panel pleaded Not Guilty.

James Thomson, chimney-sweeper. — One day in the beginning of June witness and panel had been sweeping vents together. About four o'clock in the afternoon, the panel proposed to go to Albany Street, where the panel's brother was cleaning a vent, with the assistance of Fraser, whom he had borrowed from the panel for the occasion. When witness and panel got to the house in Albany Street, they found Fraser, who had gone up the vent between eleven and twelve o'clock, not yet come down. On entering the house they found a mason making a hole in the wall. Panel said, what was he doing? "I suppose he has taken a lazy fit." The panel called to the boy, "What are you doing? what's keeping you?" The boy answered, that he could not come. The panel worked a long while, sometimes persuading him, sometimes threatening and swearing at the boy to get him down. Panel then said, "I will go to a hardware shop and get a barrel of gunpowder, and blow you and the vent to the devil, if you do not come down." Panel then began to slap at the wall; witness then went up a ladder, and spoke to the boy through a small hole in the wall previously made by the mason, but the boy did not answer. Panel's brother told witness to come down, as the boy's master knew best how to manage him. Witness then threw off his jacket, and put a handkerchief about his head, and said to the panel, "Let me go up the chimney to see what's keeping him." The panel made no answer, but pushed witness away from the chimney, and continued bullying the boy. At this time the panel was standing on the grate, so that witness could not go up the chimney; witness then said to panel's brother, "There is no use for me here," meaning that panel would not permit him to use his services. He prevented the mason making the hole larger, saying, "Stop, and I'll bring him down in five minutes' time." Witness then put on his jacket, and continued an hour in the room, during which time the panel continued bullying the boy. Panel then desired witness to go to Reid's house to get the loan of his boy Alison. Witness went to Reid's house, and asked Reid to come and speak to panel's brother. Reid asked if panel was there. Witness answered he was; Reid said he would send his boy to the panel, but not to the panel's brother: witness and Reid went to Albany Street; and when they got into the room, panel took his head out of the chimney, and asked Reid if he would lend him his boy; Reid agreed; witness then returned to Reid's house for his boy, and Reid called after him, "Fetch down a set of ropes with you." By this time witness had been ten minutes in the room, during which time panel was swearing, and asking what's keeping you, you scoundrel; when witness returned with the boy and ropes. Reid took hold of the rope, and having loosed it, gave Alison one end, and directed him to go up the chimney, saying, "Do not go farther than his feet, and when you get there fasten it to his foot." Panel said nothing all this time. Alison went up, and having fastened the rope, Reid desired him to come down; Reid took the rope and pulled, but did not bring down the boy; the rope broke: Alison was sent up again with the other end of the rope, which was fastened to the boy's foot. When Reid was pulling the rope, panel said, "You have not the strength of a cat;" he took the rope into his own hands, pulling as strong as he could. Having pulled about a quarter of an hour, panel and Reid fastened the rope round a crow-bar, which they applied to the wall as a lever, and both pulled with all their strength for about a quarter of an hour longer, when it broke. During this time witness heard the boy cry, and say, "My God Almighty!" Panel said, "If I had you here, I would God Almighty you." Witness thought the cries were in agony. The master of the house brought a new piece of rope, and the panel's brother spliced an eye on it. Reid expressed a wish to have it fastened on both thighs, to have greater purchase. Alison was sent up for this purpose, but came down, and said he could not get it fastened. Panel then began to slap at the wall; after striking a long while at the wall, he got out a large stone; he then put in his head and called to Fraser, "Do you hear, you sir?" but got no answer: he then put in his hands, and threw down deceased's breeches. He then came down from the ladder. At this time the panel was in a state of perspiration; he sat down on a stool, and the master of the house gave him a dram. Witness did not hear panel make any remarks as to the situation of the boy Fraser. Witness thinks, that, from panel's appearance, he knew the boy was dead. Reid's wife came to get her husband away to a job, and the panel went with him, This was between six and seven o'clock. Panel's brother enlarged the hole, but still could not get in. Witness then went in with difficulty. He found Fraser lying on his belly, with his hands stretched above his head. He was lying at a turn in the vent, and his head jammed at the head of the turn; had a towel about his head, and a shirt all about his neck. Witness tore off the shirt bit by bit, and threw it on the floor; then brought down the boy: there was a little heat in the body; got spirits and washed the boy's temples, but in vain. Witness went for Dr. Poole, who came, and applied a bellows, but in vain. Witness knew the deceased twelve months past in May used to come to witness's house. Witness always gave him a piece or a halfpenny. Boy complained that his master used to starve him, strike him, and use him badly. Witness stopped in prisoner's house for some time in May, 1816. One Saturday night, heard panel's wife say, "You are done now, there's your ladder and materials away;" whereupon panel made the deceased strip himself. Boy applied to witness to save him. Witness asked panel to forgive him. Panel said if it were God Almighty himself speaking from the heavens, he would not forgive him. The boy was told to strip himself perfectly naked; panel beat him on the back with the single end of a sweep's ropes, apparently with all his strength. The boy cried much. About ten o'clock at night the panel took the boy to a back room, and made him go naked up and down the chimney, till one o'clock Sunday morning. — Panel afterwards acknowledged that the ladder and materials were in the house all the time; boy was a fine boy; witness has stuck in a vent himself, but never saw ropes used; did not remonstrate, because boy's master was the principal. The mason said that panel was killing the boy, and that he could get him aid, but was hindered by the panel. Witness thinks that the expressions used by the panel to the boy while in the vent were from revenge; panel seemed in anger at the boy: did not hear deceased speak after panel had left the house.

James Stalker, publican and grocer in Albany Street, in most respects corroborated the preceding witness. He stated, that before panel left the house, he (witness) said to him, "Sir, you have killed him;" and either Reid or panel said it was not the case — it was the boy's cunningness. Witness again said, he might depend upon it he had killed him; panel said it was not the case, — he would not wonder if he were in a faint.

John Cameron and James Steel, porters, also corroborated the statements of the preceding witnesses.

James Alison, apprentice to Robert Reid, a boy of

eleven years of age, stated, that he had fastened the rope to Fraser's leg by the direction of the panel. — Examined by the prisoner's counsel: has known deceased remain a long time in vents when he might have come down: once in Gayfield Square, witness and deceased were both sent up to clear a vent; witness went up first and deceased followed, but deceased would not come down till another boy was sent for to take him down; upon this occasion he kept witness in the vent from seven in the evening till near three next morning: witness has known him stay long in other vents.

Thomas Marwood lived in panel's house along with deceased: saw panel tie deceased to a chest, gag his mouth with a stick, and beat him with ropes till the blood came, and then put saltpetre on him; has seen panel make deceased eat the vilest offal.

James Bryce, surgeon, was sent for to examine the body of the deceased 36 hours after his death; found some abrasion on the skin in the front of the breast — no particular appearance on the face — no fracture — no contusions — greater mobility in the neck than would have been expected so long after death. As first, supposed this mobility might proceed from dislocation, or a fracture of the deltoid process; dissected the muscles from the bones of the neck; discovered no fracture of the bones; then severed the head from the body, and found the deltoid process in its place perfectly entire; thinks the death must have happened in one of three ways: 1st, By the head getting into a certain angle with the neck, and permitting such a pressure on the spinal marrow as to prove fatal; 2d, All the clothes getting round the head and producing suffocation; 3d, The clothes getting round the neck, and being attached to some stone in the vent, and producing strangulation from the force applied below. — Dr. Farquharson stated, in addition to the above, that he observed the skin off one of the legs, as if occasioned by a ligature. — Dr. Poole corroborated the above statement. He also described the situation of the deceased an hour after the body was taken from the vent; the jaw was firmly locked; uncommon facility of motion of the neck: had no doubt that forcible extraction of the boy had produced some fatal effect on the neck; concurred in the three modes mentioned by Mr. Bryce, but declined giving any opinion as to which of them caused the death.

The Lord Advocate addressed the jury on behalf the Crown, and had no doubt but that they would return a verdict of guilty. Mr. M'Neill addressed the jury on behalf of the prisoner, and contended, that the evidence failed to make out a case of murder. — Verdict, Culpable Homicide. — Panel transported for 14 years.

MARY DAVIS.

A TRUE STORY.

The Truth of the following Relation, which appeared, in substance, in the Boston Gazette, of 1*st September,* 1812, *is attested by Mr. C. E. Welbourn, of Folkingham, himself a witness, in part, of the circumstances, and the writer of the original account as it appeared in the aforesaid paper.*

On the evening of August 25th, 1812, a poor yet interesting young woman, with an infant about six weeks old in her arms, came with a pass billet to remain all night at the Greyhound inn, at Folkingham, in Lincolnshire. Apparently sinking with hunger and fatigue, she unobtrusely seated herself by the kitchen fire to give that sustenance to her baby, of which she appeared to be in equal want herself. Silently shrinking from observation, she neither solicited nor obtained the notice of any one. The sons of intemperate mirth neither ceased their riotous tumult, nor relaxed their hilarity to soothe her sorrows. The bustling servants brushed past without regarding her, and the rustic politician continued to spell over again the thrice conned paper, without casting his eyes upon her.

There is, however, an eye that never slumbers, there is an ear that is ever open to the supplication of the afflicted, and there is a hand which is ever ready to be stretched out to succour and to support them in their necessities.

That eye now beheld her unobtruded sorrows, that ear was listening to her silent prayers, and that hand was supporting her apparently sinking frame, and preparing for her the cup of consolation. Hers was indeed a tale of many sorrows!—*This*, the following slight sketch of her story previous to her arrival at Folkingham will serve to evince. Her name was Mary Davis; she resided with her husband and one child, a boy about seven years of age, in the city of Westminster. Her husband, who is a private in the 2d Regiment of Foot Guards, was compelled to leave her big with child, in the beginning of the present year, to accompany the regiment to fight the battles of his country under the gallant and victorious Wellington. Impelled by poverty and maternal affection, poor Mary (though in a situation, in which the daughters of affluence often find every accommodation and consolation which riches and friends can afford, unequal to banish despondency,) was under the necessity of leaving her darling boy, now her only remaining comfort, to the care of strangers, whilst she went out to wash for his maintenance and her own.

She however repined not; her toil was lessened, and her cares were enlivened by the reflection, that she could, after the labours of the day, return to her beloved boy, gaze on the reflected features of his father, give him smile for smile, press him to her maternal bosom, join him in his sports, enlighten his understanding, and teach him to know, to fear, and to love his God. With these delightful enjoyments, even the poor, labouring, widowed Mary could not be termed unhappy; but these were the *only* sweet ingredients in her cup of bitter sorrows. Let those, then, who have feeling hearts, and know the force of parental affection, when confined to one object, judge, if they can, what must be the agonies of poor Mary, when, on returning from her daily task, only eight days after the departure of her husband, she learned that the woman (if she deserves that name) in whose care she had left her darling boy, had absconded with him. nobody knew whither. *Now then* she might indeed be termed unhappy, for hope itself could scarcely find admittance to her bosom, so entirely was it occupied by affliction and despondency. View her seated after the toils of the day, in her cheerless apartment, exhausted with exertions beyond her present strength, solitary and friendless, a childless mother and a widowed wife; awaiting in silence and solitude, in grief and despondency, her painful trial; her gloomy imagination figuring and dwelling upon a dying husband and a famished child.

Could a weakened, human, female frame, support all this and live? yes! through all these sore afflictions, these accumulated evils, did her God support her, and even after the birth of her child, shed a ray of hope on her returning strength.

Soon after that event she was informed, that it was discovered that the wretch who had stolen her child was a native of Leeds. This truly, to those who bask in sunshine, would appear a feeble ray, yet *this* on Mary's midnight gloom, shed a glimmering, cheering light. *This*, faint as it was, aroused and animated her desponding soul; it seemed to her as sent in mercy to direct her to her son, and she lost no time in taking the path to which it pointed. Five weeks after the birth of her child did she set out in her weak state, without money, on foot, to carry her infant nearly four hundred miles (thither and back again,) on a road and to a place with which she was totally unacquainted. O Nature! how powerful are the feelings which thou hast implanted in the maternal bosom! how do they set at defiance all opposing difficulties and dangers! how do they grasp at, or create, objects to which hope may cling, or on which it may rest to spurn away despair! Never, perhaps, were those feelings more strongly evinced than in this instance; never, perhaps, were their exhilarating and beneficial influence more powerfully experienced.

An object, apparently, more truly wretched than poor Mary, as she pursued her journey, could, one would think, scarcely be imagined: weak, languid, poor, and friendless,; plodding, with an infant in her arms, through the alternate vicissitudes of heat and wet, of dust and dirt; now sinking beneath the sun's oppressive rays, now dripping with the driving storm; without a husband to support her; a beggar and an unwelcome obtruder wherever she came.

And yet, with all these aggravating circumstances, poor Mary was, in reality, perhaps less miserable than many, even of the sons and daughters of affluence. So little does happiness depend upon external circumstances; so comparatively impartially has God distributed good and evil amongst his creatures, even in this life, that the most miserable are not without their consolations, nor the most prosperous without their sorrows. Mary, it is true, seemed to have only *one* hope, one animating expectation, but it was one which appealed to and warmed the heart; it was one in which the whole faculties of her soul and body were embarked; it was one which nature, conscience, and God approved. It set difficulties at defiance, and it penetrated, or dispersed the deepest gloom that despondency attempted to cast around her. But what is the hope? what is the source of consolation, to the *unnatural mother, who forsakes her sucking child?* who abandons her offspring to the guidance and the care of others, or initiates them *herself*, into scenes of frivolity, vanity, and vice;—who smothers every maternal feeling, and flies to scenes of tumult and dissipation, in search of that happiness which they cannot bestow! Listless and dissatisfied with herself and all around her, possessing no source of consolation, no object to arouse and stimulate to spirited exertions, her conscience upbraiding and the world failing her, she is an object much more demanding our pity than poor Mary, under all her external sufferings.

Labour and sorrow are the lot of humanity, and *they* must be unhappy indeed who, from a mixed company, cannot select those with whom they would be unwilling to exchange situations. So, perhaps, thought poor Mary, as she sat by the side of the kitchen fire of the Inn at Folkingham, regarding with looks of attention and pity two poor chimney sweepers' boys, who were getting their frugal supper, before the same fire. They had been sent for from a distance, to sweep some chimneys early in the morning, and were now taking their scanty meal, before they retired to obtain, by a few hours sleep, a short respite from their sufferings. Mary long viewed them attentively; perhaps the sufferings of her lost boy might be connected with the commiseration which she felt for these poor oppressed children. However that might be, she continued to gaze upon them, till the younger, who sat with his back towards her, turned his sooty face, and fixing his eyes upon her, regarded her for a few seconds with attention, then springing up he exclaimed, "*MY MOTHER! that's MY MOTHER!*" and in an instant was in her arms. The affectionate and astonished Mary, on hearing his voice, in a moment recognised her boy, and clasped him to her bosom; but she could not speak, till a flood of tears having relieved her almost bursting heart, she gave utterance to her feelings.

After the confusion and the agitating sensation, which this unexpected rencontre had occasioned amongst both actors and spectators, were in some degree subsided, the master of the boy, who was present, was particularly questioned how he came by him. His account was as follows:—He was walking on his business, in the neighbourhood of Sleaford, where he resides, when he met a ragged woman with a little boy, whom she was beating most unmercifully. On enquiry, she told him, that "she was in great distress, that she had a long way to go, that the boy, her son, was very obstinate, and that she did not know how to get him along with her." This led to further conversation, which ended in her offering to sell the boy to him as an apprentice, for two guineas. The bargain was soon struck, and the lad was regularly bound, the woman making oath to his being her own son. There did not appear to be any reason for questioning the account of the master, especially as it was corroborated by the boy, with this addition, that the woman was beating him so unmercifully, as she had frequently done before, because he would not call her mother.

The story soon became generally known in the place, and, through the exertions of Mr. Welbourn and others, a subscription was raised for poor Mary, and the little chimney-sweeper, who was soon cleaned, clothed, and transformed into a very different looking little being,—

> "And restored to his mother, no longer needs creep
> Through lanes, courts, and alleys, a poor little sweep."

After they had stopped for some time to rest and refresh themselves, the mother and son had places taken for them in the coach to proceed to Loudon. Thither they departed, with hearts overflowing with gratitude both to their heavenly and earthly benefactors.

THE

CHIMNEY SWEEPER'S BOY.*

SIXTH EDITION, NOW CONSIDERABLY ALTERED.

Thrice had returning Flora, with her train,
Chased the hard-hearted tyrant from the plain;
Thrice had she scatter'd wide her leaves and flowers,
Fann'd them with zephyrs, and refresh'd with showers;
Thrice summon'd all the songsters of the groves
To pour their praises, and declare their loves;
Since first the new-born Edwin smiling prest,
And stirr'd strange transports in his mother's breast;
Since first his parents, doating on his charms,
Clasp'd the young stranger with enraptured arms;
Gaz'd on the ripening beauties of their boy,
And left no place to yield to other joy:

* Though this poem is not a literal relation of facts, it is nearly such.

For though possessing every earthly bliss,
The rest were all absorb'd and lost in this;
While each returning season served to prove
How well the child deserved the parent's love.

The mother's daily pleasing task had shed
Unwonted knowledge on his infant head;
Had taught him, morn and eve, his voice to raise
In supplicating prayers and hymns of praise;
Instinctively he seem'd to tune his voice
To every air, but this his constant choice:—

"Father! heavenly Father! hear
Infant praises, infant prayer;
Let me, heavenly Father, raise,
Morn and eve, my voice in praise.

Heavenly Father! please impart
Love for thee to this my heart;
May that love be ever mine,
May that heart be wholly thine.

Father! heavenly Father! hear
Infant praises, infant prayer;
Let me, heavenly Father, raise,
Morn and eve, my voice in praise."

It was a simple, pleasing, plaintive air,
Which when he sung, his mother loved to share,
While to her side the gentle boy would creep,
And, as his hand she prest, they both would weep.

At early dawn, oft, with elastic tread,
He traced the lawn which round the mansion spread,
Wild and delighted as a lamb at play,
As meek, as innocent, as light and gay.
There as he once enraptured chanced to spy
The gaudy beauties of a butterfly,
With eager haste he strove the prize to gain,
And chased it on from flower to flower in vain,
Till to the lawn's extremest verge he prest,
Where the deep fence and mound his feet arrest;
Sad on the brink he disappointed stands,
The fly escaping from his outstretch'd hands.
A wandering gipsy passing saw the boy,
Gazed on his costly dress with looks of joy;
His aim she saw, and stretch'd her wither'd arm,
He seized the proffer'd aid without alarm;
Then sprung away, as by her hand he held,
And as her cheering voice to speed impell'd.
They quickly gain'd the confines of the wood,
Nor long the gipsy hesitating stood,
Clasp'd in her arms she bore, without delay
Through briers and thorns her trembling prize away,

Nor stopt till, in the woods profoundest shade,
She reach'd a rocky dell, by torrents made:
A fearful place, by human steps untrod,
The croaking raven's undisturb'd abode.

The struggling Edwin shriek'd and shriek'd again,
Vain were his shrieks, and all his struggles vain;
Stript of his clothes, in filthy tatters drest,
He sobb'd till worn out nature sunk to rest.
When the deep shades of night around were spread,
Far with the sleeping child the gipsy sped.
From parents, home, and every comfort torn,
To other scenes the wretched child was borne;
A wandering outcast, doom'd, half-clad, to roam,
And heat and cold endure without a home;
With want, and sin, and misery to abide,
While all the vagrant train his griefs deride;
Taught and compell'd to beg from door to door,
To feel, indeed, distress, yet feign much more.

But who shall paint the wretched parents' woe?
The world a blank, no joy, no peace they know;
Profusion spreads for them in vain her store,
E'en nature smiles in vain, — she charms no more.
The restless, tedious day brings no relief,
The night no sleep to mitigate their grief:

Yet still they cry, with piercing anguish torn,
At morn, "Would God 'twere night!" at night,
"Would God 'twere morn!"

Meanwhile a vagrant life poor Edwin led,
Through three long years he begg'd his daily bread;
Till as the beldame led from street to street,
A chimney-sweeper there they chanced to meet;
The iron-visaged tyrant eyed the boy,—
His active step, his slender frame, — with joy;
He saw him fitted for his dreadful trade,
And soon the price of life and freedom paid,
He bore him, weeping, to his deep-sunk cell,
Midst gloom and filth, and rags and want to dwell.

Poor wretched sufferer! is this freedom's shore?
Are there no slaves in England? Never more
Let Britain boast that her's is freedom's land,
While foot of infant slave pollutes her strand.
The innocent, the helpless, native poor
Are bought and sold, e'en at our very door!
Are scourged, are wounded, crippled, maim'd, and
driven
To tasks more horrid than were ever given
To other slaves! to climb where brutes would die,
Through smothering soot, to rocking turrets high;

Through rugged flues, that tear the tender frame,
Through death's most hideous portal, scorching flame;
To hang, close wedged, immoveable, where none
Can aid impart till life itself is gone;
Or waste away, with festering sore on sore,
Till outraged nature can support no more!
And are there slaves like these? There are! But where?
In every street their piercing cry we hear,
Yet heed it not, — because 'twas always there.

Such was poor Edwin now, a hopeless slave
Where other slaves are free, — no law to save
A free-born Briton from a tyrant's power;
A slave to passion's slave; doom'd, every hour,
To eat affliction's bread, and, from the cup
Of woe, to drain the dregs and drink them up.
His fearful task t' explore, from day to day,
The chimney's horrid, dark, and rugged way;
And blindfold through obstructing soot to climb,
With bleeding wounds from lacerating lime.
Oft were the tyrant's secret blows and scourge
Applied, the infant's trembling limbs to urge
Along the untried way, — but all in vain:
Down, down he fell, o'ercome with fear and pain.
At length he reach'd a part which sloped away,
And there, involved in soot, he panting lay,

The big black drops fast rolling from his eyes,
Midst bursting sobs and plaintive stifled cries;
By desperation urged, resolved to lie
In that secure retreat unreach'd, and die.

New threats and promises in vain assail,
Nor threats nor promises to move avail;
At length the blazing straw's thick smothering smoke
Deprived of breath and strength,—his senses took,
And down he fell; with scorn the tyrant smiled,
And, with his blows, to life restored the child.
Restored to misery, want, disease, and pain!
Sore was the conflict, ere he could attain
The dreadful art; nor did he find success
One comfort gain, or make one trouble less:
Still doom'd through heat and cold, through frost and snow,
O'er cutting ice barefooted oft to go;
And, long ere morn, to pace the silent street,
Through drifted snow, while hail and driving sleet
Against his naked bosom keenly beat.
Such was poor Edwin's task till evening's close,
Rejoiced if that glad hour could give repose;
But, if he fail'd the stinted sum to gain,
His cries for food at eve were all in vain;
Tired, hungry, shivering, wretched, and forlorn,
Stretch'd on a sooty sack, he wept till morn.

When six long, lingering months had crept away,
One winter's morn, long ere the break of day,
He, with another shivering wretch, was sent
To good Alcander's, and with joy they went;
The way was tedious, but full well they knew
None cold or hungry ever thence withdrew.
With joy they went, though deep the drifted snow,
Though cold and loud the whistling wind did blow;
For all Alcander loved, but most the poor,
Who, if deserving, never left his door
Unblest; his feeling generous heart
Was always prompting comfort to impart;
His chief delight to mitigate distress,
To aid, advise, encourage, praise, and bless;
Such too, Nerina, tender-hearted fair
Deserving such a husband's love to share.

When to Alcander's hospitable dome
The shivering Edwin and his partner come,
Barefooted on the marble hearth they stand,
The spacious room extends on either hand,
The glimmering taper sheds a feeble light,
And faintly shows the gilding glittering bright;
The distant mirrors long perspectives throw,
And other far-off sweeps, and glimmering tapers show.
The wondering Edwin silent stood, and threw
His eyes around, struck with the splendid view;

Strong recollections rush'd upon his mind
Of scenes like this, though faintly now defined;
Scenes once beloved, and still to memory dear:
Poor Edwin sigh'd, and check'd the starting tear.

Now from his back the cumbering rags he threw,
And o'er his face the sooty cap he drew,
Then up the dark and dismal flue ascends,
The soot, in clouds of dust, his course attends;
The room he pass'd (as up the flue he crept)
In which Alcander and Nerina slept.
His clattering brush beat loud from side to side,
The good Nerina heard, and hearing sigh'd;
Then thus she spoke: "Alcander, hark! how loud
The wintry tempest howls, from every cloud
Thick fall the sleet and snow, while, by the frost
Fast bound, the snow-clad lake is lost;
Yet here we in security are blest,
And, though the tempest rages, safely rest:
Then let us feel for those exposed to all
The season's fury,—let us hear the call
Of those who need our aid,—of yon poor boy,
Whom we with thoughtless cruelty employ,
(Our comfort to promote) even in a task
Unfit for him to ply, or us to ask.
Oh, my Alcander! let us ne'er again
Afflict the *infant* poor with needless pain!

How my heart bleeds to think, that in a morn
Like this the child hath been from slumber torn,
And forced, at such an hour, through frost and snow,
Barefooted, loaded, and half-clad to go, —
Perhaps unfed, — perhaps, — but let me hold,
Too horrid are such miseries to unfold.
We, my Alcander, never should oppress,
We should, *above all others*, seek to bless :
For we have known distress, distress severe,
Yet found a hand to wipe away the tear,—
The hand of God ; yet had we greatly err'd !
For we to HIM an earthly child preferr'd.
Then let us bow with reverence to his will,
And his commands with grateful hearts fulfil."

Now all within was hush'd, for Edwin now
The room had pass'd, and found the chimney grow
More choked with soot as more it sloped away ;
'Twas warm, and here the wearied Edwin lay ;
His head and arms he clear'd, that he might rest,
And, while of silence undisturb'd, possess'd,
Commune with God : to pray he never fail'd
Or morn or eve, howe'er by toil assail'd.
The sooty cap from face and head he drew,
He raised his sable hands, his eyes of blue ;
To Him who is the friendless infant's friend,
Who sends relief when none besides can send.

Poor Edwin's little heart o'erflow'd with love,
He felt he had a friend, — a friend above;
He felt, and wept with joy; he raised his voice,
And sung aloud the hymn so long his choice.

"Father! heavenly Father! hear
Infant praises, infant prayer;
Let me, heavenly Father, raise,
Morn and eve, my voice in praise.

Heavenly Father! please impart
Love for thee to this my heart;
May that love be ever mine,
May that heart be wholly thine.

Father! heavenly Father! hear
Infant praises, infant prayer;
Let me, heavenly Father, raise,
Morn and eve, my song of praise."

A sweeter voice than Edwin's never flow'd
From any human lips; he raised it loud,
And, though the wind was raging wild and high,
His heavenly notes were heard, as from the sky.
Nerina heard; — 'twas fancy first she deem'd;
She raised her head, — she heard it still; — it seem'd

The hymn of spirit in the midway air,—
The spirit of her Edwin *might* be there;
The voice, the notes, the words, were his; they all
Her dear, lamented Edwin's form recal;
Strong palpitations agitate her heart,
A tremor seized her frame, with sudden start
She grasp'd Alcander's arm,—"Hark! hark!" she cried.
"It is the sweep," Alcander said, and sigh'd.
"The *sweep!*" Nerina shriek'd, with transports wild,
"Alcander! 'tis my *child! my* child! my *child!*"
It was indeed her son, her Edwin dear,
The source of all her joys, her griefs, her fear;
Her long-lost child, now rescued from distress,
Again his parents' longing arms to bless.

Oh! ye who are the guardians of the state!
From whom her laws proceed, — ye wise and great,
Permit not this oppression in the land.
On you these infants call; extend the hand
That can protection give; of all the slaves
That base, unfeeling, sordid avarice craves,
These are the most oppress'd; they loudest call
For that which *Britons* should extend to all,—
Nor will their cry be vain; for there is near,
One friend who loves, and will not fail to hear:
The greatest monarch on an earthly throne
Hath pledged his word to make their cause his own:

Though senators may laugh, and lords may jest,
At infant sufferings, infants yet shall rest
In peace and safety;—GEORGE THE FOURTH their
friend—
Their needless sufferings soon will have an end.

S. R.

THE

Following Extracts from a Work of the late Dr. Buchan,

ENTITLED

"ADVICE TO MOTHERS,"

Deserve particular attention.

"But there is another set of devoted beings more pitiable still than those which I have now described — I mean the children that are bound apprentices to chimney-sweepers. If any creature can exist in a state of greater wretchedness, or is a juster object of commiseration than a boy who is forced to clean chimneys in this country, I am very much mistaken. Half naked in the most bitter cold, he creeps along the streets by break of day, the ice cutting through his feet, his legs bent, and his body twisted. In this state, he is compelled to work his way up those dirty, noisome passages, many of which are almost too narrow for a cat to climb. In order to subdue the terror which he must feel in his first attempts, his savage master often lights up some wet straw in the fire-place, which leaves the poor creature no alternative but that of certain suffocation, or of instantly getting to the top. I have witnessed still greater cruelty: I have more than once seen a boy, when a chimney was all in a blaze, forced down the vent, like a bundle of wet rags, to extinguish the flame.

"Perhaps I shall be told, that boys so trained are necessary. I deny the assertion. Chimneys are kept clean without such cruel and dangerous means, not only in many countries on the Continent, but even in some parts of our own island, where the houses are much higher than in London. In North Britain, for instance, a bunch of furze or broom answers the purpose, and does the business cheaper and better. One man stands at the top and another at the bottom of the chimney, when a rope is let down by means of a ball, and the bunch of furze or of broom, being properly fastened on, is pulled up and down till the chimney is quite cleaned. The little trouble and expense attending the operation are the strongest incitements to repeat it so often as to preclude the possibility of a chimney's ever taking fire. Is this the case in London, though hundreds of lives are every year sacrificed to the most barbarous method of preventing danger? How vain shall we find the boasts that are made of mighty improvements in the metropolis of the British empire, if we fairly consider that it is at least a century behind the meanest village in the kingdom, in almost every thing that regards the preservation of human life.

"My late worthy friend, Jonas Hanway, who literally went about doing good, used all his influence to ameliorate the condition of those unhappy creatures; which, in a certain degree, he effected. But there are some customs that can be thoroughly mended, only by being completely abolished. While boys are forced up chimneys they must be miserable, whatever laws are made for their relief. A law prohibiting the practice altogether, would be at once laying the axe to the root of the tree; and the evil admits of no other remedy.

"Had Mr. Hanway taken up the matter upon this ground, he had spirit and perseverance sufficient to have carried it through, and to have obtained an act of parliament for the effectual relief of the most wretched beings on the face of the earth. He confined his benevolent exertions to a partial alleviation of their miseries, because it had never occurred to him that the *climbing boys*, as he calls them, were wholly unnecessary. What a pity that he did not carry his views a little farther, as, in that case, he certainly would not have remained satisfied with any thing short of their total emancipation from such cruel and useless bondage!

But surely there is humanity enough in both houses of parliament to take up this subject, without any other appeal to their feelings than a bare representation of facts.

Many touches more would be necessary to finish the melancholy picture of the wretchedness of young chimney-sweepers. It is enough for me to sketch the principal outlines, in hopes that some person more at leisure may be induced to lay on the internal colouring. In addition, however, to the miseries already described, I must not omit the malignity of the disorders with which those poor creatures, if they live long enough, are almost sure to be afflicted. They are not only deformed and stunted in their growth, but, in consequence of having their pores clogged, and the surface of their bodies continually covered with a coat of dirt composed of soot, sweat, &c., they are subject to various maladies unknown to the rest of mankind.

I need only give an instance of one of those diseases, which is called by the sufferers the *Soot-wart*, but which the late Mr. Pott has very properly named the *Chimney-sweepers' Cancer*. He describes it as a ragged, ill-looking sore, with hard and rising edges,—rapid in its progress, painful in all its attacks, and most certainly destructive in its event. Extirpation by the knife, on its first appearance, and the immediate removal of the part affected, he looks upon as the only chance of putting a stop to, or preventing the fatal issue of the disease. His reflection on the subject does equal honour to his heart and to his understanding. " The fate of these people," says he, " seems singularly hard. In their early infancy they are frequently treated with great brutality, and almost starved with cold and hunger. They are thrust up narrow, and sometimes hot chimneys, where they are bruised, burned, and almost suffocated; and when they get to puberty, they become peculiarly liable to a most noisome, painful, and fatal disease."

EXTRACTS FROM

A LETTER, BY J. C. HUDSON,

TO THE MISTRESSES OF FAMILIES.

LADIES,

I AM not fastidious or over sensitive, far from sentimental, very far from puritanical; yet I own that I am shocked at your continued apathy on a subject so very exciting as that of the employment of young children in sweeping chimneys. I should be sorry to have reason for believing that this apathy exists, but by the want of reflection on the subject. On the contrary, I feel convinced that want of reflection is your only crime: you deem the matter one of no importance, and refuse to look into it; or perhaps you give way to a false delicacy which bids you shun a subject so entirely vulgar, filthy, and uninteresting. On this side at least you are vulnerable. You will not have it said that false delicacy deterred you from the performance of any one of the duties of humanity. Here, then, let me fix my attention. In the midst of this mass of filth, squalidness, poverty, and sufferings of every kind, behold an object which to your regard prefers the claim of helpless infancy, frequently of unprotected orphanage, and sometimes of that still heavier misfortune, illegimate birth and total absence of parental cognisance. Will you turn away? will you let the very magnitude of the evil and of the necessity for interposition be the cause of your refusing to interpose? I feel confident that you will not, and that you will hear me in this cause, not only with patience, or even with attention, but with deep interest.

We have been so long used to the morning cry of the chimney-sweeper, and to the sight of the grim, black, brawny master, carrying a little brush or scraper or other light implement in his hand, and followed by a shivering half-naked boy, stooping and shuffling as well as his old shoes will let him, under the weight of a bag full of soot; that we are apt to forget, or rather we are not apt to remember, that these are human creatures; that, that little creeping object is a child of almost the tenderest age; and that his bare legs, and often bare feet, though concealed from our view by their sable vesture, are but thinly partitioned from the frosty air and the snow-covered ground. He partakes in some degree of the fate of the negro: we lose, in his sooty complexion, all sympathy with him as a fellow-creature; forgetting that he was ever one of ourselves, or that a single plunge into a bath would restore the relationship.

"A little water clears him of the deed."

I really believe that to his filthy disguise is to be attributed all the indifference which is manifested towards the miserable condition of infant chimney-sweepers. I feel almost assured that were one of these unfortunate little children to be washed and presented in the undisguised beauty and simplicity of childhood, as the person intended to perform the frightful task of climbing up a foul chimney forty or fifty feet high by means of his knees and shoulders, no person would have the brutality to let him be so abused. It is habit indeed which has reconciled to us a practice, abhorrent under any disguise; but habit could never have conquered nature, had not the efforts of the latter been weakened by the distance at which the excessive filth, and complete disfigurement of the victims in whose behalf those efforts should have been made, placed them from us. If I may be allowed a tristful kind of pun on the subject, their disgusting and painful profession has thrown them into the *shade*.

My own way in all such matters is to call to mind my own sensations and reflections when the subject first came before me. I remember well, that, when a boy, the exercise of the chimney-sweeper's function was an affair which engaged all my curiosity. I never missed getting up at the same time as the servant did, on such an occasion; and witnessed the performance with a most intense interest not unmixed with a feeling of horror. In winter I could not help remarking, at the very first, that the atmosphere of the fireless kitchen, which made me shiver, seemed to be a relief to the poor boy, just come in from the street. There was often a dreadful harshness in the voice and manner of the master-sweep, as the little boy prepared for his work, by slipping off his upper garment, and drawing a sooty cap all over his face. The mysterious cloth was appended to the mantle-piece by means of two forks, and the boy, with a scraper in one hand, and brush in the other, slipped behind it and disappeared. I used to listen for the sound of his body rubbing against the sides of the chimney, and catch with eagerness every sound of his half-stifled voice as it answered the gruff call of the master from below; and when I thought him near the top, I used to run out into the street to see him emerge. At first the rattling of his scraper was heard against the sides of the chimney-pot, and then his shrill voice announcing the success of his achievement. Then appeared his brush, and immediately afterwards the little hero himself, waving it victoriously, and shouting, so that the whole neighbourhood might know that he had arrived in safety at the top of his chimney. Resting himself for a moment, I have seen him take off his cap, with the air, and with some portion, perhaps, of the feeling of a warrior of old, relieving his aching brow from the pressure of the ponderous casque, and taking a refreshing draught of cool and wholesome air.

But if in this picture a spectator should discover one spot more luminous or rather less sombrous in comparison than the general aspect, some little reflection of that sun of divine benignity from which no earthly lot is so wretched as to be wholly excluded, let it not be pleaded in extenuation of a practice which almost obscures every ray of that sun from the horizon of a human creature's existence. Let the question be fairly stated: are not these poor children most barbarously sacrificed? and is not the sacrifice wholly unnecessary? For what, in the first place, but a most perfect sacrifice of every thing which sweetens life, as it regards the individual, and of the life itself, as it regards society, is the taking of a child at the age of six or eight to initiate him in the business of sweeping chimneys by means of his own body? In this service only, the very worst of all that a huge and crowded metropolis requires, are children employed at such a very tender age. Destined to any other occupation than this, however vile or laborious, the human creature has, in its childhood, a few years of freedom and of pleasure; but the unhappy being, selected for the trade of a chimney-sweeper, must enter upon it almost as soon as he arrives at the free use of his limbs. No interval of untasked life is permitted him: his very dawn of life is overcast; and that period which has been held by some philosophers to be the happiest of human existence, is to him a period of the greatest suffering; of suffering unrequited and unrelieved. Do you think that I represent the cruelty of this practice in too strong a light? The facts which I shall shortly detail will, I am sure, convince you that my picture is poor and spiritless in comparison with the reality. But imagine for a moment, let any woman, though she may be the most inflexible of housewives, imagine, a child of from five to eight years of age first made to climb a chimney; to ascend a perpendicular aperture (to say nothing about its foulness) thirty, forty, or fifty feet high, by no other means than the sticking of his shoulders, knees, and elbows against the sides of the chimney, and the shifting of them upwards alternately (no matter for the tenderness of his skin or the rugged hardness of the brickwork). Can the stoutest hearted man think of making such an attempt without shuddering? what, then, must be the agony which a child endures, when compelled to enter on this frightful task! what the cruelty, the torture he undergoes, sufficient to overcome his dread, and make him yield to this as the less of two evils. And when these poor children have gone through their course of instruction, a series of horrors which shun the light, except when, as occasionally happens, they comprise the immediate death of the victim, and fall under the notice of the coroner, what have they attained? an art, which their youth alone qualifies them to practise, which is full of danger, degradation, disgust, and the keenest of suffering, and which, after all, in ninety-nine cases out of every hundred, might be effectually superseded by the use of a broom!

Is it possible that women, whose love of infants is said to be so strong and so general, can persist in employing little children for this purpose, even if there were good reason for preferring their performance to the effect of the sweeping machine. If the latter were costly, attended with trouble, clumsy, and ineffectual, still who would not put up with some inconvenience and expense, rather than be the means of continuing a practice so brutal as the use of climbing boys? While there was any other mode by which this necessary operation could be performed, I should almost have supposed it impossible that a woman could bear her own reflection as she heard the little wretch working his way at the hazard of life and limbs, through a cold, stinking chimney, perhaps the tenth that he has climbed that morning, and without any other hope at the conclusion of his day's labour than that of resting his wearied little frame in a dark loathsome cellar among soot and cinders, ill fed and half naked; until the chillness of daybreak should summon him to take his shivering rounds, calling with his weak treble voice for fresh opportunities of exercising his painful skill, for the benefit, not of himself, but of his sordid and too frequently brutal master.

Perhaps you think that I dwell too long on what all must admit, the wretchedness, the misery, the disgusting nature of this employment. But I will not be so readily satisfied with your admission of these parts of the subject. I will not spare you the examination of even the most shocking details. If your heart be made of penetrable stuff I will make an impression on it, which shall frequently embitter your hours of quiet reflection, until effaced by a consciousness of having done all that lies in your power to remove the evil which caused it.

Now that the sweeping of chimneys by the machine is found to be such a practicable and even simple operation, it appears surprising that it should not have been resorted to long ago, for the purpose of abolishing the cruel method of sending up climbing children; but that surprise vanishes before the still more extraordinary fact, that now when the matter has undergone discussion, when the horrors of the child-abusing system have been exposed, when the equal advantages and almost universal adaptation of the machine have been proved beyond doubt, and when all that remains is with housekeepers themselves, generally speaking with the mistresses of families, to make their election between the broom and the child.

INTRODUCTORY ADDRESS

TO A

PAMPHLET ON THE SUBJECT OF CLIMBING BOYS.

By Mrs. Alexander, of York.

The author of this tract, having, from early life, felt a degree of commiseration for climbing boys, which has seldom allowed her to pass one of them unnoticed or unpitied; it was cause of rejoicing to find, by "Tales of the Poor," and through some other means, that this degraded class of society had become the objects of public attention, particularly in London and Sheffield.

This afforded a convincing proof, that "He whose tender mercies are over all his works" had heard the secret cries of many of those who might be said to have no human helper, and was about to effect their deliverance from the hard and cruel bondage with which many of them are still made to serve. But as their situation, does not yet seem to have awakened that general feeling, which their abject state, on investigation, will no doubt appear to demand, the circulation of a small pamphlet, delineating their sufferings, seemed a primary step to pursue, for promoting that amelioration of their condition, which has, for some years, deeply interested the feelings of the writer, and has very frequently cláimed her serious consideration.

With this object in view, leave has been obtained from the author of "Tales of the Poor *," to make a selection of such parts as are adapted to the present purpose; to which are annexed, extracts from other sources of information, and observations which have occurred to the author. A hope is cherished, that if the facts and statements relative to these objects of Christian compassion can but obtain the careful perusal of persons of different religious denominations, their case will not long remain unregarded by a benevolent public.

In all places where the Society of Friends have any influence, it is particularly desirable, that they should ascertain, if it is not in their power to excite the attention and feelings of other benevolent characters, and to assist them in devising means for mitigating the sorrows of these poor, oppressed children,

* Tales of the Poor may be had of the publisher and venders of this tract at 1*s*. 6*d*. in boards.

of the one great Father of the Universe, till the cause of humanity may become so far triumphant, as to provide means for cleansing our chimneys without endangering the lives, or injuring the health of any of our fellow-creatures.

Though little more may appear necessary to introduce the consideration of the subject, yet a few hints suggest themselves to some classes of society who may be most capable of feeling sympathy for these objects of pity, by endeavouring to make their cases, as much as may be, our own.

Let us, then, who are mothers of children, reflect what would have been our feelings if, like many poor widows, we had been left with sons to provide for, and that no situation had offered more eligible than placing them out to be climbing boys. Could we have endured the idea, that those who had been nursed at our bosoms, with all a mother's tenderness; those who had repaid the toils of maternal solicitude with the sweet smiles and endearing actions of unconscious innocence; should, at the early age of from five to seven years, when probably their natural or acquired dread of darkness was in full operation, be forced into the rough and obscure recesses of a chimney, in the manner described in this pamphlet?

Though the dangers of the first attempt should happily be got over, and time have somewhat blunted the keenness of the feelings attendant on the first outset, could we support the reflection, that nearly all their days, during seven years' servitude, were to be dragged over in a degree of filth and wretchedness which make them " as the offscouring of all things," and their nights passed on a bag of soot, probably with very little covering; while, at the same time, many children, equally poor, have the enjoyment of mixing with others in the daytime, and, in the night, of reposing themselves on beds of comparative ease and indulgence? Where is the mother that can " think of these things" and not be willing " to do what her hands find to do" towards preventing such accumulated suffering, or lessening its pressure upon those who are still labouring under it.

And you, young men, who are placed as apprentices to those who furnish you, as is meet they should, with every necessary comfort, shut not your ears against the cry of the oppressed. Consider, they are your brethren — the offspring of the one Universal Parent. Read the account of their abject condition, and, when contrasting it with your own situation, reflect, I entreat you, if you can, in any way more acceptably, show your gratitude for unmerited mercies, than by contributing all in your power towards carrying into effect such plans as may be devised for their help and assistance. This you will no doubt be inclined for, if, while viewing, as you often have opportunities, these objects of commiseration wandering our streets, you are disposed individually to query — "Who made me to differ from another? and what have I that I did not receive?"

But it is not their bodily condition alone, however deplorable that may be found, in a great number of instances, which claims the attention and redress of their fellow-professors of that religion which teaches, so far as its Divine Author's example is followed, "to seek out and to save that which would otherwise be lost." There is every reason to conclude their state of mental degradation bears a full proportion to their outward appearance of wretchedness. *

As climbing boys are brought up under those who had their feelings of tenderness early blunted by their disgusting profession, and who, probably, have received little, if any, education themselves; what means of improvement can we therefore suppose such masters will provide for their apprentices? The employment of climbing boys, however, is usually accomplished while others are reposing in their ceiled houses, by

* The author was witness, about two years ago, to a proof of the correctness of this observation. Two poor climbing boys, on a very slight provocation, gave vent to their rage, not only in the most abusive conduct, but by uttering a strain of foul and horrid language, that evinced a state of depravity, at which it could have scarcely been supposed their youthful minds had arrived.

which they are more at leisure than most others, for attending day or evening schools, were they not excluded this advantage by their want of cleanliness. Indeed, their continuing for six days out of the seven in a filthy condition, is one principal cause of their present state of degradation; and it is supposed to be the origin of the painful and dangerous disease mentioned in this little work.

Thus, while others of their age can fill up their time in some useful occupation, or, at least, may be allowed to mix with their associates in innocent recreation, the poor climbing boys, like the Chandalas of our eastern hemisphere, are, in effect, daily insulted with the language of "Stand off, I am better, if not holier, than thou!" and through summer's heat, and winter's cold, drag out their days, shortened, it is true, by accumulated sufferings, in idleness and misery, ignorant of the means of rendering themselves useful and happy in this life; and, it is to be feared, generally speaking, lamentably ignorant of the important means of preparation for that which is to come.

ANN ALEXANDER.

York, 11*th Month*, 1816.

RESOLUTIONS

Unanimously agreed to at a General Meeting of the

INHABITANTS OF LONDON AND WESTMINSTER,

Held by public Advertisement, at Freemasons' Hall, on Saturday, the 7th of June, 1817,

HIS ROYAL HIGHNESS THE DUKE OF SUSSEX IN THE CHAIR.

---

1. THAT the employment of climbing boys to sweep chimneys is a cruel and unnatural practice, and ought, as soon as possible, to be abolished.

2. That this practice, which is of comparatively modern date, and only partially adopted in this country, is as unnecessary as it is inhuman, the work being capable of being performed, in all cases, as effectually by mechanical means as by climbing boys.

3. That though it appears to this meeting to have been the uniform plan of the Society to supply the established chimney-sweepers with machines, and to afford them every encouragement in the use of them; and though it also appears that they would be essentially benefited by the adoption of them; yet, that from the prejudices of master chimney-sweepers, and of many servants and others, against the use of the machine, this meeting is convinced, by experience,

that they can never be fully and beneficially introduced so long as the employment of climbing boys shall be tolerated by the Legislature.

4. That this meeting, therefore, deems it expedient to petition Parliament to pass an act entirely prohibiting master chimney-sweepers from taking any more apprentices to be used as climbing boys; and also from using their own offspring, or any other children, for that purpose.

5. That the petition to the Honourable the House of Commons, now read, be adopted by this meeting, of which the following is a copy:—

"Sheweth,

"That your petitioners, being deeply impressed with a sense of the sufferings experienced by the children employed as climbing boys, for the purpose of cleansing chimneys, the helpless victims of a trade most justly stigmatised by the Legislature as fraught with various complicated miseries, are desirous that such inhuman practice should be totally abolished.

"That various circumstances of cruelty and oppression appear to your petitioners as inseparable from the trade as now carried on, and which would be altogether obviated by the substitution of machinery for the purpose.

"Your petitioners, therefore, most earnestly request of your Honourable House, to take into consideration the situation of these unfortunate children, and to adopt such measures as in your wisdom may appear most proper for speedily and effectually preventing any children from being so employed in future."

6. That the offer of the Honourable H. G. Bennet, one of the Committee of the Society for superseding the Necessity of Climbing Boys, to present the said petition, be accepted; and that the representatives of London, Westminster, and Southwark, and of the counties of Middlesex, Essex, Kent, and Surrey, be respectfully and individually solicited to support the same.

7. That this meeting strongly recommends to the country at large to form auxiliary societies for promoting the objects of this meeting.

8. That these resolutions be published under the direction of the Committee.

9. That, in the event of the Legislature being induced to pass an act for prohibiting the use of climbing boys, it be a recommendation to the Society to take into consideration the situation of such infant children as may be thrown out of employment, and to

promote their welfare by attending to their health, and to their future prospects in life.

His Royal Highness having quitted the chair:

10. Resolved, That the cordial and grateful thanks of this meeting are in an especial manner due, and are hereby given, to His Royal Highness the Duke of Sussex, for his condescending and ready acquiescence in the application of the Committee, by taking the chair on this occasion, and by his gracious and able conduct in it.

Signed by order,

W. JONES, Secretary.

PETITION

OF THE

COMPANY OF CUTLERS WITHIN HALLAMSHIRE, AND OTHER INHABITANTS OF THE TOWN AND NEIGHBOURHOOD OF SHEFFIELD,

TO THE HONOURABLE HOUSE OF COMMONS,

IN 1817.

WE, &c., humbly represent to your Honourable House, That during the last century the practice of cleaning chimneys by means of young children being sent up them, has become almost general in this country.

That your petitioners are of opinion that the said practice is inimical to the prosperity of the state, being destructive of the morals, the health, and often the lives of the children so employed; compelling them in their tender age to the performance of a daily task which is cruel and unnatural, and which at the same time prevents them from obtaining that learning, and enjoying that relaxation, which are essential to their afterwards becoming useful and respectable members of the community.

That your petitioners are of opinion, that if the poor children apprenticed as climbing boys had the same chance for life as other children have, there would not be employment for more than one in twenty of them at their own trade when grown too big to get up chimneys; and that they therefore must either learn other trades, or what is more probable, become pests and burdens to society.

That your petitioners are decidedly of opinion, that there is no occasion whatever to employ children as climbing boys, because the practice, even in this country, is but of modern date; because they are at this time very little, if at all, employed in another part of the United Kingdom, in which the houses are frequently much higher, and, consequently, the chimneys much more difficult to sweep by mechanical means than in England; and, because that in this town one man, with a comparatively imperfect machine, in the course of twelve months, swept nearly 1300 chimneys, in spite of a considerable degree of prejudice which then prevailed with many, against the use of machines.

The chimneys of the poor, your petitioners are of opinion, may be swept with machines, even cheaper than by climbing boys, as they are generally very easy to clean, and may be done at the convenience of the sweeper, when he is not employed at larger houses.

That though your petitioners are thus fully convinced, both by the experience of themselves and others, that the cleansing of all chimneys may be readily and effectually performed by mechanical means, they are nevertheless persuaded that climbing boys will never be generally discarded without a parliamentary enactment, entirely prohibiting the use of them. This persuasion rests on the experience of ten years, which has shown them that whoever undertakes to sweep chimneys with machines will soon (if permitted by law) lay them aside and take climbing boys. The machine he must work himself, the boy being only his assistant, by taking apprentices (regardless of the law, which restricts the number to six,) he can have an unlimited number. These he can send in all directions to take their own way; satisfied if they do but bring back every day a certain sum of money and a certain quantity of soot. He may all the time be enjoying himself at his ease. On this account the master will never use the machine but where it is possitively required; and in those instances he will so use it, as to disgust the servants, and thereby prevent its being again required.

That your petitioners are well convinced, that so long as climbing boys are allowed by law, all chance of improvements being made in the construction and working of machines is precluded. Such improvements can only be looked for from the ingenuity of those who are anxious to use them, and who will therefore endeavour to render them as perfect as possible.

That your petitioners are decidedly of opinion, that all attempts materially and permanently to improve the condition of climbing-boys will prove unavailing. During ten years, a committee from among your petitioners have been endeavouring, in vain, to accomplish this. The nature of the trade, and the circumstances of the children, seem effectually to preclude it.

That your petitioners are fully convinced, that if none but mechanical methods were permitted, these would afford a regular, reputable, and profitable employment, both for apprentices and adults. The former, if not put out too young, would be likely to be as well treated, as well taught, and as healthy, as the children apprenticed to other trades. When out of their time they would have learnt an employment which they could continue through life.

That your petitioners believe, that if a law were enacted, prohibiting the binding of any more apprentices to chimney-sweepers to be employed as climbing-boys, and the use of their own offspring or any children as such, this cruel and unnatural practice would be relinquished, without much inconvenience to the public or loss to the present master-chimney-sweepers. The boys already apprenticed would serve to continue the trade for several years till the masters had procured the machines and become expert in the use of them; in the management of which the boys would be also instructed, before the expiration of their apprenticeship.

That your petitioners, therefore, do most earnestly implore your Honourable House, to take this subject into your early and serious consideration.

PETITION

MASTER CHIMNEY-SWEEPERS

OF

LONDON AND WESTMINSTER.

To the Right Honourable the Lords Spiritual and Temporal, of the United Kingdom of Great Britain and Ireland, in Parliament assembled.

The humble Petition of the several Persons whose names are hereunto subscribed, Master Chimney-Sweepers, Householders of the Cities of London and Westminster, and the Vicinity, on behalf of themselves and others,

SHEWETH,

THAT your petitioners served apprenticeships as climbing-boys, to the trade of chimney-sweeping, and have since carried on the same for several years as journeymen or masters.

That your petitioners have lately, upon full experience and conviction of its practicability and efficacy, adopted the use of machinery, and discontinued the employment of climbing-boys.

That your petitioners, with great humility, beg leave to confirm, from their own knowledge, the several statements contained in the Report of the Committee of the Honourable House of Commons, and in the evidence therein referred to, as to the cruelty and danger inseparable from the employment of climbing-boys, in cleansing chimney flues.

That your petitioners are well convinced that the machine invented by Mr. George Smart, will sweep, on an average, at least ninety-five flues out of one hundred, and that the remaining flues may be swept by the ball and brush, or other simple expedients. And that few, if any, flues will require any alteration therein, or fixed apparatus.

That your petitioners, from their own knowledge and experience, are enabled to assert, that such flues as are the most difficult for the machine to ascend, are the most hazardous to the life and limbs of the climbing-boy.

That your petitioners are satisfied, that the miseries of the climbing-boy will not be mitigated or alleviated by any measure short of an absolute prohibition of the employment of them, from a time to be limited.

That your petitioners are of opinion, that the bill now pending in your Right Honourable House, for that purpose, will have the most beneficial effects on the trade in general, by putting it, for the first time, on a level, in point of respectability, with other reputable callings, below which it has hitherto been degraded, by the diseases and sufferings necessarily occasioned to the young children of both sexes employed in it.

Your Petitioners therefore most humbly pray your Right Honourable House, that the said bill may pass into a law.

And your Petitioners shall ever pray, &c.

Signed by a considerable number of master chimney-sweepers, householders of the cities of London and Westminster and the vicinity.

N.B. Petitions, numerously signed by householders, in favour of the bill, have been presented to the Houses of Lords or Commons, from the following, among other places: —

London and Westminster
Parishes of St. Andrew, Holborn, and St. George the Martyr
St. Mary, Islington
St. James's, Clerkenwell
York
Sheffield
Birmingham
Chester
Bath
Bristol
Liverpool
Stockton-upon-Tees
Sunderland
Chelmsford
Walthamstow
Hackney
Stoke Newington and Stamford Hill
Malden
Yarmouth
Ipswich
Durham
Lancaster
Wellington, Shropshire
Hertford
Woolwich
Master Chimney-Sweepers of Kingsland, Dalston, and Shacklewell.

PETITION

OF

WILLIAM SAMPSON,

A CHIMNEY-SWEEPER.

From the Sheffield Iris, July 15, 1823.

On the 30th of June, Lord Milton presented to the House of Commons a petition from William Sampson, a chimney-sweeper of this town, setting forth the hardships endured by climbing-children (we say children, because *girls* as well as *boys*, even in Sheffield, are so employed,) who are bound apprentices, or used by their unnatural parents as such, in this shocking trade. The petition was read in the usual manner, then laid on the table, and ordered to be printed. This was all the notice, which a statement of grievances, not less real than revolting, yet daily and almost hourly practised in this country, at that time obtained from the representatives of the British people. If similar atrocities, among the barbarous customs of Hottentots and Hindoos, were recited at any of our missionary meetings, the audiences would shudder with horror: yet we tolerate them at home, and it seldom occurs to the most humane or reflecting among us, that towards one class of children at least, we ourselves are as coolly, deliberately, remorselessly cruel as the most depraved and ignorant heathen,—and that, not from mistaken notions of *piety*, but out of tenderness to our fine carpets, or veneration for our crooked chimneys. Let any reader of this uncharitable sentence confute it, if they can. Under the circumstances of the case, we do not at all complain that the gentlemen of the House of Commons could not afford more of their "valuable time" to the petition, because it was clearly too late in the session for any effectual measure to be taken to remedy the evil; and because, by ordering it to be printed with their votes, they have placed it upon a permanent record, so that it will neither be lost in the House nor out of it.

In the House, we trust that the subject will be taken up again, at an early opportunity, by the Noble Lord who introduced it, for there is little fear of the claims of humanity and justice being laughed out of credit *there*, whatever may be apprehended from a higher quarter. We only regret, that the rules of Parliament did not allow the petitioner himself to present his prayer and complaint, and give evidence by word of mouth, at the same time, of all that he has witnessed, and all that he has suffered,—perhaps, too, of what he has been forced to inflict on others,—in the way of his profession. The very sight of him would have created an interest, which no eloquence from Honourable or Right Honourable lips, dropping manna, could awaken in behalf of the innocent victims of good housewifery in this land of sense and sentiment; for poor Sampson is as perfect a model of what this villainous trade can make of a human frame, naturally stout and noble, as the Belvidere Apollo is of another disposition of limbs and features. We have known him many years, and can never forget our first acquaintance, when he was rescued by the Committee for the Relief of Climbing-Boys, in this town, from a condition of wretchedness, which must soon have plunged him into a premature grave, had it not been abated.

Out of the House, we hope that this petition will be copied and circulated by the newspapers, from one end of kingdom to the other, to prepare the public mind for the abolition of this species of *infanticide*, which is as much and as rationally legalised here as the burning of widows in India. Nothing short of abolition will do; we have, therefore, long ago ceased to plague our readers with urging upon them the use of that machine which is partially in vogue; for while climbing-boys are allowed, no apparatus is likely to be invented, which chimney-sweepers will chuse to employ, because they must work it themselves; or which housekeepers will approve, because the former will work it so negligently or so perversely as to prejudice their customers against it.

"A petition of William Sampson, of Sheffield, chimney-sweeper, was presented, and read; setting forth, That the petitioner, impressed with a deep sense of the privilege, thus most gratefully avails himself of the right, which the humane laws of his country afford the very lowest member of the community, to state his grievances and his requests to the House; that the House has long been alive to the sufferings of that degraded and oppressed class of human beings to which the petitioner formerly belonged, namely, chimney-sweepers' climbing-boys, is evident from the attention which the House has frequently paid to their peculiar case, particularly in the Session of the year 1819, when a bill to prohibit the use of them was referred to the patient and strict investigation of a Committee, at whose recommendation the said bill finally passed the House; that the petitioner has no personal favour to solicit of the House; that the petitioner comes forward as an advocate of an oppressed class of helpless and unoffending children, with whose sufferings he is, by experience, too well acquainted; that the petitioner was born of very humble but industrious parents, of the township of Sheffield; that hard times, a large family, and frequent sickness, compelled them to apprentice him at an unlawful age (not eight years old) to a chimney-sweeper; that an attempt to describe one-tenth part of the sufferings which the petitioner endured in those tender years would be painful in the extreme, and would take up too much of the valuable time of the House; that during several years the petitioner had scarcely ever had an opportunity of resting his wearied and wounded limbs in a bed; that the floor of a cold, damp, ruinous stable, was his customary lodging-place till three or four o'clock in the morning, the usual hours of rising; that when, from not having been able, during the day, to procure a sufficient number of jobs, he durst not venture home, a shed in the street, or any open outhouse which he could find, has been his only shelter during many a cold and rainy night; that the food with which the petitioner was fed was often such, both in quantity and quality, as to be scarcely sufficient to sustain nature; that the knees, the elbows, and the shoulders of the petitioner were, at first, for a long time, in such a raw and ulcerated state, as to render the misery of climbing up a rough chimney almost insupportable; that the effects of these complicated unceasing sufferings were such as to produce weakness and debility in a naturally strong frame, so that the knees of the petitioner (who was frequently compelled to carry very heavy loads) failed, and by degrees got distorted, in which state they have continued ever since; that the petitioner was continually subject to the brutal violence of both his master and the different journeymen whom he attended, and that one of the latter at one time so kicked and beat him for some trivial fault, that the petitioner's hip was dislocated, in which condition, to avoid further beating, the petitioner crept into an obscure corner, where he was found, after a long time, insensible and nearly dead; in that state he was taken to the Infirmary, and at length recovered; that the petitioner has remained dreadfully deformed ever since; that the petitioner's parents frequently remonstrated with the master, but without effect, till the establishment of a Society for the Relief of Climbing-Boys in Sheffield, when, by the exertions of the members, the petitioner's sufferings were greatly lessened; that the petitioner was at one time for two hours suffocating in a chimney, totally unable to extricate himself till a part of the slates and the wall had been removed; that the petitioner has since been greatly injured by falling down a very high chimney; that the petitioner had once a great part of his skin scalded off by steam, produced by a servant throwing water into the fire below while he was in the chimney; that the petitioner by these and manifold other sufferings has been rendered greatly deformed and weakened, so as not to be able even to stand long together without great pain; that from the strength of the natural constitution of the petitioner, and the appearance of his body and upper limbs, it seems probable that if put to any other calling he would have been tall and stout, — the petitioner now, though 29 years of age, being little more than four feet high; that the petitioner being too weak to work a machine, too bulky to ascend a chimney himself, and too poor to obtain and keep a boy, has frequently, with a wife and three children, been nearly famished for want of necessary food; that though the petitioner is resolved to persevere, with God's blessing, in struggling to keep from the parish, there is little chance but that he must eventually be compelled to resort to it; that the petitioner mentions these things to convince the House of the necessity of taking some further steps for stopping the source of such frequent and dreadful misery, the petitioner's case, afflictive as it is, being exceeded in degree of suffering by many hundreds of others; that the petitioner is fully convinced that either an Act of Parliament to prohibit the taking of any more apprentices as climbing-boys, (with leave to employ these already bound till of age, and no other,) or an Act, either assessed or parochial, laying a tax of forty shillings on all chimneys, which, after the passing of such Act, shall be swept by a climbing-boy, would gradually do away with the practice altogether, without any great inconvenience being experienced by any one; that the petitioner humbly craves the House to pardon this seeming presumption, and to take the matter into the serious and speedy consideration of the House; and the petitioner, with many thousands of poor helpless children rescued from misery, will ever pray."

COPY OF THE REPORT

OF THE

SURVEYOR-GENERAL OF THE BOARD OF WORKS,

OF THE

Experiments made for the purpose of ascertaining the Practicability of superseding the Necessity of employing Climbing-Boys in the Sweeping of Chimneys, by means of the employment of Machinery.

Ordered, by the House of Commons, to be printed, February 1, 1819.

Office of Works, 14 January, 1819.

SIR,

I HAVE the honour to acknowledge the receipt of your letter, dated the 14th of March last, directing me, by command of Lord Sidmouth, "to ascertain, by experiment, how far it is safe and practicable to supersede the practice of climbing-boys in sweeping chimneys, by the use of machinery;" and I beg leave to acquaint you, for his Lordship's information, that upon the receipt of your letter, I proceeded, with as little delay as possible, to secure, by every means in my power, a fair and impartial trial of all the different machines that had been collected, for the purpose of sweeping chimneys without the aid of climbing-boys.

From the many difficulties I had to encounter at

the commencement of this undertaking, I found it necessary, in order to secure a faithful execution of the commands I had received, to appoint Mr. Davis, an active and intelligent clerk in this office, to superintend, personally, the progress of each separate experiment, and to give such directions and assistance, in the use of the different machines, as circumstances and situation might require.

It will not, I conceive, be necessary for me to enter into a detailed statement of all the numerous trials made by Mr. Davis, to sweep chimneys without the aid of climbing-boys; and I shall therefore only submit, for his Lordship's information, the following list of experiments, where machinery has succeeded in effectually cleaning such chimneys, as presented particular difficulties in sweeping, from the size, situations, and peculiar construction of the flues.

	Swept by the Machine.	Swept by the Ball ad Brush.	TOTAL.
At Kensington Palace - -	5	2	7
— the Queen's Palace - -	43	34	77
— Windsor Castle - - -	20	...	20
— the Royal Mint - - -	5	5	10
— the Speaker's house - -	4	...	4
— Mr. Huskisson's house -	13	4	17
— Mr. Nash's house - - -	1	2	3
— Lord Liverpool's - - -	9	2	11
	100	49	149

This statement contains, I believe, with some few exceptions, specimens of nearly every difficult description of chimney that can be met with in the generality of either old or newly constructed buildings, and will afford, in my humble opinion, sufficient evidence, that even at present by far the greater proportion of the chimneys throughout the country, can be effectually swept by machinery, without the aid of climbing-boys. There were, however, many chimneys, that, from their very confined and horizontal construction, Mr. Davis could not succeed in sweeping, either with a machine or with the ball and brush; but this difficulty he thinks might be overcome, by inserting iron registers or doors in some convenient parts of such flues, where machinery might be used with ease; and, if these registers are properly constructed and fixed, without either danger or inconvenience. The best constructed registers for this purpose, that I have seen, were exhibited here by Mr. Thomas White, of Air-street, Picadilly, and by Mr. William Feetham, of Ludgate-hill. And the danger to which climbing boys are so constantly exposed when employed in sweeping narrow and intricate flues, would, in my opinion, in a great measure be obviated, were such iron registers or doors directed to be made at proper and convenient distances in every flue of this construction. The machinery that principally succeeded in the above experiments, was the invention of Mr. Smart, and has proved far superior in utility to any that have been submitted for trial upon the present occasion. This machine is simple in its construction, easily worked, can be repaired, when out of order, with little trouble or expense, and may be carried by a single person from place to place without any difficulty. During the progress of these experiments, I have had every possible assistance and advice, that the abilities and experience of Mr. Browne, the assistant surveyor-general, and of Messrs. Nash, Soane, and Smirke, the architects attached to this department, could afford me upon this very interesting subject; and, from the information I have obtained from these gentlemen, as well as from the observations I have been enabled to make in attending to several of the trials made with the different machines, I beg leave to offer it to his Lordship, as my most decided opinion, that the total abolition of climbing-boys in the sweeping of chimneys, is at present impracticable, and could not be attempted without incurring much risk of danger to the general safety of the metropolis.

I shall beg leave to annex, for Lord Sidmouth's further information, copies of three letters, which I have received from the attached architects, upon the subject of superseding the use of climbing-boys in sweeping chimneys; together with a copy of Mr. Davis's report to me, upon the several experiments he has made, to promote this very desirable object.

And have the honour to be,

Sir,

Your most obedient servant,

B. C. STEPHENSON.

Dover-street, 31st December, 1819.

SIR,

Having attended to several experiments made to sweep chimneys of intricated construction by machines, without the use of Climbing-Boys, I am of opinion, that though it will be difficult, and perhaps impossible, to construct a single machine which will clean every chimney, yet by the use of various machines, almost any chimney may be swept clean; and that experience would, in a short time, render the operation quite easy: but I do not think the use of Climbing-Boys can be wholly dispensed with; the pargetting or plastering of flues will require repairing; new buildings will require to have the mortar and knobs of bricks which stick to the plastering cleared away, which I think cannot be done by any other means than Boys. I beg also to observe, that till the use of machinery shall by experience be made easy, and the adopting of the most efficacious form of the different machines shall be ascertained, much damage will be done to the plastering or pargetting of the flues, which will require Climbing-Boys to repair. I should advise also, that a clause be inserted in the Building Act, that all chimney funnels hereafter to be built, or old chimneys when taken down and rebuilt, should have the flues made circular in form; there would be then little difficulty in cleaning them with any machine; and if tubes like chimney pots were worked upon the walls as funnels for the smoke, they would be a great security against fire, having few joints and no plastering to require repair.

I have the honour to be,

Sir,

Your obedient Servant,

(Signed) JOHN NASH.

The Surveyor-General of the Office of Works.

Lincoln's-Inn Fields, 4th of January, 1819.

MY DEAR SIR,

In reply to your letter respecting Climbing-Boys, I beg leave to state, that as far as my experience goes, a very large portion of the chimneys now constructed may be cleaned with machines; but that it will not be possible to do away entirely the service of Climbing-Boys.

I am, dear Sir,

Your very obedient and faithful Servant,

B. C. Stephenson, Esq. &c. &c. &c. (Signed) JOHN SOANE.

Albany, November 17th, 1818.

SIR,

In compliance with your desire that I should report to you my opinion upon the question of how far it is practicable to supersede the practice of Climbing-Boys, in sweeping chimneys, by the use of machinery, I beg leave to say, that I am not able to give an opinion founded on much personal observation upon the subject; but the result of the very particular inquiries, and of the numerous experiments which you have caused to be made, prove, that machines, upon the principle of Smart's, may be employed with success in all common cases; but that the ball and brush let down from the upper part of the chimney flue is the only process which has answered in every instance.

I have however learnt, from intelligent workmen in Scotland, where it has long been employed, that much injury is often occasioned by this operation at the turning of flues, especially where they are separated only by a thin wall; and I do not think it would be practicable, by any regulation, to provide for the construction of chimney flues in such a way as to obviate this important objection.

I am therefore led to believe, that, although the use of machines may be very generally adopted, there is none hitherto invented which is so far free from objection in all cases, as to render it possible wholly to dispense with the use of Climbing-Boys.

I have the honour to be,

Sir,

Your obedient and faithful Servant,

Lieut. Col. Stephenson. (Signed) ROBT. SMIRKE.

Office of Works, 11th January, 1819.

SIR,

In obedience to the instructions, at various times received from you, on the subject of superseding Climbing-Boys by the use of machines, I hereby enclose the result of the experiments made in consequence, with some observations and suggestions naturally presenting themselves in the detail.

It appears that the whole of the flues at present in use, may be comprised in four classes; the first and most numerous are those which are carried up in a perpendicular stack, the only bend in these flues being just sufficient to clear the opening of the flue above. The second, far less numerous, are those in which the fire-place is in a wall not continued higher than the next floor, and turning off with one bend (making two angles in the elevation) to a partition wall, in which the shaft is continued to the top. The third, still less numerous, are those in which the shaft is at some distance from the fire-place, having at least one angle on the plan, and which of necessity forms two bends in the elevation. The fourth class, which forms a very small proportion of the total number already constructed, are those having more than one angle on the plan, and being, for a part of the length, entirely horizontal.

For the first class, the machines already in use are quite efficient; they are also competent to sweep part of the second class; for the remainder of the second class the ball and brush is perfectly efficient, unless any error in the construction has given the only bend in them a dip the contrary way. In the third class, where the ascent is at all preserved, the ball and brush still acts effectually; as it will also do in the fourth class, where there are no parts entirely level. The remainder of the fourth class comprehends those flues, which have several bends, and are frequently horizontal; and in these cases it is alike necessary to let in registers or doors, whether they are swept by Boys or Machines, there being no other security for the safety of the Boys than this measure; which when done, actually presents the means of sweeping by a common machine.

As far as my experience has led me, I consider the proportions of the different classes nearly as under; out of 1000 flues, 910 of the first class, 50 of the second, 30 of the third, and 10 of the fourth.

For the first and second classes, the machinery has been proved, at Kensington Palace, the Queen's Palace, the Mint, The Speaker's House, Lord Liverpool's, Mr. Huskisson's, Mr. Nash's, and at the Office of Works; but a case has occurred at the Queen's Palace, where a flue of the second class could not be swept by the ball and brush, and upon examining the external part of the chimney, by going between the timbers of the ceiling and lead flat above, that part of the flue was out of a level, the end nearest the shaft being lower than that next the fire-place.

I have not seen a machine that will sweep many flues of the third and fourth classes; but have succeeded with the ball and brush at the several palaces and places above enumerated; and in the last week a chimney was swept at the Tower with the ball and brush in half an hour, which a boy was five hours sweeping a short time since, and in which I am informed, a boy was once confined 28 hours.

The necessity of putting doors in the remainder of those classes, has been proved at The Speaker's House, where, for want of them, they are obliged to cut out tiles or take down part of the stone work every time the servants' hall chimney is swept by a boy; as well as at Somerset Place, where they have put doors in consequence of accidents occurring. Much has been stated by the parties interested, about the injury done to the pargetting by the use of the machinery and the ball and brush; but so far as the closest observation has enabled me to form an opinion, this is entirely without foundation; for in the use of the common machine less compression is required than is exerted by the boys to sustain their own weight; and with the ball and brush, unless there is a level, and the ball is wantonly thrown down instead of being lowered carefully, there can be no injury done. In the course of my own experience, I have never met with an instance of the necessity of employing a climbing-boy to repair the pargetting of a chimney; and with respect to the coring of new chimneys, it requires only a determination on the part of the bricklayers to avoid the necessity of it.

It will appear, that the result of my experiments is, that all the really difficult flues to clean, are met with in large mansions or public offices, and that the middling and lower classes of houses are entirely free from them. The doors introduced in the flues can certainly be constructed to answer, by their locality, all the purposes of convenience, safety, and cleanliness.

The machines I have seen used are Messrs. Smart's, Bean's, Mumford's, Skinner's, Lee's, and the Bath; and these are nearly the same in principle and effect.

Smart's being most used in London, possesses from that circumstance advantages the others have not; practice being required to give confidence to the men employed.

The ball for conducting the brush is susceptible of improvement, inasmuch as making it lighter and larger, is found to increase its utility.

The machine from Scotland is not yet ascertained to possess more advantages than the others; but that being different in principle, it may be found capable of improvement.

I have the honour to be,

Sir,

Your most obedient humble Servant,

(Signed) Geo. Davis.

B. C. Stephenson, Esq.
Surveyor-General,
&c. &c. &c.

THE

SPEECH OF DR. LUSHINGTON,

IN SUPPORT OF THE BILL

For the better regulation of Chimney-Sweepers and their Apprentices, and for preventing the Employment of Boys in Climbing Chimneys, before the Committee in the House of Lords, on Friday, the 13th of March, 1818.

I HAVE the honour to attend your Lordships' Committee in support of this Bill. It is incumbent on all who seek a legislative enactment, purporting to remedy an evil, to show first the existence of the evil; secondly, the inadequacy of the present laws to restrain it; and thirdly, that the proposed remedy is practicable and efficacious. It seems agreed, on all hands, that the employment of boys in climbing chimneys, is in itself an evil; but it is alleged, that it is irremediable, and necessary for the well-being of society, that the good of the great majority requires that all these sufferings should be accumulated on the heads of a few hundred individuals. Of the hardships to which climbing boys are exposed, some are the necessary effect of the occupation, and must always take place so long as boys are so employed; others are incidental only. From the events which have occurred within the last thirty years, I trust I shall be able to show your Lordships, by reference to evidence produced before the Committee of the House of Commons, and by other testimony from witnesses to be examined here, that the same hardships continue in the same degree as they existed thirty years since, when the legislature deemed it necessary to interfere.

My Lords, that there is a necessity for some alteration in the existing system of the law, I think there will scarcely be found any one so hardy as to deny, more especially when, by referring to the Appendix to the Report of the Committee of the House of Commons, I find that the whole meeting of Master Chimney-Sweepers seem to have recognised the existence of that fact: Your Lordships will find that the first resolution of that meeting of Master Chimney-Sweepers states, "That this meeting is anxious the condition of climbing-boys should be taken into immediate consideration, and that the legislature may be pleased to enact such laws as will secure to the children employed in this necessitous business, a mild and humane treatment." And the fourth resolution is, "that the Act relative to Chimney-Sweepers is inefficient for the purposes for which it was intended, and that it is expedient the said Act should be amended." Your Lordships therefore must be satisfied, — as far as the opinion of the petitioners against the Bill can avail, and they are persons who from their habits must necessarily have ample and complete knowledge of all the facts, — that the provisions of the former bill have been found wholly inefficient for the purposes for which it was intended; and, therefore, that it is necessary that some legislative measure should be adopted for preventing the recurrence of the inhumanities which have taken place. This, my Lords, I make out, in the first instance, by reference to the admissions of those who now appear to oppose the present Bill: but it is not enough for me, or for your Lordships sitting here, to be satisfied even with their admissions. I must show your Lordships also, by positive evidence, that the facts on which I shall endeavour to satisfy your Lordships' minds that this Bill ought to pass, are satisfactorily proved.

My Lords, amongst the provisions of the 28th of the King, there were clauses for the purpose of preventing boys being employed in this occupation, until they had attained the age of eight years; it was intended, doubtless, by the legislature, that no boy whatever should be employed either as an apprentice or as a servant, or in any other manner, in climbing chimneys, until he had reached that period of life when he might be supposed to have attained sufficient strength to enable him to undergo the hardships incident to such an employment. Now it is proved by the evidence before the House of Commons, and I shall show it to your Lordships by further evidence, that this most material provision of the Bill has been entirely nugatory.

My Lords, we must first see in what manner boys are procured for this trade: your Lordships will find in the evidence, that there exists a considerable difficulty in procuring boys to be employed; and it is not to be wondered at, I think, my Lords, that persons are not easily to be procured for a trade of this description. Then, my Lords, how has this difficulty been surmounted, and in what manner are they obtained? The whole of the evidence before the Committee of the House of Commons shows, that the climbing-boys are procured in three different modes: they are procured, first, from the parishes; they are procured, secondly, from their parents, by purchase: I shall not trouble your Lordships by pointing out minutely the evidence, because I know I assert that which the evidence proves, and which cannot be denied, and a detailed reference would occupy too large a portion of your time. My Lords, the purchase appears to vary from the price of two, to three, four, and five pounds; and sometimes parents have been found, who, for the love of lucre, have thus sold their own children. It is also in evidence, from Mr. Cook, who is a master chimney-sweeper, and himself has had thirty-two years' experience in this trade, that the smaller a boy is, the larger the price he fetches; so that in proportion as the infant is less capable by nature of undergoing the hardship, so much more valuable is he as an instrument in the hands of those who purchase him. Now, my Lords, there is one other mode left yet; and your Lordships will, I think, be rather surprised to hear that it should have become a frequent and an ordinary practice in this country, to kidnap and steal boys for the purpose of employing them in this trade, without the knowledge or consent of any parent, relation, or friend. My Lords, it is in evidence from Cook, it is in evidence from all the master chimney-sweepers, that this is an ordinary practice; and in particular it is stated that several individuals have been so carried off, and that their parents have not known for some time, indeed in one instance for some years, what had become of them.

Now let us see at what time of life it is that they first become initiated in this mystery. The Act of Parliament has said eight years of age; "to be employed as apprentices or servants," are the terms of the 28th of the King; there is no peculiar prohibition as to parents employing their own children, and the consequence is, that parents have employed their own children from the age of even five years; and Allen, who is one of the witnesses whose evidence is contained in the Report of the Committee of the House of Commons, states himself to have been apprenticed to his uncle at the age of five years and a half. My Lords, Mr. Tooke, a person who has taken very great pains in investigating the nature of this trade, expressly says, in answer to a question put to him in folio 8, "Do you know whether it has been the custom for parents to employ their own children as chimney-sweepers? They do, and consider themselves entitled so to do without their being apprentices, owing to an ambiguity in the Act; and they do not consider themselves bound by the Act as to the age of the child who is not apprenticed." My Lords, Cook, in answer to the question, "At what age have you known climbing-boys taken as apprentices?" states, "Why, seven years old. — Have you ever known a boy taken under the age of seven? No, I do not know that I have. — Is it not the practice for parents to employ their own children under that age, particularly the smaller master-chimney-sweepers? They often do it." Your Lordships find from this evidence what the practice has been.

Now, my Lords, how is the age ascertained? The Act of the 28th of the King directs that a certificate of the boy's register shall be produced where it is practicable; Cook, when he is examined, says in answer to the question, "How do you ascertain the age of the boy when he is offered to you as an apprentice, do you take the parents' word for it? The parents will often say that he is older than what he is. — Are you in the habit of getting any other evidence of their ages than the parents' own words? No. — Do you ever get a certificate of their age, or is it the practice of other masters to get one? No, I cannot say that I ever heard of it." Your Lordships therefore perceive that the wholesome regulation of the law, for preventing the employment of persons in this trade till the age of eight years, has proved entirely inefficient; that parents, and indeed there is the evidence of Fisher, who himself is a father, that he has been in the habit of employing his own boy, though he has not attained the age of eight years. Your Lordships therefore must be satisfied that in that respect there is a necessity for legislative interference.

My Lords, we have now then, somehow or other, either from the parish, from the parents, or by the means of kidnapping, procured the boy, let us then see what becomes of him, and in what way he is initiated into the occupation.

My Lords, it is really painful to be under the necessity of pointing out to your Lordships the severity which it is necessary, absolutely necessary to inflict, in order to induce infants of this age to undertake the hardship of originally learning to climb the chimney. Mr. Cook being asked, "Do you find many boys show great repugnance to go up at first? Yes, most of them. — And if they resist and refuse, in what way do you force them up? By telling them we must take them back again to their father and mother, and give them up again; and their parents are generally people who cannot maintain them. — So that they are afraid of going back to their parents, for fear of being starved? Yes, they go through a great deal of hardship before they come to our trade. — Do you use any more violent means? Sometimes a rod. — Did you ever hear of straw being lighted under them? Never. — You never heard of any means being made use of, except being beat and being sent home? No, no other." — Then in answer to another question; "Of course you must know that there are persons of harsh and cruel disposition;

have you not often heard of masters treating their apprentices with great cruelty, particularly the little boys, in forcing them to go up those small flues which the boy was unwilling to ascend? Yes, I have forced up many a one myself. — By what means? By threatenings, and giving them a kick or a slap." In folio 19, my Lords, there is the evidence of a person who has had some experience in the manner in which they are taught. The evidence of Fisher, in page 23, your Lordships will find, corroborates all that this witness has said. I will just advert to one answer of his; "Have you known many instances in which masters have ill treated their children, to force them up chimneys? Many masters are very severe with them. — What methods do they use to make them go up? I have seen them make them strip themselves naked, and threaten to beat them; I have been obliged myself to go up a chimney naked, but I do not like to see my children do so." Not an unnatural observation, my Lords, from a person who had been under the necessity of submitting to such a hardship.

Your Lordships see from this evidence what is the mode in which they are taught to climb. Now I will pray your Lordships to see what is the consequence of being so taught, and what the sufferings are with which these infants commence their initiation. Your Lordships will find in the evidence of Cook, page 19,

"Are not persons employed as climbing-boys, particularly children, subject to sores, and bruises, and wounds, and burns on their thighs and knees, in consequence of ascending chimneys? Yes, they are subject to that, because learning very fresh boys makes their knees and elbows very sore; but when they have properly learnt their trade, their knees and elbows get hard, and they very seldom get sore again." Now, my Lords, that is the first statement which this witness gives, but this is not all. In folio 21, the witness, speaking to the same point, says in answer to the question, "You said that the elbows and knees of the boys, when they first begin the business, become very sore, and afterwards get callous; are those boys employed in sweeping chimneys during the soreness of those parts? It depends upon the sort of master they have got, some are obliged to put them to work sooner than others; you must keep them a little at it, or they will never learn their business, even during the sores. — Is the skin broke generally? Yes, it is." A little way further on, my Lords, there is this question, "Do those persons still continue to employ them to climb chimneys? Some do, it depends upon the character of the master. — Do you imagine that many keep them till they get well, of that class? No, none. —

So that they are obliged to climb with those sores upon them? Yes."

My Lords, the evidence of Harding, at page 43, in speaking of accidents when they are taught to climb, is very nearly to the same effect.

Now, having shown your Lordships how the boys are taught to climb, and what the immediate consequences are, and the great sufferings they must undergo in learning their trade, let us see what the ultimate necessary consequences are of such climbing. Your Lordships will find at folio 20, in answer to a question put to Cook, "Does not the custom of sending those little boys up the chimneys produce crooked deformed limbs, and stunt the growth of the children? I do not know about the growth; I think it may sometimes, because now they have their chimneys sometimes built round, and as they climb up them they are obliged to be as a corkscrew, and this will turn the cap of their knees; this I know has often been the case." So that your Lordships see it is not an accidental injury to the limb, which time may repair, but even the cap of the knee itself becomes turned, and the limb permanently distorted; and this is often the case.

My Lords, at folio 25, your Lordships will see the evidence of Mr. Wright, who is a surgeon; and he states, "I am well persuaded that the deformity of the spine, legs, arms, &c. of chimney-sweepers, generally, if not wholly, proceeds from the circumstance of their being obliged not only to go up chimneys at an age when their bones are in a soft growing state, but likewise by that of being compelled by their too merciless masters and mistresses to carry bags of soot (and those very frequently for a great length of distance and time) by far too heavy for their tender years and limbs; such circumstances I have unfortunately too often been an eye-witness to; the knees and ancle joints mostly become deformed." My Lords, Harding, who is also a chimney-sweeper, in folio 45, states, that the deformity proceeds very often from the heavy loads the boys are compelled to carry.

Now your Lordships will observe that these are calamities which are absolutely inherent in the nature of the trade; no care, nor caution, nor humanity, on the part of the master chimney-sweepers, can by possibility protect the boys from those sufferings; they must be inured, in the first instance, to climb chimneys by means of great corporal suffering, by means of the sores which are made upon various parts of their body. In the second instance, the exertion in clinging to the sides of the chimneys is so great, that it must and will necessarily produce distortion of the limbs, and deformity of the body; and when your Lordships are satisfied that such are the necessary consequences, a strong case must be made on the other side, before your Lordships will be of opinion that any number of our fellow-creatures should be detained in such an employment.

The next question, my Lords, is, What accidents they are peculiarly subject to, which may not happen to the individual often, or but very seldom? My Lords, suffocation is an event far from uncommon; far from uncommon, even so as to produce the death of the victim, and so as to produce great agony; and the necessity of cutting him out of the flue is still more usual. Can your Lordships be surprised at it when you find, in the evidence of Thomas Allen, that boys are sent up flues of seven inches square? flues of seven inches square, my Lords, these boys are compelled to ascend! and I see not how that could by possibility be effected, except at the imminent risk of human life. My Lords, is that all? Your Lordships will find in the evidence of Allen, that some of those flues are of such immense extent, that it requires a great number of hours to perform the duty. Allen states, in folio 47, having been a chimney-sweeper for twenty-two years, that he had been in the habit of sweeping the chimneys at Goldsmiths' Hall, and that there is a flue, the size of which he does not think was above nine inches; it was a long one; he had swept it five or six times: "How long were you in it? I went in at eight, and came out at two." My Lords, this requires no comment from me; what must be the state of a human being incarcerated, with all the accumulated soot and filth, in a space of nine inches square, for six whole hours, I will leave to your Lordships' judgment, and not to any representation of mine, with one suggestion only; that the unfortunate child on whom this office was imposed, was subjected not only to the endurance of great suffering, but the imminent risk of life. Think that in this long flue, which is represented, in the evidence of Mr. Tooke, to be nearly two hundred feet in length; if a boy had been stopped in any one part of it by the accumulation of soot and filth, what must have been almost the inevitable consequence — he must have perished miserably; he could not have been extricated from that situation in time to save his life.

My Lords, Cook, who has been a practical chimney-sweeper for many years, states, in his evidence, that he has been many times in risk of his own life: your Lordships will find, that there are in the evidence before the House of Commons, several instances of this occurring. In folio 36, your Lordships will find, that two boys at one time were suffocated, at a baker's in Lothbury: your Lordships will find, in folio 37, the death of a boy of the name of Holt, by sticking in another chimney; and the verdict of the Coroner's jury is recited at the end, which states, that he died of suffocation from that cause. My Lords, it is not only from suffocation that they lose their lives, but in the very next page your Lordships will see two instances where they have died from being sent up chimneys which were still so much heated as to cause their death by fire! In folio 38, it appears that Joseph Fisher was, on the 20th of May, in the year 1801, burnt to death, by having been shut up in one of those flues. At the bottom of the same folio your Lordships will find, that in the brewhouse of Calvert and Co. in Thames-street, Thomas Pitt also met his death by burning. There are many other instances, my Lords, detailed in evidence, and some of which it will be necessary for me also to produce before your Lordships, showing the extreme danger to life, as well as the many accidents which have already occurred. It would be very unbecoming in me to trespass on your Lordships' time, by going minutely into these circumstances; it is sufficient for me to have shown to your Lordships, that the danger does exist, that it very often has occurred, and that many lives have been lost.

My Lords, these are accidents which may happen,

more or less frequently, to the individuals who are engaged; but there are also other calamities incidental to this occupation, peculiar to this trade, which it is right to bring before your Lordships' consideration. My Lords, there is a disease called the chimney-sweeper's cancer, a disorder which, I believe, has seldom been found in any individual whatsoever, save in those who have been subjected to this employment. In the evidence of Mr. Wright, who is a surgeon, he says that this calamity generally seizes hold of the scrotum, and that it is necessary, where once it has taken possession of the individual, that an operation should be performed, or death will ensue. It has, in some few instances, attacked them in the lip and in the mouth, but these instances are but rare. My Lords, in his evidence, he states that this disease is so peculiarly well known, that the treatment of it forms a part of surgical education; and that no person is supposed to be competent to perform his general duty as a surgeon unless he has received instructions upon this very disorder. Being asked, whether it is necessary to make it a part of surgical education? he says, "Most assuredly."

My Lords, the late Mr. Pott, who was, as your Lordships know, a very eminent surgeon, wrote an Essay expressly on this very disorder; and I believe

I shall have this day an opportunity of examining before your Lordships, Sir William Blizard, who will confirm all the evidence Mr. Wright gave before the Committee of the House of Commons, and also produce some additional facts. This disorder, therefore, is peculiar to persons in this trade; and Mr. Wright states, that the soot and the dirt are the sole cause of the disorder: it is a disorder fatal, if no operation be performed; and it appears, in the evidence of Fisher and of Mr. Wright, that in several instances persons are so afraid of undergoing an operation, that they decline submitting to it, and consequently their lives must be lost.

My Lords, this is certainly a most dreadful disorder; but there are others, which, though not so dangerous as it respects the extinction of life, yet do entail upon those who endure them considerable sufferings: they are peculiarly subject to blear eyes, as your Lordships will find from the evidence of all the master chimney-sweepers who have been examined upon this occasion; of Cook, of Fisher, of Harding, and of Allen. The nature of the employment then, my Lords, has subjected the boys to these calamities, and I conceive that more or less they would still continue to be exposed to them, whatever care may be employed on the part of the masters. However, we find that in point of practice these are not the only effects, but almost every other hardship which human nature is capable of undergoing has somehow or other fallen to the lot of these unprotected children. In the early part of the morning they go out to their labour, and the occupation generally closes about mid-day. It appears from the evidence of Fisher, Mr. Tooke, and several others, that the middle of the day they spend in idleness; and at night, my Lords, when the hour of rest comes, they betake themselves to the cellar, with straw to lie on, and the filth and dirt which they have accumulated in the day, all placed in the same identical place. My Lords, it is quite afflicting to think that human beings should be subjected to such a degradation; but when one considers the consequence to health, that any persons, particularly that boys at this early age, should have to sleep in a damp cellar, and, by way of aggravation, be surrounded with the noxious vapours which arise from all this filth and dirt — I ask your Lordships, whether the necessary consequences must not be, that their constitutions will be most materially injured, and their strength, even at a very early period of life, essentially impaired. My Lords, this is the ordinary mode in which they are lodged; in some instances it may happen about twenty of the master chimney-sweepers afford them better accommodation; but your Lordships will observe, these are exceptions from the general usage, not the general usage itself.

My Lords, the next point will be, What species of clothing have these boys? I think I might almost content myself with referring to your Lordships' observation upon this head, whether, in walking the streets, you have not seen these infants, in the most inclement seasons, almost universally without stockings, very often without shoes, with only a jacket to cover them. This is the state in which we usually see them; and all the evidence, without referring your Lordships to it more particularly, goes to show, that in point of clothing they are most inadequately provided.

My Lords, to persons who are engaged in an employment so filthy as this is, washing * is most essential; now I find, in the evidence of Fisher and of Harding, that these boys are not washed from holiday to holiday, from Easter to Whitsuntide; the whole filth accumulating during that period, it is not to be wondered that they are a prey not only to that disease particularly known by the name of the chimney-sweeper's

* It has been observed, that if chimney-sweepers' boys were to wash every day, their skins would be kept so tender, that they would be unable to perform their hard work, for they would be sore all over.

cancer, but that every other disorder of the like kind should afflict them. Your Lordships will find, in the evidence of Mr. Wright, that in consequence of this want of washing, they are peculiarly subject to sores, and those sores difficult to be cured. Upon this subject I will not go into detail, because I know that every part of the evidence completely corroborates the statement I have made; and I should detain your Lordships at greater length than I consider myself warranted in doing, if I pointed out each particular passage bearing upon this point; but as I have the success of this Bill at heart, I think I may venture to say, I have not on any one occasion carried my representation beyond the fair effect of the evidence on any one position I have submitted to your Lordships.

My Lords, there is one other consideration: We have seen what hardships they have undergone in their persons; now, what provision is made for their instruction, their education, their religious information? My Lords, Mr. Tooke, in his evidence, is asked, "Do you know whether chimney-sweepers in general have any care taken of their education by their masters? I believe none: the Association in 1800 had that object in view, and several respectable chimney-sweepers attempted to promote it among the trade; but I never understood that any progress had been made, but that, in fact, the apprentices of chimney-sweepers have not had any education whatever." My Lords, the fact makes this out: it appears that there are journeymen and apprentices to the number of 750, out of which it appears in Mr. Tooke's evidence, that only about twenty were able to write their names, and the greater proportion of them unable to read. Now, my Lords, what must be the necessary consequences of boys being thus brought up without any moral education, without having the principles of religion instilled into their minds, left, after their labours are performed in the middle of the day, without the care or protection of a parent or any other person to bestow the slightest attention upon them? Your Lordships observe, that as to the greater number of them, they are parish children, or they are children of parents who have sold them, or they are kidnapped children: what must be the consequences upon their morals, and what their future conduct in life must necessarily be, your Lordships may, I think, fairly infer from these circumstances. The boys having commenced their servitude at the earliest age at which nature has rendered the frame capable of enduring it, continue to undergo those severities until they have attained that age when their growth prevents their being any longer employed in climbing chimneys, until, I was going to say, they were emancipated by the course of nature; but, alas! in this case even the course of nature itself is arrested, for their growth is stunted, their very stature is diminished, and individuals in this employment do not attain the same height at the same age that ordinary individuals do.

Thus, my Lords, they have gone through these sufferings for eight or nine years, what is their reward at the period of sixteen or seventeen years of age? How are they to employ themselves? What is the recompense of all they have endured? Have they become initiated into a lucrative trade, where a large reward for labour may compensate them for their sufferings? Your Lordships know, that in ordinary trades the amount of the recompense accommodates itself to the severity of the employment; that a coal-heaver, for instance, will earn his six or seven shillings in a morning, whereas a common labourer cannot earn more than his two or three. Now, my Lords, the very reverse takes place in this case; the ordinary principles by which labour and reward are governed in all other trades, are here uprooted and overthrown. Your Lordships will find, that Mr. Cook states that there is not a living for above half of those *who have gone through all these severities during their apprenticeship**, and he states, that that is the reason which

* Probably two-thirds have died or been disabled before the expiration of their apprenticeship.

makes him adhere to the machines. There is the same evidence given, my Lords, by Fisher ; and there is the same evidence from Mr. Tooke ; therefore, my Lords, the reward of these youths is, that they shall be turned out upon the world with emaciated constitutions, with injured frames, without education, without information, without any means of supporting themselves after all they have suffered! The consequences to the individual are most severe. I doubt whether, in any ordinary case, the Legislature would be justified in sacrificing even five hundred individuals to a misery so accumulated, unless indeed an absolute and irremediable necessity should be demonstrated. But, my Lords, what are the consequences also to society, the necessary consequences: *there never was cruelty to an individual that was not detrimental to the interests of society.* My Lords, they have no subsistence or employment, they cannot beg, they must have recourse to robbery and plunder; and so at last, by crime and by violation of the law, that subsistence is extracted from society which they have unjustly been denied. If, therefore, the prevention of crime be a matter of most essential importance in the consideration of legislators, your Lordships will, I trust, see that the abolition of climbing-boys, and the establishment of a new system, is absolutely necessary in order to carry such objects into effect.

My Lords, is it possible that any legislative measure short of the abolition of climbing altogether could insure these most desireable objects — the protection of the boys, and the prevention of their being thrown upon the world in future? My Lords, *past experience shows us, that it is not possible:* the violation of all the provisions of the 20th of the King — the admitted inefficiency of all those measures, shows that it is useless to attempt to legislate in detail, if you allow the principal evil to continue. And for what reason is it so? Because those boys must necessarily be in the power of those whom they serve, and they have no opportunity (for they have no knowledge, information, or friends) of bringing their complaints for redress before the magistrates or a court of judicature in this country: the consequence, therefore, necessarily is, that the severity of their treatment is for the most part confined within the limits which the cupidity and interest of their employers may think fit to impose. *As to a great part of the evils, your Lordships, I trust, are satisfied that they are inherent in the system, and that even the humanity of the best masters never could have removed them.**

I proceed now, my Lords, to show your Lordships

---

* This is the grand and unanswerable argument against the practice; it cannot be mended.

that these are not necessary evils; that they are not evils which the good of society imperiously calls upon your Lordships to continue: I trust I shall do this; and by reference to the former evidence, and by that also which I am about to produce, show to your Lordships, that you will not be justified in permitting the continuance of this trade, because of the slight expense to certain individuals who may happen to have houses of a peculiar construction. I think your Lordships will not weigh against the happiness and comfort of hundreds of individuals a small pecuniary consideration. I should be very sorry if I thought it was my duty to go all the length of showing that no difficulty whatever occurred in the abolition of this practice: I am prepared to admit, that in certain cases certain remedies must be proposed and must be adopted, but also to show that those are easy and of slight expense.

My Lords, it is proposed by the present act in substance to abolish the use of climbing boys on the first of May, 1819. I do not think it is necessary for me now to trouble your Lordships with the other provisions of the act; they all tend to this one great end: but if the use of boys is to be abolished on the first of May, 1819, I must now show your Lordships, that there does exist some means of performing, in another mode, the work which has been imposed upon them.

Now, my Lords, how are we to try this question? How am I to show to your Lordships, that it is practicable to sweep chimneys by the use of mechanical inventions? I know no other way than by showing that *practically it has been done for many years;* by showing, from the opinion of eminent architects, that they conceive it may still continue to be done, except in a very few instances; and that even in all those instances, at a small expense, machinery may be successfully substituted.

My Lords, the first evidence to which I will refer your Lordships, as to the practice, is in folio 12, the evidence of Mr. Smart, who is the inventor of one of the machines, and who for *fourteen years* has been in the constant habit of employing it, and he states there is not above one flue in a hundred which he is not able to sweep with the machine; and that he says from the experience of *seventeen years*, and many thousand experiments.

A Lord.— You perceive that Mr. Cook, who Mr. Smart says uses it the most honestly, does not agree with him in the number.

Dr. Lushington.—Certainly, my Lord, he says three out of four; but Smart has used it himself. But I shall produce housekeepers whose chimneys have been swept for eleven, twelve, or thirteen years, and who have never experienced the slightest inconvenience, or matter of complaint. My Lords, the evidence of Mr. Cook is, that he conceives about three out of four may be safely swept. He says the common class of chimneys may be so swept. He afterwards is asked whether by alteration, which may be made by means of registers, they all could not be swept: he is of opinion that they might. Your Lordships will observe, that the ordinary species of flues may be swept by means of the machine being inserted from the bottom: there are some, but very few cases, in which it might be done by means of a jack chain from the top; in the remainder of the cases, which I think I shall be able to satisfy your Lordships will not amount to two in an hundred, it might be done by means of the invention of registers. I shall produce before your Lordships Mr. White, who is a district surveyor, in the parish of St. Mary-le-bone; and from his testimony, confirmed by his great practical experience, I hope to be able to satisfy your Lordships, beyond all doubt, upon this part of the case.

Your Lordships will observe that Snow, who practically has used the machine, is of opinion, that it is only one out of one hundred and twenty, that cannot be swept by it. Edmonds also deposes, that in one year he swept by it 1313 chimnies, and that he can do ninety-nine out of a hundred; so that taking the general run of the evidence, I apprehend, if we were to take precisely an accurate calculation, the number would not amount to above five in an hundred which there would be any difficulty in sweeping in the proposed mode. Now, my Lords, those chimneys exist, according to the evidence of Mr. Edmonds, in the houses of the opulent only; and I am convinced your Lordships will think, that, if by the means of a small alteration, at a trifling expense, the use of climbing boys can be superseded, there is not an individual of opulence who would not readily submit to the sacrifice.

I will now refer your Lordships to the evidence of Mr. Bevans, who is an architect of considerable eminence; it appears, in folio 48, (he is also in attendance here, and may be called in for the purpose of affording further information):—"Have you seen the different machines that have been constructed for the purpose of sweeping chimneys, to be substituted in the room of climbing boys? Yes, I think I have seen most of them.—Do you, as an architect, think that they are applicable to all the chimneys in the metropolis? By far the major part, I may almost say to all, in fact.—Can you state to the Committee in what proportion out of a hundred, the machine would be applicable? I should think to ninety-five out of a hundred.— Have you ever seen that improvement which has taken place, called a register or shutter, which is applied to the angular departure from the perpendicular shaft, by which the horizontal part can be swept? I have never seen a model; but no doubt such a plan would answer well enough, because the machine itself will turn an easy angle.—Do you think that by the invention of the machine, from its flexibility, that nearly all the chimneys might be swept? With shutters, at their turnings, every chimney could be swept." My Lords, this description of flue which it is difficult for a boy to sweep, is that description which is there represented; that is, what is called a dead flat, and it is hardly possible for any boy to go with safety along that dead flat: *the greater the difficulty for the machine to perform its office, the greater the risk of human life to the boy who encounters it.* Will your Lordships have the goodness to refer to a most important passage at the bottom of folio 48:—"Where there is nearly an horizontal flue, does it not require a great deal of clearing to get the soot out? Yes; but it is equally bad for the boy as for the machine: the boy as he comes down has an accumulation of soot about him which stops up the circulation of the air necessary to support life.—So that it is evident in all those chimneys where the machine cannot be used, the hazard is proportionably increased to the life of the boy who sweeps them? Certainly." Upon being further asked, "Do you think as an architect and as a mechanic, supposing there were to be a legislative enactment, that no chimney should be swept by means of climbing boys, that easy substitutes could be found that would sweep every chimney that now exists?" he says "*Necessity* * *is the mother of invention, and we are sure it would be done: I have no doubt of it at all.*"

My Lords, in addition to this evidence, strong as it is,—and perhaps some of your Lordships may know by character that Mr. Bevans is an architect of very considerable eminence, and has been occasionally employed in giving in plans of different descriptions for Committees of the other House of Parliament,—there is also the evidence of other surveyors and builders, which your Lordships will find in the Appendix annexed to the Report: they all certify, "that the chimneys in houses already built may, with few exceptions, be effectually cleansed by machines from below; and that by proper attention being given to the construction of chimneys in future, all in new buildings may be cleansed with ease by machines worked from below."

My Lords, I have now gone through all the circumstances of this case which I think it necessary to trouble your Lordships with. It will be my duty, in proceeding to the task I have to discharge, to call

* And, it may be added, encouragement or demand.

witnesses in order to corroborate all the statements I have made. I have made no statement which is not justified by the evidence already produced; but still I will show your Lordships that every one word I have now addresed to you will be completely proved by further testimony; and I trust therefore your Lordships will be of opinion, that as no absolute and imperative necessity any longer exists for continuing the employment of climbing boys, it is high time some legislative provision should be made which should relieve the country from the disgrace which has hitherto attached upon it, from having subjected so many individuals to such severe and unmerited hardships. I trust that your Lordships will find that the practicability of the machine sweeping the generality of chimneys, and all with a slight alteration, will be so completely established, that your Lordships will not entertain the minutest doubt that the practice which I have characterized as contrary to humanity needs no longer be continued.

A Lord. — Do you know whether any calculation has been made how many of these boys die in a year?

Dr. Lushington. — I am not aware, my Lord, that that fact has been ascertained; nor do I apprehend that it is possible to ascertain it correctly.

EXTRACTS

FROM THE

REPORT

FROM

THE COMMITTEE

ON

Employment of Boys in Sweeping of Chimneys;

TOGETHER WITH

THE MINUTES OF THE EVIDENCE

TAKEN BEFORE THE COMMITTEE:

AND

AN APPENDIX.

Ordered, by The House of Commons, *to be Printed,*
23*d June,* 1817.

Society for superseding the Necessity of Climbing Boys, by encouraging a New Method of Sweeping Chimneys, and for improving the Condition of Children and others, employed by Chimney-Sweepers. Instituted Feb. 4, 1803.

At a Meeting of the Committee of the Society, held at the City of London Tavern, on the 10th day of July, 1817,

Resolved,

That the Report of the Committee of the Hon. the House of Commons, on the Employment of Boys in Sweeping of Chimneys, be printed for general Information, with Notes and Observations, under the direction of the Treasurer.

Signed by Order,

W. JONES, Secretary.

Society for superseding the Necessity of Climbing Boys by encouraging a New Method of Sweeping Chimneys, and for improving the Condition of Children and others employed by Chimney Sweepers.

PATRON:

His Royal Highness the Prince of Wales.

PRESIDENT:

The Honourable and Right Reverend the Lord Bishop of Durham.

VICE-PRESIDENTS:

His Grace the Duke of Bedford,
Earl Grosvenor,
Lord Somerville,
Hon. and Right Reverend the Bishop of Oxford,
Right Hon. the Lord Mayor,
Sir T. Baring, Bart. M.P.
Sir Charles Bunbury, Bart. M.P.
William Wilberforce, Esq. M.P.
John Julius Angerstein, Esq.
Patrick Colquhoun, Esq.

TREASURER:

William Tooke, Esq.

COMMITTEE:

Right Hon. Earl of Morley,
Hon. Richard Bagot,
Hon. H. Grey Bennet, M.P.
Hon. P. D. Burrell, M.P.
Sir F. Burdett, M.P.
Robert Barclay, Esq.
James Belloncle, Esq.
W. H. Burgess, Esq.
Henry Cockfield, Esq.
T. J. Clarke, Esq.
Joseph Dimsdale, Esq.
Charles Elliott, Esq.
D. Fernie, Esq.
C. Francis, Esq.
B. M. Forster, Esq.
T. Forster, Esq.
W. Fry, Esq.
Gabriel Gillett, Esq.
Thomas Heaver, Esq.
Mr. W. Jones,
Stephen Lushington, LL.D.
P. Martineau, Esq.
Captain M. Montagu, R.N.
George Reveley, Esq.
Richard Sanderson, Esq.
R. Stainforth, Esq.
Adams Smith, Esq.
John Smith, Esq.
Jas. Soper, Esq.
R. Smith, Esq.
C. H. Tatham, Esq.
John Temple, Esq.
T. F. Forster, Esq.
William Vaughan, Esq.
John White, jun. Esq.
Wm. Wigram, Esq. M.P.
W. Williams, Esq.
Frederick Webb, Esq.
Rev. Mark Wilks,
Mr. W. P. Sundius, Secretary,
No. 39, Threadneedle-street.

ADVERTISEMENT.

In conformity to the preceding resolution of the Society, a few explanatory observations have been introduced by way of notes on the evidence attached to the following Report; and it is hoped that a short statement of the circumstances that have led to Parliamentary inquiry on the subject, may not prove unacceptable.

The history of the origin of the Society, and a detailed statement of the measures adopted by it for promoting the object for which it was instituted, will be found in the Reports published from time to time by its Committee *; of which a brief summary, by

* A short account of the proceedings of the Society to June, 1816, may be had of Messrs. Baldwin, Cradock, and Joy, Paternoster Row; J. Hatchard, Piccadilly; and Henry Colburn, Conduit street; Price 6*d*.

way of narrative, is also introduced in the evidence referred to by the Committee of the House of Commons.

In June, 1816, the Right Honourable the Lord Mayor, was kindly pleased to accede to the wishes of the Society for reviving the public interest towards the completion of an object they had so long been labouring to attain, by convening a meeting of the inhabitants of London and Westminster, to take into consideration the best means of superseding the use of infants in cleaning chimneys by climbing.

Such meeting, most numerously and respectably attended, was accordingly held at the Mansion House on the 12th of June, 1816, at which the Lord Mayor presided; and, among other resolutions unanimously agreed to, was one recommending immediate application to Parliament for such legislative enactment for prohibiting the use of climbing boys, and promoting the substitution of the machine, as might be deemed most expedient.

The Society availed itself of the increased interest thus excited, by publishing resolutions recommending public meetings in all the principal cities and towns throughout England, for the purpose of co-operating with the Society by petitioning Parliament for remedy of the grievance complained of.

The recommendation was generally attended to,

and meetings were accordingly held in several places, and more particularly in the populous towns and villages in the environs of the metropolis, for discontinuing the employment of climbing boys, and for promoting the use of the machine.

The credit of presenting the first petition to Parliament for those purposes is due to the town of Sheffield, where a society had been formed in aid of, and soon after, the institution of the one in London. An account of the Sheffield meeting, held on 14th April last, has been published, containing a copy of the petition, and the substance of a speech made by Mr. Samuel Roberts on the occasion, containing a comprehensive view of the subject, and an animated and argumentative appeal in favour of the emancipation of the poor helpless children employed as chimney-sweepers' climbing boys, denominated by Mr. Roberts the worst, the most oppressed of slaves; adding, "that the West India slavery, excepting only the middle passage, has not a feature comparably horrid, and disgustingly repulsive, with the slavery of these poor creatures."

The Sheffield petition was presented by Lord Milton, with an appropriate statement of his sentiments in support of it, with a view merely to its being received and laid upon the table; but the whole House appeared so favourably disposed to an early investigation of the subject, that his Lordship availed himself of the intimation, and that Committee was forthwith appointed to whom we are indebted for the subsequent Report.

The beneficial effect of the meeting at the Mansion House having been thus exemplified, his Royal Highness the Duke of Sussex was induced, at the request of the Society, to preside at a similar meeting at the Freemasons' Tavern, which was held on the 7th of last June, and was sanctioned by the presence, and animated by the speeches, of several distinguished characters, in favour of the petition to Parliament, which was unanimously agreed to at such meeting, and will be found in a subsequent page of this work, among the resolutions of that meeting.

The London and Westminster petition was presented to the House by the Hon. H. G. Bennet, the Chairman of the Committee, to whom this, and the several petitions from Sheffield, Bath, and other places, were referred.

The Committee of the House of Commons, which was attended by some of its most distinguished members, lost no time in proceeding on the reference; and, owing to the intelligence and indefatigable zeal and attention of the Honourable Chairman, the following able Report was prepared; and, in consequence of the impression made on the Committee by the weight of the evidence, so concisely and perspicuously stated in that Report, the Committee concluded by recommending the immediate introduction of a bill for abolishing the employment of children in climbing flues; thus anticipating the intention of the Society, who contributed their assistance, by causing a draft of the proposed bill to be prepared.

A bill was accordingly, on June 25, brought in to amend the Act of the 28th Geo. III. by limiting the age of apprentices to fourteen; and for prohibiting all climbing of flues by persons under 21 years of age, after the 1st day of May next; but on the eve of the second reading of it, a doubt was suggested, whether it should not be considered as a private bill, purporting as it did, to amend an act which was a private one, and, therefore, subject to fees; in addition to which it was apprehended that sufficient time could not now be found to pass the bill in either case, into a law, during the short remainder of the session.

This consideration, and an anxious desire to avoid any appearance of precipitancy in a public measure of so much importance, induced the Society to consent to withdraw the measure, in the certain expectation that they have nothing to fear, but, on the contrary, every thing to expect, from the increased publicity of their intention; with a view to which they have directed this publication.

With regard to the expediency of legislative enactment on the subject, it may be necessary to observe, that this cannot be considered as any undue interference with the freedom of trade, but only as a proper interposition of Parliament for the protection of those who, for the most part, are foundlings or orphans, who have no other guardian than the State; who have no option in the selection of their trade; who are oppressed because they are helpless; who labour because they are weak; who perform the hardest service at a period when they are least able to endure it, and with whom every principle of beneficial employment is reversed; thus constituting at once a stigma on our humanity, and a humiliating limit to the boasted fertility of our mechanical resources.

The result of the inquiry thus instituted by the House of Commons has more than confirmed the statements made in the several publications of the Society; by whom the utmost care has been taken to avoid the language of declamation, or to work upon the public feeling by exaggerated statements. The error, if any, has been of a contrary description; but it will be compensated ultimately by the confidence to which it entitles them from a judicious public, who will have to acknowledge, that, in renouncing a vicious system, they have not yielded to the clamour of visionary enthusiasts, but have given their reasonable assent to the proposed alternative, in consequence of the conviction produced by the steady and persevering efforts of the Committee of the Society; who, as men of the world, and men of business, studied to mature for practice what they had long felt desirable in theory.

In conclusion, the Editor trusts he will not be deemed presumptuous in stating his full conviction,—by which he abides, and from which he has never deviated, founded as it is on an unremitting attention to the plan commenced in all the fervour and buoyancy of youth, and only more concentrated towards its object by the lapse of fourteen years,—

That machines, upon Smart's construction, are capable of cleansing a very large majority of common chimney flues;

That all other flues, of every description, admit of being cleansed by mechanical means, more or less expensive and complicated, according to circumstances;

That the flues most difficult for the machine are

precisely those which are the most dangerous for the climbing-boy;

That, therefore, the employment of them in the former case is unnecessary, in the latter barbarous.

W. TOOKE.

Bedford Row,
August 1, 1817.

EXTRACTS

FROM

MINUTES OF EVIDENCE.

Mercurii, 11° *die Junii*, 1817.

The Honourable HENRY GREY BENNET, in the Chair.

William Tooke, Esq. called in, and examined.

I BELIEVE you are secretary to the society whose object is to supersede the necessity of employing climbing boys?—I am the treasurer of that society; but I have, in point of fact, executed the office of secretary; that is, I have conducted the whole correspondence.

How long have you had the direction of the affairs of the Society?—From its formation in February, 1803.

Have you made it your business to inquire into all

the details connected with the object of the society?—I have.

Shall you be able to give the Committee information in the way of narrative?—I think I can, from the papers I have.

[*The witness commences his narrative.*]

The public interest was first excited towards the condition of climbing boys in the year 1788, when Mr. Jonas Hanway (1)*, with some other gentlemen, prepared a bill to be brought into parliament, for the purpose of protecting these boys in the conduct of their trade. The bill contained a variety of provisions for that purpose, but the principal ones were rejected in the House of Lords; and the existing act of 28 Geo. III. c. 48. was the result.

What were the clauses in the act which the Lords rejected?—I understood that those clauses were for licensing all master chimney-sweepers, having an accurate register of the names and ages of their apprentices, and for preventing the calling of the streets, as it is termed.

What is meant by the "calling of the streets?"—Giving notice to housekeepers of their being prepared to sweep chimneys, by crying "Sweep;" and by such

* This and the subsequent figures throughout the evidence refer to the corresponding number of the notes in the original.

proposed act the hours prescribed were later in the day than they are in the existing act.

[*Narrative resumed.*]

In the year 1800, the Society for Bettering the Condition of the Poor took up the subject; but little or nothing appears to have been done upon that occasion, except that the most respectable master chimney-sweepers entered into an association and subscription for promoting the cleanliness and health of the boys in their respective services. The institution of which I am treasurer, and which is now existing, was formed in February 1803. In consequence of an anonymous advertisement, a large meeting was held at the London Coffee House, and the Society was established. Immediate steps were then taken to ascertain the state of the trade; inspectors were appointed to give an account of all the master chimney-sweepers within the bills of mortality, their general character, their conduct towards their apprentices, and the number of those apprentices. It was ascertained, that the total number of master chimney-sweepers within the bills of mortality might be estimated at two hundred, who had among them five hundred apprentices; that not above twenty of those masters were reputable tradesmen, in easy circumstances, who appeared generally to conform to the provisions of the act; and which twenty had upon an average from four to five apprentices each. We found about ninety of an inferior class of master chimney-sweepers, who averaged three apprentices each, and who were extremely negligent both of the health, morals, and education of those apprentices; and about ninety, the remainder of the two hundred masters, were a class of chimney-sweepers recently journeymen, who took up the trade because they had no other resource: they picked up boys as they could, who lodged with themselves in huts, sheds, and cellars, in the outskirts of the town, occasionally wandering in the villages round, where they slept on soot bags, and lived in the grossest filth.

Can you give the Committee any information with respect to the ages of the climbing boys?—The apprentices of the respectable part of the trade we found to be generally (I believe in all instances) that prescribed by the act, namely, from eight to fourteen; but even among the most respectable, it was the constant practice to borrow the younger boys from one another, for the purpose of sweeping what are called the narrow flues. Of the apprentices of the other classes of the trade it was found impracticable to obtain accurate accounts of the ages; but they had the youngest children, and who, in many instances, it was ascertained, were much below the prescribed age:

thus the youngest and most delicate children were in the service of the worst class of masters.

Did you ever know of any cases in which a child so employed was not older than four, five, or six years? —I have known one instance of a child under six years, and you will have evidence before you from other persons of children under five.

Are you acquainted with the manner in which those children are bound apprentice, whether by the master giving a premium, or, as in most trades, the parents giving a premium?—I cannot state of my own knowledge; the large proportion at the time we undertook the inquiry were apprenticed by the parishes, under indentures.

Does that practice still prevail?—It has been very much diminished of late.

Have you heard that it has been the common practice for parents to sell their children for three, four, or five guineas?—In many instances.

Do the parents receive that sum for the purpose of having their children bound apprentices?—Yes.

Do you know whether it has been the custom for parents to employ their own children as chimney-sweepers?—They do; and consider themselves entitled so to do, without their being apprenticed, owing to an ambiguity in the act; and they do not consider themselves bound by the act as to the age of a child who is not apprenticed.

Have you ever heard of cases in which children, even younger than those that have been mentioned, have been so employed by their parents?—Chimney-sweepers have told me themselves(2), that they were sent up chimneys by their parents at five years of age.

Have you ever heard of female children being so employed?—I have heard of cases at Hadley, Barnet, Windsor, and Uxbridge; and I know a case at Witham, near Colchester, of that sort.

Were those children you have been speaking of, of a very tender age; that is, were they within the act?—I cannot say: they were young and small; but there is great difficulty in ascertaining their ages, where they are not regularly indentured, in judging from appearances; and there being so much equivocation in the masters giving the ages of their apprentices, that it renders it next to impossible to ascertain the ages of the apprentices; but for the common purposes of sweeping chimneys, there must be a large proportion of them small enough to ascend flues from nine to twelve inches diameter, and who must consequently be either very delicate in their frame, or within the age directed by the act.

[*Narrative resumed.*]

From the information derived of the characters of

the masters, and of the condition of their apprentices, by the reports of the inspectors, the committee of the Society proceeded immediately to advertise premiums for the discovery of a machine to supersede the use of boys; and in the meantime brought in a bill for the protection of the climbing boys, until such a machine should be produced. The object of that bill was to appoint and incorporate certain gentlemen as guardians and trustees, for the purpose of licensing and registering all chimney-sweepers within ten miles of the Royal Exchange, and imposing penalties upon all persons exercising that trade, without being so registered; and to require that the apprentices should be bound until the age of twenty-one years, subject to a proviso for cancelling such indenture at the age of sixteen, with the approbation of the guardians and trustees, who were to see to the putting out in the world of such apprentice, either to some other trade or in such other way as they should determine at such age of sixteen. There were also clauses for preventing the employment of any but apprentices as climbing boys, and also for preventing masters from borrowing, purchasing, or selling the services of their apprentices. Such, with some regulations of detail, were the objects of the bill which passed the House of Commons, and a committee of the House of Lords, but was rejected at the third reading in the

Lords. Since that period the Society have used their best endeavours to promote the invention of machines for effecting the purpose, and have found that the one invented by Mr. Smart has in most instances been found to succeed; the proportion of instances in which it has failed, as far as upon rather a loose calculation we have been able to ascertain, has been as one in an hundred.

Can you give the Committee any information how these boys are in general treated by their masters; first as to their lodging?—With the exception of the few respectable tradesmen, the rest had no better lodging than the cellars in which the soot was deposited; the boys sleeping on the soot bags.

How were the apprentices of the better class of masters lodged?—They slept in attics, two, or three, or more together; and even in their cases they were not washed or cleaned more than once a week.

Did they sleep on beds, or on matrasses?—They sometimes were found sleeping on pallets; and in one very respectable situation they had nothing but straw; and that was the case in most instances even of the respectable ones.

Had you any information how often they were washed, or if any care was taken that they should be washed, by those persons who were not considered as respectable masters?—We found that among the less respectable class of chimney-sweepers the boys were taken to the New River on a Sunday morning, in the summer season.

During the winter months, do you know whether any care was taken with respect to their washing?—We had reason to fear there was not, and which would account for the disorders generated by remaining longer than the week in their filthy garments.

What disorders do you particularly allude to?—The principal complaint to which they are liable is the cancer, which generally affects them in the scrotum.

Has it not sometimes been known to affect them within the lip and in the eye?—Yes; but the affection in the scrotum is the most general, and by medical men is technically termed the chimney-sweeper's cancer.

Do you know whether that disease is common?—I have been informed cases of that sort are very common in the hospitals.

Have you ever heard of boys of a very tender age having that disease?—I have heard of one; the medical persons at St. Bartholomew's considered that they had had a boy under seven, but they had no means of ascertaining his age; and that boy got liberated by a magistrate from his indentures.

Are they subject to an inflammation in the eyes?

—I have seen many with a disorder commonly called blear eyes.

Is their appearance then of a stinted growth; can you give the Committee any information upon that subject?—Their general appearance is certainly more of knock-knees and an emaciated countenance, than any other description of children about the metropolis.

So that from appearance a boy of seventeen will continue to be able to ascend chimneys?F requently.

Do you know any thing of the mortality of chimney-sweepers, contrasted with other trades in the metropolis?—No; I have no facts to warrant any information upon that subject.

Is there not in general a prejudice against children who have been brought up in that trade, when they have grown too big to be employed in it?—Unquestionably; they are totally incapable, from previous habits of education or strength of body, to make themselves useful in any other vocation.

So that a boy who has outgrown his fitness for that business must be thrown upon the parish?—Certainly.

Do you know whether chimney-sweepers in general have any care taken of their education by their masters?—I believe none. The association in 1800 had that object in view, and several respectable chimney-sweepers attempted to promote it among the trade; but I never understood that any progress was made, but that in fact the apprentices of chimney-sweepers have not had any education whatever.

Do you know whether any of them attend the Sunday schools?—I understand some of the masters who are well disposed send the boys to Sunday schools; and that, I understand, is the only means of their deriving any instruction whatever.

Do you know whether the chimney-sweepers, when they are bound apprentices, keep up their connection with their friends; or are they not discarded by them, and left entirely to associate with their fellow chimney-sweepers?—I believe entirely; it cuts them off from all society; and what I before stated, as to their sports, only applies to dissipation in the public streets, having nothing else to do from an early hour in the morning, when their labours, generally speaking, are suspended.

Do you know whether the boys are allowed any perquisites for their labour? — So far from it, that I have been informed by boys themselves, that they are called upon to account for the pence and small sums given to them by benevolent individuals in the pubiic streets.

Are there any master chimney-sweepers who use

this machine, or other machines? — Several masters have applied for the machines, and had them from the Society; but I know of but one or two who have faithfully used them.

What objection do you imagine they have to the use of the machine? — General prejudice, together with the increased labour that it demands on their part, or that of their journeyman.

But do you think, in point of fact, by means of these machines they would be able to earn as much as at present? — More; and we have constantly endeavoured to persuade them upon that point.

Then the trade would be quite as good as it is now? — Better; and we have always endeavoured to keep it within the trade, without introducing a new set of chimney-sweepers with the machine.

You think the prime cost of the machine would not be so much as the cost of the boy? — Certainly not; Mr. Cook, of Windmill Street, is the only one I know who uses the machine honestly. (4) I would incidentally mention one circumstance, and that is, the use of the machine in extinguishing fires in chimneys; for by dipping the brush with cloths round it, in a pail of water, and sending it up the chimney, it completely effects its purpose, and thus obviates a great deal of that risk to which children have been hitherto exposed, by being sent up too soon after a chimney has been on fire, and which has very often been attended with fatal or dangerous consequences.

Mr. *George Smart* called in, and examined.

Where do you live? — At the foot of Westminster Bridge, on the Surrey side.

What are you by profession? — I am a carpenter and builder, and sometimes act as a surveyor.

Are you the proprietor of the machine now produced, for sweeping chimneys without the necessity of employing climbing boys? — Yes; I have received two medals from the Society of Arts. (5) It is perhaps fourteen years since I invented the machine; I have here a complete model, that I made since last Saturday.

[*The witness exhibited a model in wood of the plan upon which houses are built in the present day.*]

Could you not give the Committee a drawing of that plan from the model which you now exhibit, with the names and descriptions in the margin, of the machine? — Yes.

[*The witness exhibited another model of a chimney flue, of which he also promised to furnish a plan.*]

Witness.—This sort of flue is of the most difficult kind.

That model which you have given of a flue is the most difficult that you know of in houses now existing? — Yes.

How many flues of that description do you think there are in proportion to the ordinary chimneys in the metropolis? — I should suppose not one in a hundred, only where there are detached kitchens across a yard; but they are dangerous flues.

In all other chimneys with which you are acquainted, there is no impediment to the use of the machine? — None, except from awkwardness in a person not understanding the principle of the flue; then there is great difficulty. I have known instances of the sweeps breaking the machines, and coming to me with the sweat running down their faces, when I have put them to rights with the greatest possible ease.

Then in those cases where the machine has been broke, it has been by the awkwardness of the person who has used the machine, and not from any real impediment in the flue to prevent its being so used? — It is from that circumstance.

You say you have invented this machine 15 years? — About 14 years.

What do you think has been the reason why, if it

would so easily sweep chimneys, it has not been generally adopted? — There has been a general objection to it, as it respects the interest of the sweeps: I have found, in many instances, the servants equally obstinate; they were in league with the sweep.

Has the use of this machine increased of late years? — Very much.

Can you state to the Committee in what proportion? — Since the last meeting at the Mansion House I think I have made about 200 (6), which I think was in last July or August.

You said that servants were opposed to the use of the machine, being influenced by the sweeps? —Yes.

Do you know what arguments the sweeps use with the servants to influence them? — The first winter I went out with this machine, I went to Mr. Burke's in Token-house Yard, who was a friend of mine, with a man to sweep the chimneys, and after waiting above an hour in a cold morning, the housekeeper came down quite in a rage, that we should presume to ring the bell or knock at the door; and when we got admittance, she swore she wished the machine and the inventor at the devil: she did not know me. We swept all the chimneys, and when we had done, I asked her what objection she had to it now. She said, a very serious one; that if there was a thing by which a servant could get any emolument, some damned invention was sure to take it away from them, for that she received perquisites.

From whom did she receive those perquisites? — The master sweep.

In another instance, a number of ladies and gentlemen had been invited to see the chimneys swept by our machine; my foreman put the cloth before the chimney, and put the brush inside, and it stood there waiting till the company should collect. The gentleman of the house sent the valet out to let the company know all was ready. The valet came in and took a towel to show the effects of the machine; that every thing would be covered with dust, when the machine had not been up. The gentleman and his lady enjoyed the thing very much; but when it was put up there was not the smallest appearance of dirt or dust. The result of my experience is, that the servants have set their faces against the use of the machine.

Veneris, 13° *die Junii*, 1817.

The Honourable Henry Grey Bennet, in the Chair.

John Cook called in, and Examined.

What trade are you? — Chimney-sweeper.

Are you a master chimney-sweeper? — Yes.

How long have you been in that trade? — About thirty-two years; rather better, I think.

As master? — No: my indenture, which I have with me, shows when I served my time.

How long have you acted as master? — Twenty years.

How many apprentices do you keep? — Only two at present, because one is out of his time.

How many apprentices do you generally keep? — I have had five; but I have not, for some years, kept more than three. I could have had one a little time ago, but I thought something would be done to stop climbing boys.

What age was the boy you refused to take the other day as an apprentice? — I only refused to take him because I thought something would be done; he was about eight years, just within the limits of the act of Parliament.

Were his parents living? — Yes.

Do parents give a premium to you for taking their children, or do you give them a premium? — Neither the one nor the other.

Is it customary in the trade, for the sake of security, for those things to be done? — It is; I have had boys with me a fortnight, and something longer, and because I would not give the parents the money they asked for, they have taken them away again, and apprenticed them to another man in the trade.

What sum of money is generally given for those children to the parents by the master sweeps? — Two or three pounds; it depends upon circumstances, sometimes more, and sometimes less.

Do you give more for children that are delicately formed, and who therefore are better calculated for ascending small chimneys? — The smaller they are the master generally likes them the better, because they are generally more serviceable to them.

So that a small boy bears a better price than a full-grown boy? — Yes, if he is strong enough to do the duty, and is a hearty-looking boy of his age.

How many chimneys are you in the habit of sweeping daily upon an average? — Some days we have a dozen to do, and other days we have not above three or four, and some days not one.

Of the days you have a dozen, how many do you sweep with the machine? — This morning we swept three out of seven.

Then you mean to say, that you generally sweep one-third of the chimneys which you sweep, with the machine? — Yes, I think we do one-third; that is as near as can be: I think one-third.

Is the machine used, within your knowledge, by many master chimney-sweepers? — Yes; but many do not like it, and give it as bad a name as they can: they will not use it but where their customers insist upon it; merely keeping it to save their custom, and generally make some complaints about it, that they may not take it there again.

Your own opinion is favourable to the machine? — Yes.

Do you think that you could sweep every chimney, even that of peculiar construction, such as you have described a short time back, with this machine, without the use of climbing boys at all? — Yes, with the alteration suggested in the model made by Mr. Smart.

To what alteration in the model do you allude? — If ever so high a house, there is some part of the house where you generally may find a stack of chimneys which unite; it may be near the top, or even in the middle of the house, where a hole or register might be made to work the sticks, through which we should be able to drop a ball attached to a cord; and when that comes to the bottom, you may easily fasten on your two brushes, and the machine may be worked without difficulty.

Then you think that if those alterations took place, as shown to you by Mr. Smart's model, that there is no chimney in London which might not be swept by mechanical means? — There are none but what might be done in that way.

At what age have you known climbing boys taken as apprentices?—Why seven years old.

Have you ever known a boy being taken under the age of seven?—No, I do not know that I have.

Is it not the practice for parents to employ their own children under that age, particularly the smaller master chimney-sweepers?—They often do it.

Eight years old is the time specified in the act of Parliament; but the Committee have been informed that the parents do not consider themselves bound by the act of Parliament, thinking it is applicable only to masters: what we want to know from you is, at what age you have ever known children to be employed to ascend chimneys?—About seven years.

You have never heard of children being employed as young as four, five, or six?—I have heard as young as six, but I do not know the boy; I was very young when I came to it.

How young were you?—I really cannot say; but I believe I was between six and seven.

Is it not the practice of some masters to advertise themselves as being in possession of small boys for the purpose of ascending flues?—Almost every one has got it in their bills, that they keep small boys for register stoves, and such like as that; I do not recollect ever seeing it in the newspapers, but they do it in their bills.

How do you ascertain the age of the boy when he is offered to you as an apprentice; do you take the parents' word for it?—The parents will often say that he is older than what he is.

Are you in the habit of getting any other evidence of their ages than the parents' own words?—No.

Do you ever get a certificate of their age, or is it the practice of other masters to get one?—No, I cannot say I ever heard of it.

Do you not know that the act of Parliament required it?—I do not know that it does.

Then you think it never is attended to?—I think that it is never attended to; that is, the certificate.

You say you have two apprentices in your employ; do those two apprentices live with you?—Yes.

Where do they sleep?—In the cellar.

Upon their soot bags?—No; they have blankets and a bed.

A matress?—Yes.

Is the soot kept in the cellar too?—Yes.

Do you give them any wages?—Not the apprentices.

Do you give them any perquisites?—No.

What is the food that they daily have?—They have bread and butter and tea for breakfast, and what we have for dinner; and for supper they generally have bread and butter.

They have the remains of your dinner, whatever it may be?—Yes.

Are not persons employed as climbing boys, particularly children, subject to sores and bruises, and wounds and burns on their thighs and knees, in consequence of ascending chimneys?—Yes, they are subject to that; because learning very fresh boys makes their knees and elbows very sore; but when they have properly learnt their trade their knees and elbows get hard, and they very seldom get sore again unless they meet with an accident; sometimes they get burnt by chimneys partly on fire.

The Committee understand, by use, that the extremities of the elbows and of the knees become as hard as the heel of the foot of a person who walks without shoes?—Yes, it does.

What time does it take before those parts get cartilaginous? — Six months.

What mode do you adopt to get the boy to go up the chimney in the first instance?—We persuade him as well as we can. We generally practise him in one of our own chimneys first: one of the boys who knows the trade goes up behind him; and when he has practised it perhaps ten times, though some will require twenty times, they generally can manage it. The boy goes up with him to keep him from falling; after that, the boy will manage to go up by himself, after going up and down several times with one under him: we do this, because if he happens to make a slip he will be caught by the other.

Do you find many boys show great repugnance to go up at first?—Yes, most of them.

And if they resist and reject, in what way do you force them up?—By telling them we must take them back again to their father and mother, and give them up again; and their parents are generally people who cannot maintain them.

So that they are afraid of going back to their parents for fear of being starved?—Yes; they go through a deal of hardship before they come to our trade.

Do you use any more violent means?—Sometimes a rod.

Did you ever hear of straw being lighted under them?—Never.

You never heard of any means being made use of, except being beat and being sent home?—No; no other.

You are aware, of course, that those means being gentle or harsh, must depend very much upon the character of the individual master? — It does.

Of course you must know that there are persons of harsh and cruel disposition; have you not often heard of masters treating their apprentices with great cruelty, particularly the little boys, in forcing them to go up those small flues which the boy was unwilling to ascend?—Yes; I have forced up many a one myself.

By what means?—By threatenings, and giving them a kick or a slap.

Are there not peculiar diseases under which chimney-sweepers suffer?—Yes, I have seen them; what are commonly called the sooty warts, a kind of cancer.

On what part of the person are those sooty warts, as you term them?—On the scrotum.

Are they ever on the face or lip?—I have never seen them there, nor heard of them.

Is not the effect of soot on the eyes very prejudicial; and are not many of the chimney-sweepers blear-eyed? —Yes, there are many so.

Does not the custom of sending those little boys up the chimneys produce crooked, deformed limbs, and stunt the growth of the children?—I do not know about the growth; I think it may sometimes, because now they have their chimneys sometimes built round, and as they climb up them they are obliged to be as a corkscrew, and this will turn the cap of their knees: this I know has often been the case.

Is not lameness a very common effect of the system of climbing chimneys?—I do not know many instances of boys getting lame through being of the trade: it is not often the case; it is but very seldom.

In general, are they not more stunted and deformed than any other class of children in any other trade?—Yes; but there are a great many deformed a little before they come to it, though certainly working at the trade so young deforms them more.

When a boy has served his apprenticeship to a master chimney-sweeper, and is out of his time, if he is too big to be employed in your trade, what becomes of him?—That is a very great evil in the trade; there is not always a living for all who serve their time.

What then generally becomes of them?—It is a hard thing to say; some go to sea, and some have got parents, who will take them and learn them something else, and some have got none. I had no parents, and I was obliged to remain in the trade. We cannot tell what becomes of them, but there is not a living for above half who serve their time at it.

Then for the other half, for whom there is not a living, they are thrown upon the world at the age of about sixteen, without having been taught any trade, or having any means of earning a livelihood?—Yes; that is one thing that makes me hold with the machines.

Supposing that a law was to be passed that was to prohibit climbing boys to be used, do you think, from the mechanical inventions at present known, all the chimneys in London could be swept?—I have no doubt of that; though it would be a great confusion in some of the public buildings, because many of the chimneys would require alteration.

Suppose a certain number of months were allowed between the passing the act and the time in which it should be put into execution, would there then be any difficulty in carrying the law into effect?—No, not if a certain time were allowed.

Is it the practice of the journeymen to correct the boys?—Yes.

Do they correct them with a stick, or in what way? —When I was an apprentiec, they often used to keep a cat in their pocket; but I think it is not carried on so much now as it used to be; they are used better now than what they used to be formerly.

The cat of which you were speaking, for the purpose of flogging the boys, do you think it is ever used now?—Yes, I think it is sometimes used now.

What sort of a cat is it?—It is made of rope, and hard at each end, and as thick as your thumb.

Have you ever known a journeyman use any of the children very ill?—Yes; for very little faults they will frequently kick them and smack them about; the boys are more afraid of them than of their masters.

You said that the elbows and knees of the boys, when they first begin the business, become very sore, and afterwards get callous; are those boys employed in sweeping chimneys during the soreness of those parts? — It depends upon the sort of master they have got; some are obliged to put them to work sooner than others: you must keep them a little at it, or they will never learn their business, even during the sores.

Is the skin broke generally?—Yes, it is.

Can they ascend chimneys during the sores without very great pain?—The way that I learn boys is, to put some cloths over their elbows and over their knees till they get the nature of the chimney, till they get a little used to it; we call it padding them; and then we take them off, and they get very little grazed indeed after they have got the art; but very few will take that trouble. Some boys' flesh is far worse than others, and it takes more time to harden them.

Do those persons still continue to employ them to climb chimneys? — Some do; it depends upon the character of the master.

Do you imagine that many keep them till they get well, of that class? — No, none.

So that they are obliged to climb with those sores upon them?—Yes.

Are the boys ever washed?—Yes, I wash mine regularly; but some of the lower class are not washed for six months.

Do they receive any education?—Many do not.

Is it a general practice to attend divine worship?—

Great numbers are neither washed nor attend on the Sunday.

Are they sweeping on the Sunday?— No, I do not think they are.

Is there not a prejudice existing among the children of other persons in the same station of life, against the associating with young chimney-sweepers?—Yes.

Is it not considered as one of the most degrading trades in the metropolis?— I think it is.

Have you any difficulty in obtaining children?—Very often.

It is then of the very lowest class that you have them? – Yes.

Is it not the practice for thieves, and bad people of that description, to get hold of the chimney-sweepers whose servitude is over, and who are turned loose in the world without parents or means of gaining a livelihood, and associate them with their gangs?—It is hardly possible to tell; but I am convinced that not above half that are employed can get a livelihood after they are out of their time.

Of course they may become a prey to the first person who wants their services, whether good or bad?—I should think it may be so.

I think you have stated that you have known many parents sell their children; did you ever know a child whom you suspected to be stolen?—I have heard talk of such things, but never knew it myself.

Have they not frequently taken children from persons whom they did not know to be the parents of these children?—They entice them sometimes out of schools and parishes, and get them apprenticed.

But at the same time their parents know where they are?—They frequently do not know where they are.

Is it often the case?—Yes, it is often the case; one of my fellow apprentices was at the trade three or four years before his friends found him out.

Did he know where his friends were?—No.

Did he come from a workhouse?—Yes.

Do you recollect what workhouse?— St. George's workhouse.

Is he alive now?—I do not know.

Did his friends remove him from the trade when they found him out?—Yes, they did.

John Fisher called in, and examined.

Are you a master chimney sweeper?—Yes.

Have you any apprentices?—No, only a child of my own.

How old is that boy?—Eight years.

How long has he been in the trade?—Nearly two years.

Do you work on your own account, or as a journeyman for others?—I work on my own account.

Is your boy small of his age?—Yes, he is small of his age.

Do you employ him in ascending small flues?—Yes, because I have only got him; I am obliged to get my living by him, or else I must go without.

Are you at all lame yourself?—No, but I am "knapped-kneed" with carrying heavy loads when I was an apprentice.

That was the occasion of it?—It was.

In general are persons employed in your trade either stunted or knock-kneed by carrying heavy loads during their childhood?—It is owing to their masters a great deal; and when they climb a great deal, it makes them weak.

Have you known many instances in which masters have ill-treated their children to force them up chimneys?—Many masters are very severe with them.

What methods do they use to make them go up?—I have seen them make them strip themselves naked, and threaten to beat them; I have been obliged myself to go up a chimney naked, but I do not like to see my children do so.

How long have you ever known children remain unwashed in the trade?—Some go two or three months.

How long have you ever gone yourself when you were an apprentice ?—Sometimes a month.

Were you washed of your own accord, or by your master's order ?—Sometimes by my own accord, and sometimes my master made me be washed.

What sort of bed had you to sleep upon, when you were apprentice ?—Most boys sleep upon a straw bed.

What becomes of those boys who get too large to go up chimneys ?—They get into a roving way, and go about from one master to another, and they often come to no good end at last.

What becomes of them at last ?—They sometimes go into the country, and after staying there some time, they come back again ; I took a boy of that sort very lately, and kept him like my own, and let him go to school ; he asked me one Sunday to let him go to school, and I was glad to let him go, and I gave him leave ; he accordingly went, and I have seen nothing of him since ; before he went he asked me if I would let him come home to see my child buried ; I told him to ask his schoolmaster, but he did not come back again.

Can you tell what is become of him ?—I cannot say ; he was to have served me for twelve months.

Who did you take him from ; from the parish ?—No, he came to me.

Did he give any account of his parents?—No, he said they were dead.

What do you think is the effect of that roving habit of the large boys when they become too large to climb?—They get one with another, and learn bad habits from one another; they never will stop long in any one place.

What becomes of them at last?—They frequently go into the country and get various places; perhaps they stop a month at each; some try to get masters themselves, and some will get into bad company, which very often happens.

Do they turn thieves?—Yes, they get lazy, they won't work, and people do not like to employ them lest they should take any thing out of their houses.

Do you think that the generality of them ever settle in any steady business?—No, they do not.

They generally turn loose characters, then?—Yes, when they get linked with these bad characters, people will not employ them, lest they should take any thing out of the house.

Mr. *Richard Wright* called in, and examined.

You are a medical person, I believe?—I am a surgeon.

Where do you live?—At Rotherhithe at present.

Have you paid particular attention to the complaints that climbing boys are subject to?—Not being aware of its becoming a public question, I did not attend to them more particularly than others; whilst I was attending Guy's and Bartholomew's Hospitals, I had three or four cases particularly under my care.

What is the nature of the particular diseases?—The diseases that we particularly noticed, to which they were subject, were of a cancerous description.

In what part?—The scrotum, in particular: I think I recollect two cases of that sort, and one was cured, the other not; but I remember three or four cases operated on, in which we found the testicles equally diseased with the scrotum, and when the operation was performed we were obliged to remove the testicles. I cannot exactly say when that was, but I think it was in the year 1794 or 1795; but I am not quite prepared for so close an answer to that point.

Did you ever hear of cases of that description that were fatal?—No, I do not think them as being altogether fatal, unless they will not submit to the operation; they have such a dread of the operation that they will not submit to it; for when they do not let it be perfectly removed, they will be liable to the return of it; but when the operation has taken place, the bag or scrotum being gone, there is then no danger.

To what cause do you attribute that disease?—I think it begins from a want of care, because if people are careful, they are not so liable to such bad sores that will not heal rapidly.

Should you consider it to arise from that part being wounded and not being attended to?—No, I do not consider it to arise from a wound of the part, but the bag or scrotum being in so many folds or crevices, the soot lodges in them and creates an itching, and I conceive that by scratching it and tearing it the soot gets in and creates the irritability; which disease we know by the name of the chimney-sweepers' cancer, and is always lectured upon separately as a distinct disease.

Then the Committee understand that the physicians who are entrusted with the care and management of those hospitals think that disease of such common occurrence, that it is necessary to make it a part of surgical education? — Most assuredly; I remember Mr. Cline and Mr. Cooper were particular on that subject, and having one or two cases of that kind in the hospital, it struck my mind very forcibly. With the permission of the Committee I will relate a case that occurred lately, which I had from one of the pupils of St. Thomas's Hospital; he informed me that they had recently had a case of a chimney-sweeper's cancer, which was to have been operated on that week, but the man brushed (to use their expression) or rather walked off; he would not submit to the operation: similar instances of which I have known myself. They dread so much the knife, in consequence of foolish persons telling them it is so formidable an operation, and that they will die under it.

Without an operation there is no cure? — I conceive not; I conceive without the operation it is death; for cancers are of that nature, that unless you extirpate them entirely they will never be cured.

You went to see, the Committee understand, a little boy of the name of William Hatton, at one of the hospitals; in what state was he? — He was then recovering very fast; he had got two wounds, I think, but I believe they were those that had been inflicted upon him: this was my reason for going to see him; at which time they were nearly well.

I think you said you considered these cancerous diseases to arise from the filth and dirt of the soot? — I have not the least doubt that is the whole and sole cause of it; I was always taught so, and have been since confirmed by my limited observations.

[*The witness delivered in the following letter, which was read:*]

"Dear Sir,

"Agreeably to your request relative to the diseases,

accidents, &c. incidental to chimney-sweepers, I take the present opportunity of enumerating a few of their complaints, as far as my practice has afforded me an opportunity of observing, and which I trust you will (on comparing them with those of the different authors who have written on this subject) find tolerably correct; at the same time I beg you will make every allowance for any inaccuracy you should observe, and which I shall be obliged by your pointing out to me at any future opportunity.

"To proceed, I shall begin with deformity. — I am well persuaded that the deformity of the spine, legs, arms, &c. of chimney-sweepers, generally, if not wholly, proceeds from the circumstance of their being obliged not only to go up chimneys at an age when their bones are in a soft and growing state, but likewise by that of being compelled by their too merciless masters and mistresses to carry bags of soot (and those very frequently for a great length of distance and time) by far too heavy for their tender years and limbs: such circumstances I have unfortunately too often been an eye-witness to. The knees and ancle joints mostly become deformed, in the first instance, from the position they are obliged to put them in, in order to support themselves, not only while climbing up the chimney, but more particularly so in that of coming down, when they rest solely on the lower extremities, the arms being used for scraping and sweeping down the soot in the mean time: this, in addition to that of carrying heavy loads, confirms the complaint.

"Sore eyes and eyelids, are the next to be considered. Chimney-sweepers are very subject to inflammation of the eyelids, and not unfrequently, weakness of sight, in consequence of such inflammation. This I attribute to the circumstance of the soot lodging on the eyelids, which first produces irritability of the part, and by the constantly rubbing them with their dirty hands, instead of alleviating increases the disease; for I have observed in a number of cases, when the patient has ceased for a time to follow the business, and of course the original cause has been removed, that with washing and keeping clean they were soon got well.

"Sores, for the same reasons, are generally a long time in healing.

"Cancer is another and a most formidable disease, which chimney-sweepers in particular are liable to, especially that of the scrotum; from which circumstance, by way of distinction, it is called the 'chimney-sweeper's cancer.' Of this sort of cancer I have seen several instances, some of which have been operated on; but, in general, they are apt to let them go too far before they apply for relief. Cancers of the lips are not so general as cancers of the scrotum. I never saw but two instances of the former, and several of the latter.

"Cough and Asthma. — Chimney-sweepers are, from their being out at all hours and in all weathers, very liable to cough and inflammation of the chest; and which are generally increased by the wretchedness of their habitations, as they too frequently have to sleep in a shed exposed to the different changes of the weather, their only bed a soot bag, and another to cover them, independent of their tattered garments.

"Burns. — They are very subject to burns, from their being forced up chimneys while on fire, or soon after they have been on fire, and while over-heated; and however they may cry out, their inhuman masters pay not the least attention, but compel them, too often, with horrid imprecations, to proceed. And there are several instances where the poor sufferer has fallen a victim to the harsh treatment he has already experienced, and the fear of future punishment if he disobey his master's mandates, so that he has remained as long as he possibly could until the excessive heat and his exhausted strength have compelled him to let go his hold, and he has fallen down, perhaps not to rise again, or if he has, it has been only to linger out a miserable existence, and that for a short period.

"Stunted growth, in this unfortunate race of the community, is attributed, in a great measure, to their being brought into the business at a very early age, so early even as five years. And I have heard of instances of children of four years and a half old being compelled to go up narrow chimneys.

"Short life is very common among them, frequently from their being exposed to colds, coughs, and from the poor miserable and half-starved manner in which they generally live, as many of them are not allowed any thing to eat, except what they obtain through the generosity of the inhabitants whose chimneys they sweep; and in many cases they come off very scantily, so that in order to procure food they take every opportunity of purloining any article which may be worth their while, if it should come in their way; and which, when they take it home to their master or mistress (for they seldom know how otherwise to dispose of it), they are rewarded perhaps with some cold and broken victuals, or a little money to procure some. This is another calamity, as it initiates them at early life in acts of depredation, a disposition which increases with their years, and for which several unfortunate creatures have paid the forfeit with their lives.

"Accidents they are very liable to from several causes, and among the rest, that of getting fixed in a chimney, so as not to be capable of extricating themselves; and there are several instances wherein part of a chimney has been obliged to be taken down before the unhappy sufferer could be relieved.

"Clothing. — The clothing of these poor creatures is, in general, very wretched; not that they require good clothes, but it is essentially necessary for their health and comfort that their clothes should be entire, and not a bundle of rags half stitched together, and half torn to pieces.

"Diet. — In cases where the masters or mistresses provide the food for their apprentices, it is in general not only of the coarsest sort, but, what is worse, mostly of the poorest and stalest meat they can get, and at the most inferior price, which lays a foundation for scurvy, general debility, loss of limbs, and often consumption, by weakening the organs of life.

"Time. — I think it very prejudicial to the health of the poor creatures, to be sent out at all hours of the night and morning, without regard to weather, as it subjects them to most violent colds, &c.; and they are exposed to this for no other reason than because it is customary for them to come early, as if a chimney could not be much better swept in the day than during the night, or that part of the morning when it is necessary to have a light in the room, the chimney of which is to be swept, as is constantly the case during the winter months, when the sweep comes long before day-light.

"Should the foregoing ideas be worthy your attention, I shall feel myself exceedingly happy in having penned them, and remain,

"Dear Sir,

"Yours, most respectfully,

"(Signed) RICHARD WRIGHT.

"289, Rotherhithe, July 16, 1816."

Jonathan Snow called in, and examined.

Are you the proprietor and the maker of a machine to sweep chimneys? — Yes.

Have you brought either a machine or a model with you? — I have not.

In what respect does it differ from Smart's? — It differs very little from Mr. Smart's; the difference consists chiefly that I work two heads or brushes instead of one with the machine; I am perfectly convinced that chimneys can be cleansed with these machines full as well as boys can cleanse them.

How long have you used your machine? — For nearly a twelvemonth, within a few days.

How many chimneys have you swept since that period? — I will say 600 or 650.

Is your machine capable of sweeping any chimney? — Not every chimney where I have gone to; where the chimney runs with quite a flat, and rises up again directly, the machine will not sweep it.

Of the chimneys you are acquainted with in London, what proportion does that sort of chimney bear to the common chimney which your machine will sweep? — About one out of 120 or 130.

Do you ever sweep chimneys in carpenters' shops? —Yes.

Does the soot cake upon those chimneys more than others?—Yes, according to the quantity of wood which they burn; but we have a stouter machine for chimneys of that nature.

From your own experience, can you state that this brings down that soot?—Yes, it is formed of a stronger brush.

So that you do not find practically difficulties in those chimneys?—I do not find the least difficulty in the world with those chimneys.

How do you manage with the pots and the tin pipes at the top of many chimneys?—The head of the brush is made with the bristles sticking up; by constant working, it will cleanse the pot.

By constant working of this brush it will cleanse the pot sufficiently?—It will cleanse it sufficiently.

How do you manage with the tin pipe?—The machine will go up a tin pipe as well as a chimney; and if there is any tube or pot, the whalebone that is in this brush, directly it gets near the top, will strike immediately into these pipes.

Have you ever seen any mechanical invention which would enable you to sweep those flues which you have described, which your machine will not now sweep ?—Yes, a great many of them ; there is a certain thing by which, getting to the top of the chimney with a round ball, which, by letting it down, will find its way to the bottom, having a string tied to it, and the person at the bottom attaches a brush to that string.

How do you attach that cord to the ball ?—By a round hole in the ball.

Have you ever seen a chimney that you could not sweep by one mechanical process or another ?—No, I have not seen any but which by one mechanical process or another might be swept, barring those two chimneys that I saw, and which ran upon a long dead slant ; one was at right angles with the level.

Have you ever seen any plan by which that species of chimney could be swept without the aid of a climbing boy?—Yes, I have ; it may be done by altering the chimneys a little, by having a little flap door made.

By means of that small door, which has been termed a register, you think that even those chimneys could be swept ?—I do.

The ball would not pass those chimneys ?—Not

where the chimney runs slant; the ball would not find its way down.

Benjamin Meggot Forster, Esq. of Walthamstow, Essex, called in, and examined.

Do you belong to the committee who have been endeavouring to supersede the necessity of climbing boys?—Yes.

Have you paid considerable attention to the subject?—I believe it may be said I have.

Will you be so good as to state to the Committee the result of your inquiries upon that subject?—First, with respect to teaching the children to climb, one mode of which I understand to be common, though I will not say universal, is to send a greater boy up the chimney after the lesser one, who has a pin in his hand, and if the little boy does not climb properly he sticks it in his feet.

Do you happen to know this of your own personal knowledge?—I have heard of it as a practice, and when I was at Norwich I made particular inquiry upon that subject. In the whole city of Norwich I could find only nine climbing boys, two of whom I questioned on many particulars; one was with respect to the manner which they are taught to climb; they both agreed in that particular, that a larger boy was sent up behind them to prick their feet, if they did not climb properly. I purposely avoided mentioning about pricking them with pins, but asked them how they did it; they said that they thrust the pins into the soles of their feet. A third instance occurred at Walthamstow; a man told me that some he knew had been taught in the same way; I believe it to be common, but I cannot state any more instances from authority. One part of the sufferings of the children is in what is called coreing chimneys, that is, going up to clear out the rubbish which the workmen, from their slovenly mode of proceeding, often let fall into the chimney; when they are built at the outside, the mortar and little chips of brick fall in, and the clearing of these out is, as I am informed, a very painful operation; it cuts their feet, and lacerates other parts of their body.

This is then before the chimney is used?—It is; it is done to enable the smoke to have a free ascent up the chimney. Another part of their sufferings is being sent up chimneys on fire, which, though the Act of Parliament strictly prohibits their being sent up when the chimney is actually on fire, is a custom, I believe, frequently practised.

Do you know any particular instance from your own examination?—Yes; a poor boy of the name of William Hatton, who had been up a chimney on fire in Stamford-street, Blackfriars; at least, from his own account, it appears that he had been up a chimney on fire, and was injured by that circumstance. Those boys, too, that I questioned at Norwich also acknowledged that they had been up chimneys on fire. There can be no doubt of its being a common practice.

Was the boy very much burnt who was taken to Guy's Hospital?—The boy's account was, that the accident was owing to a burn, but the master denied it; when the boy was taken to the Police Office to be released, it was not substantiated to be a burn; the boy appeared to be in a bad habit of body. Another mischief is, their being stifled in a flue, which was the case in Bryanstone-street, Mary-la-bonne, lately.

From what did it arise?—From absolute suffocation, occasioned by the soot. Another cruelty is, by driving them up with lighted straw or hay.

Did you ever know that fact?—A man at Walthamstow, of the name of Hedbury, related a circumstance to me, which happened some years ago; the lad was ordered to sweep a chimney at Wandsworth when he was an apprentice: he came down after endeavouring to ascend, and this occurred several times before he gave up the point, at last the journeyman took some straw or hay, and lighted it under him to drive him up; when he endeavoured to get up the last time, he found there was a bar across the chimney, which he could not pass, he was obliged in consequence to come down, and the journeyman beat him so cruelly, to use his own expression, that he could not stand for a fortnight.

Notwithstanding he found a bar?—He might state that, but probably the man did not believe it. With respect to the age, some are put to the employment very young; one instance of which occurred to a child in the neighbourhood of Shoreditch, who was put to the trade at four years and a quarter, or thereabouts. A child in Whitechapel, whose father told me last week, that his son began climbing when he was four years and eight months old; I have heard of still younger, but as it is only what I have heard from vague report, therefore I had better not mention it.

But this you know as a fact?—The father told me so himself, and he could have no reason to make the case worse than it was; I have no better evidence than that. Another circumstance, which has not been mentioned to the Committee, is, that there are several little girls employed; there are two of the name of Morgan at Windsor, daughters of the chimney-sweeper, who is employed to sweep the chimneys of the Castle; another instance at Uxbridge, and at Brighton, and at Whitechapel, (which was some years ago,) and at Hadley, near Barnet, and Witham in Essex, and elsewhere.

Do you not think that girls were employed, from

their physical form being smaller and thinner than boys, and therefore could get up narrower flues?—The reason that I have understood was, because their parents had not a sufficient number of boys to bring up to the business.

Do you know the age of those girls?—No; I have not got that exactly. With regard to boys sticking in flues, and being compelled to be cut out, I think it would be better to examine chimney-sweepers as to those facts.

Do you find your servants complain that there is now more soot brought down and thrown into the apartment by the use of the machine, than by the old method?—Very seldom; I do not know but there may be little complaints now and then.

Then you wish to state to the Committee generally, that you are well satisfied that the machine will answer the use designed?—Certainly; and if you ask my opinion, I think chimneys may be much better swept by machines than by the use of boys.

That is, a boy may neglect his duty; but a brush, if it fits, must do its duty?—Undoubtedly; I have several times worked the machine myself, in order to introduce it into our neighbourhood.

Do your neighbours use it very much?—Yes; especially since we have had a meeting, they have taken it up very much; with the common-built chimneys, the machine is very easily worked.

Joseph Birch, Esq. a Member of the Committee, made the following Statement.

I beg to state, in corroboration of what has been stated by Mr. Snow, that we have found in my house in the country that the use of the ball being put down the chimney answered every purpose we wished for in clearing the chimneys, independent of the practice of sending up boys; we have used this method some time, it being very much my wish to avoid that practice. The chimneys at my house are peculiarly constructed, for they are all collected into the centre of the roof, and consequently the chimneys at the extremities of the house must lie in a flat direction; we therefore use, in order to get the ball down the chimney, a very heavy one; the ball we have used generally is about eighteen pounds weight; in the first instance, on using it, we put it into a canvas bag, but that I found was attended with considerable difficulty in getting it down the chimney, in consequence of the soot clogging the bag; I afterwards contrived a wire bag to put it into, and which net was somewhat larger than the ball, so as to allow it to roll backward and forward in the bag, by which means the impetus that was given to it forced it down those angular parts of the chimneys, which there was great difficulty in getting at: the necessity of the bag, however, might be superseded by having balls constructed for the purpose, with holes through them, so that a rope might be passed through the ball and fastened with a knot, which would answer the purpose much better. When the ball is got down to the bottom we affix a wisp of holly to it, the person at the bottom pulls it down, and the person at the top pulls it up; by which means we have effectually cleansed all those chimneys without employing any sweeps.

And you have found that plan universally answer? —Perfectly so for several years; I have heard of two facts in my neighbourhood, in one instance where the boy was actually lost, and in the other instance was cut out of the chimney, and saved with considerable difficulty.

Lunæ, 16° *die Junii*, 1817.

The Honourable HENRY GREY BENNETT, in the Chair.

George Reveley, Esq. called in, and examined.

Have you used any machine for the purpose of sweeping chimneys, to supersede the necessity of climbing boys?—I have, many times.

How many years have you used them?—I cannot exactly say; but I have occasionally used the machine: but owing to some difference between a part of my family, and a chimney-sweeper that imposed upon us, we have declined it for a short time, meaning, however, to resume it again when I can get a proper person to work it; as I am still perfectly convinced that the machine was very competent to effect the purpose for which it is intended.

What machine did you use?—Smart's. I beg to state to the Committee, that a great deal depends upon a man's mind of the machine, whether he is pleased to do justice to it, or willing to make dirt and confusion in a family, in order to render the use of the machine obnoxious; and I will state the grounds. It is upon this principle: I sent for a neighbouring sweep to sweep a two-pair of stairs chimney, which was perfectly straight, and which I could have swept with a hand brush myself, and he was upwards of two hours sweeping that chimney, and made a very considerable dirt which was the cause of some part of my family being put a little out of conceit of the machine: it was upon the strength of that opinion, however, which I had formed, that I sent for Edmunds, who swept it perfectly well, and who has swept another chimney with the machine, which was much more difficult to sweep from its not being so straight; and with respect to the dirt, and the objections which have been raised to the use of the machine on that account, whenever Edmunds sweeps the chimney, instead of making more dirt, there is less dirt than when swept by a boy, and done in a shorter time, and more completely, as the chimney will last longer before it wants cleaning again.

Will you inform the Committee whether your chimneys are straight, that is, if they are nearly perpendicular?—They are very old chimneys; I have never been up any of them, so that I cannot exactly tell; the house has been built nearly an hundred years.

Have you any small flues in your house?—I have, and I will relate a circumstance that happened respecting one of them; it was before I belonged to the society, of which I have the honour of being one of the committee, and which settled my opinion in wishing to get rid of so great a nuisance; a young boy was brought to my house to sweep the copper chimney, which runs nearly perpendicular to the top of the house, and is about a brick and a half in width, and pretty nearly square, so that its dimensions may be easily ascertained; there was a hole made in the side for the boy to go up, and the boy was repeatedly driven in at the hole, but the mortar and soot fell in such great lumps upon his head, and with such force, that if he had not had a cap upon his head it would have been broken. Upon seeing the boy writhing in order to get into the chimney, and being satisfied he could not conveniently get up, although the man who was his master, being without feeling, seemed to say it was mere idleness in the boy, and that he would force the boy up, I would not suffer it, and the chimney was not swept.

Have you never swept this flue, of which you have given an account, with a machine?—I never have; but I have not any doubt but it would answer, because being perfectly straight, there could be no doubt upon earth about it, only the brush would require to be smaller than that commonly used for chimneys. The cause of the masters resisting so much the application of the machines seems most extraordinary, because one would suppose, from the circumstances of not having to keep the boy, and of the expense of clothes, if they give him any, would make it an object in favour of the chimney-sweeper; but all that I can suggest upon that head is, that when they send a boy up they can make him sweep just as they please, either sweep the chimney clean or leave it half done; and I am very apt to think that kitchen chimneys are often swept in that manner, and that the person so sweeps them in order to have them to do more frequently. There is a great cruelty, as it strikes my mind, in sending the boys up, in consequence of the carelessness of servants, it being done at that time of the morning when masters or mistresses are seldom up to see what is done; the servants frequently leave a little fire in the grate, and the consequence is, the sweep coming suddenly upon them, they throw a little water upon the fire, and the boy is forced up the chimney, when it is too hot for any body to endure it; and I understand they have frequently returned very much burnt: so I have heard from others; I will not speak of it as a fact within my own knowledge.

Have you any other information to give to the Committee?—I have nothing else; excepting that I beg leave to state, that those chimneys which are the most difficult to sweep are those very chimneys up which a boy ought never to be sent; because, when we consider the smallness of the chimney, and if it has not been swept a long time, the soot comes down so suddenly, and in such quantities, that if he even calls for assistance, he becomes suffocated before it can be afforded him; of which we have an instance in our report. I enquired into the fact of the case of the boy, and I found by the report of every one that it was true. That boy who was sold for 8*l.* 8*s.* was also really a fact; I heard it in the neighbourhood of Beverley.

To what story do you allude?—It is printed in

our report; it is the case of the boy who was sold for 8*l.* 8*s.*

Was he a stolen child?—Yes, he was a stolen child. I wish to state to the Committee that case in particular, because it comes home to the better sort of persons in higher life. It seems that the child, upon being asked various questions, it appeared that he was taken away: the child was questioned how he came in that situation; he said all that he could recollect was (as I have heard it told at that time) that he and his sister, with another brother, were together somewhere, but he could not tell where; but not being able to run so well as the other two, he was caught by a woman and carried away, and was sold, and came afterwards into the hands of this chimney-sweeper.

Was he afterwards restored to his family?—He was not; but when he was shown a repeating watch, he used to say his father had such a thing; or silver forks, he used to say the same: whether his father was gone abroad, or what had become of him, could never be ascertained.

Was he advertised?—Yes: but some lady took the child and educated him. There is another case I recollect, in which, however, the child did not suffer; but I mention it to show the extreme danger that there is in ascending chimneys: it is the case of a boy whose master lived in Coleman-street, or the neighbourhood; he ascended and got into the chimney-pot, which fell with him into a stone court; but very luckily he was not hurt: the pot was broken in pieces, and the boy crawled out like a bird out of an egg. I state this to show the danger there is when a boy ascends a chimney for the purpose of cleansing a pot, which they generally make them do, and to prove that they go up to the top, they make them halloo when they get up to the top of the house.

William Tooke, Esq. again called in, and further examined.

Have you any further information to give to the Committee?—I have some few observations to make. In compliance with the request of the Committee, I have made a selection of such cases of injury or death happening to climbing boys, as have come to my knowledge in the most authentic shape: the list might have been considerably increased, but there is no disposition to attempt to affect the feelings of the public. The cases which are submitted are a selection of such as clearly prove the injury to which all climbing boys are subject, and which it is supposed will be considered sufficient for the purpose of establishing the object of the Society; namely, the propriety of substituting mechanical means instead of climbing boys. If the Committee will permit me, I will state the conclusion of my investigation upon this subject, and which is the result of thirteen or fourteen years' experience, — that nothing short of legislative enactment and provision will have the desired effect; for, although the efforts of the Society have greatly tended to alleviate the condition of the boys, and more might be done by legislative provision, yet so much misery is inseparably connected with their business, that, as I observed before, nothing short of actual prohibition will effect the purpose; and that, I conceive, could be done by an act to amend the existing act, by introducing a clause for prohibiting the use of climbing boys after the first day of May, 1818. I merely take that day because it is the chimney-sweepers' holiday, and within that period the one case out of an hundred which does not admit the use of Smart's machine might be met by the fixing (as suggested in evidence) of a register in the flue, or of the bullet and the brush, as the case may happen. Another clause I should, with deference, beg to recommend; namely, for extending the age at which the apprenticeship should commence from eight to fourteen, putting this trade upon the same footing as others which take apprentices at fourteen; the boy would have then received a previous education, or at least would have had a chance of it, and at the expiration of his apprenticeship would be enabled to carry on the same business, or be qualified by strength and previous education for any other employment. In my opinion this will be the only mode of altogether relieving the boys from the oppressions under which they now suffer, and of very much improving the general character of the trade, and being of positive benefit to the persons engaging in it.

Martis, 17° *die Junii*, 1817.

The Honourable Henry Grey Bennet, in the Chair.

Thomas Edmunds called in, and examined.

What are you by trade?—I was brought up to the carpentering business.

Are you proprietor of one of the machines for sweeping chimneys?—Yes.

You are not the inventor?—No; I am the only person who first began the use of the machine, and the person who continued it from 1804.

Whose machine do you use?—Mr. Smart's.

Have you of late years used that machine much oftener than heretofore?—Certainly I have.

Can you state to the Committee what has been the extent of the increase of business that you have had?

— I look upon it that the increase of business is nearly doubled since I first began business.

How many chimneys did you sweep last year? — Thirteen hundred and thirteen with the machine, for I use nothing else.

From your observation, how many chimneys do you think, out of a hundred, can be swept with that machine? — I look upon it we can do ninety-nine out of a hundred; I have not the least doubt of it.

The one out of a hundred are those twisted or crooked chimneys which you cannot sweep with these machines? — They are, and nothing else.

Are these chimneys common in the metropolis? — It is very seldom that we find them.

Are they principally to be found in the houses of the opulent or those in the middling classes? — In the houses of the most opulent in general.

Did you ever see an invention that is called a register, or aperture, which is opened near the angle which the flue makes, and by the use of which you could sweep those difficult flues with a machine? — O yes, certainly.

Have you seen, then, these registers, and have you swept chimneys that have them? — I certainly have.

Then you have found that you could use the machine? — Yes.

Do you meet with many objections in the use of your machine; and, if you do, from whom?—Repeatedly.

And from whom?—From the master chimney-sweepers in the business.

Do you think that some of the master chimney-sweepers have used this machine for the purpose of showing that it will not succeed, rather than for the purpose of substituting it in the room of climbing boys?—I am certain of it; and more than that, I have heard that they would do so.

Do you believe they have done so?—I am certain of it.

With the use of this machine do you sweep the chimneys as clean as by climbing boys?—We do.

Do you not throw about the dust more than they do?—Not near so much; for instance, I was called upon to sweep a chimney in a gentleman's house in Bedford-square, who placed the china on the table, and there was no soot came out of the chimney to soil it.

To confirm that, you did not take more than ordinary pains to do it cleaner?—No, I did not: I was called suddenly to do it.

Does it take a longer time than climbing boys?—Shorter than by the use of boys.

Then the Committee are to understand that it

sweeps a chimney as well, in a shorter time, and with less dust, than by the use of climbing boys?—I have not the least doubt of it.

And that is the result of your experience from 1803 to the present time?—Yes.

Do you think the machine capable of any improvement?—Yes, I do.

Have you any doubt, that by the use of this machine and other mechanical means, all the chimneys in the kingdom can be swept?—I have not the least doubt of it.

Have you, on any occasion, used the machine by sending it down the chimney in case it would not ascend?—I have.

And in this instance the machine succeeded as well as in sweeping?—Just the same.

Was it you who swept the chimneys at Guildhall?—Yes.

How many were you enabled to sweep there?—I swept twenty-three out of twenty-five; I swept at the Mansion House fourteen out of fifteen, and I did not try the other, because they were cooking their dinner.

John Harding called in, and examined.

What are you by trade?—A chimney-sweeper.

How long have you been in that trade?—About twenty-three years, since I first came to it.

Do you use now one of the machines for sweeping chimneys? — Yes, certainly, almost every day.

What sort of chimneys can you not sweep with the machine? — Chimneys that run a dead slant, flat along, such as those chimneys that run in different directions; we cannot sweep them so well with the machine.

Have you ever seen the invention of what are called registers (a species of trap-door), where the slant commences, through which you could insert the machine, and by that means sweep the chimney? — Yes; those persons' machines will sweep a chimney of that kind.

Have you ever used it to that sort of chimney? — No; it happens very seldom that we find them.

Do you not think, that in all those flues which are in what you call a slant, those trap-doors could be used, and by which means the machine could be substituted for the climbing boys? — Yes, I do think they might be swept entirely without climbing boys.

From your experience, then, as a chimney-sweeper for 23 years, you have no doubt that in the greater proportion of chimneys in the metropolis, this machine could be substituted for the climbing boys? — I am sure it could.

When you were first taught to climb as a chimney-sweeper, how were you taught? — Why the most general way; I was sent up the chimney, and another boy sent up after me to put my feet in the proper and different directions.

If you refused to climb, were any means used to force you? — Yes, they are always forced up.

Specify the sort of force used? — They are threatened when they come down; it is chiefly by threatening, and sometimes by giving them a smack or two.

In general, do children who are so employed go unwillingly to the work? — Yes, they always go unwillingly to the work.

Did you ever hear of making a boy go up by means of another following him, putting pins into his feet to quicken his progress? — I cannot say that I have heard that; but I know some of them pinch their feet a great deal to make them go up.

Do not their knees and elbows get very sore in the first instance? — Yes; I never knew one out of twenty but always was sore.

What is the common price that chimney-sweepers give for children? — There are instances of two or three pounds, or even four pounds being given.

What is the common price? — It is hard to say, for if the magistrate knows of any thing being given, he will make the indenture void; but boys are bound in many different ways.

But a sum of money is generally given? — Yes, mostly so.

Have you ever heard of girls being employed? — Yes; I have heard of an instance of that sort at Windsor.

You never heard of any instances in London? — Yes; I once heard of a man who employed his daughter; but he is now dead.

Do not accidents often happen from children being put up chimneys while they are hot, or when they take fire? — O yes; the case of the boy that was burnt at Calvert's brewhouse establishes that; I once stuck fast myself in a baker's flue, as we call it in our trade, for four hours, and was near losing my life.

Were you much burnt at that time? — Yes, I was; it happened when I was first an apprentice.

Is it an event of common occurrence for children to be scorched and burnt, in consequence of being put up chimneys when too hot? — There have been instances of that kind; I have heard of two myself.

Then it often happens that boys are burnt and scorched in going up chimneys? — Both burnt and scorched.

Have you known many cases of cancer? — O yes, a great many; it is scarce one in five but who have it.

Is it in the face? — No, it is in the private parts

generally; there are many who have undergone the operation for it.

In general there is a great unwillingness to undergo the operation? — Yes; because it is either kill or cure.

Did you ever know any person in your trade die of that complaint, who refused to undergo the operation? — O yes.

Boys or men? — Chiefly men.

Are not persons generally, in your trade, affected with sore eyes? — Yes, a great many; where they have got bad eyes, there the soot is very injurious to them, because they are apt to wipe their eyes with their sooty hands, and that inflames them.

Would you not say, in general, that people who are employed in that trade are stunted in their growth, and are apt to have deformed limbs? — Yes, I should think so; for one seldom sees chimney-sweepers, who have been regularly apprenticed, grow to the same height as other people; they are almost always deformed or lame. There was an instance of that near the London Tavern yesterday; a lad was resting himself against the pump there, who could scarcely carry the cloth: his knees were bent almost double.

What was his age? — He was a stout lad; he had been in the business many years.

Should you think he was twenty?—I should think nearly so.

Does not that deformity principally arise from being forced to carry very heavy loads upon their backs?—Yes; and partly from their weakness.

Have you known many cases of boys not being washed for months together?—I have known many instances.

Did you ever hear of a boy that had not been washed for three months?—O yes; I recollect when I was an apprentice, I was never cleaned from holiday to holiday; that is, from Easter to Whitsuntide, and so on; but there are more laws now than there used to be formerly.

Where do they sleep?—In different places; sometimes in sheds, and sometimes in places which we call barracks, or in the cellar.

At what age does that which is called soot-wart make its appearance?—In some instances when the boy is young, and sometimes not till the boy grows up to manhood.

After the boys have done their master's work, do they ever sweep chimneys for the journeymen?—O yes: there is a great deal of that. There are many masters who take five or six apprentices, and let them out to hire; they frequently hire young lads as journeymen, to prevent the penalty of the Act of Parliament: I know many instances of that now.

The Committee then are to understand, that the law only allowing of a certain number of apprentices to each master, that in order to have a greater number of boys than the law allows, they hire boys as journeymen, and let them out for that use and other purposes? — No; the boys they hire are lads who have served their apprenticeship; the journeymen use them for "queering," which is a term used in the trade, and work the younger boys; so that they know not when their work is done.

Did you ever know of masters hiring boys who had not been apprenticed to chimney-sweepers? — Yes, very frequently.

Is it a common practice? — O yes, in many parts; for they take them from those workhouses, and they will not bind them; they often have no parents, and they will go from one master to another.

Do those boys escape out of the workhouse without the cognizance of the master, or are they enticed away by the master chimney-sweepers? — Yes, they are enticed away.

What number of chimney-sweepers are employed in the trade? — I cannot exactly say.

There is no register kept any where of them? — Oh no; because there are so many frequently coming up out of the country and returning there again; there is no regularity at all.

Thomas Allen called in, and examined.

What trade are you? — A chimney-sweeper.

How long have you been in that trade? — Near twenty-two years.

At what age did you begin? — When I was between four and five years of age.

Were you taken as an apprentice, or was your father in the trade? — I was articled to my uncle, my uncle Allen; he lived at that time in Five-foot-lane, where there has not been a chimney-sweeper for more than fourteen years.

Were you articled at the age of five years and a half? — I was only taken to a house in Hatton Garden, not to a regular office, but to a public house, where the officers articled me.

You were articled at the age of five years and a half? — Yes.

Are there any other chimneys beside those with a dead slant, that cannot be swept by a machine? — There are large chimneys of a particular kind which are obliged to be swept once a year, and where stones must be taken up; it is so at Goldsmith's Hall, where, before some of the chimneys can be swept, some stones must be taken up, because I have swept a long narrow flue there myself several times.

Is it possible to sweep that flue by means of the machine? — Yes, I have no doubt but what it can be done.

How long is a boy generally in the flue to which you have alluded? — I went in at eight and came out at two.

Do you use climbing boys now? — I have only one boy, and he is nearly out of his time; he is of little use to me, he has got so stout.

What are the smallest flues up which boys are sent? — Seven inches.

Square? —Yes.

Each way? — Yes; that is the smallest we ever send a boy up.

Is it not necessary, then, to have boys under eight years of age to ascend those small flues? — Yes; I have been obliged to have boys under that age myself.

Have you ever known any accidents in consequence of boys being sent up chimneys of this kind? — I have heard of a boy sticking in those chimneys, and of many who have been obliged to be cut out several times, and they have stuck so close in the flue as to make it difficult to get them out. A boy stuck in a flue of that kind in one of the squares, some time ago.

What was the age of that boy? — I have heard he was very young, about six years of age.

Do not the pots at the tops of the chimneys very often give way? — Yes, they give way sometimes:

but do not do much injury, unless boys will carelessly go right out of them.

Have you ever known instances of boys who have been so careless, and in consequence of which accidents have happened? — I have heard of a boy who fell out of a pot in St. Paul's Churchyard, and his head was fractured.

Is there an opinion entertained in the trade, that the machines will be substituted in lieu of climbing boys? — It is the general opinion in the trade with three parts out of four, unless it comes to those very head gentlemen, who do not like the trouble of it, and who have so many boys of their own, that they do not like to dirty their fingers; some of them have eight or nine boys.

What wages are allowed to journeymen chimney-sweeps? — Two shillings a week; they give them their victuals, and that is all.

The average wages, then, in the trade are two shillings a week? — Yes, if it is a man of five and twenty years of age he has no more; or if a boy of ten or twelve years, he has the same.

He is fed, clothed, and lodged besides, is he not? No; he is not clothed — only fed and lodged in the same manner as the boys.

Are the two shillings a week sufficient to find him clothes and other necessaries? — No, certainly not;

it is hardly enough to find him with shoe-leather, for they walk over a deal of ground in going about the streets.

In what way, then, is the journeyman able to live upon those wages? — They get halfpence given them: supposing he is sixteen or twenty years of age he gets the boys' pence from them and keeps it; and if he happens to get a job for which he receives a shilling, he gets sixpence of that, and his master the other sixpence.

What do you mean by getting the boys' pence? — What the boys get after they have been doing their master's work; they get a penny or so, and the journeyman takes it from them, and "licks" them if they do not give it up.

Do the journeymen gamble with the boys for this money, by playing at chuck-and-toss? — O yes, that is frequently done; even men who are twenty-two and twenty-three years of age will play with the young boys, and win their money.

That is, they get half the money from them by force, and the rest by fraud? — Yes.

Are they not driven to this course from the low wages which the masters give them? — Certainly; because they have no other means to get any thing for themselves, not even the few necessaries which they may want; for even what they want to wash with, they must get themselves.

James Bevans, Architect, called in, and examined.

Have you ever seen the different machines that have been constructed for the purpose of sweeping chimneys, to be substituted in the room of climbing boys? — Yes, I think I have seen most of them.

Do you, as an architect, think that they are applicable to almost all the chimneys in the metropolis? — By far the major part; I may say almost to all, in fact.

Can you state to the Committee in what proportion, out of a hundred, the machine would be applicable? — I should think to ninety-five out of a hundred.

Have you ever seen that improvement which has taken place, called a register or shutter, which is applied to the angular departure from the perpendicular shaft, by which the horizontal part can be swept? — I have never seen a model; but no doubt such a plan would answer well enough, because the machine itself will turn an easy angle.

You think that by the invention of the machine, from its flexibility, that nearly all the chimneys might be swept? — With shutters at their turnings every chimney could be swept.

Where there is nearly a horizontal flue, does it not require a great deal of clearing to get the soot out? — Yes, but it is equally bad for the boy as for the machine; because the boy as he comes down has an accumulation of soot about him, which stops up the circulation of the air necessary to support life.

So that it is evident, in all those chimneys where the machine cannot be used, the hazard is proportionably increased to the loss of life to the boy who sweeps them? — Certainly.

Do you think, as an architect and as a mechanic, supposing there were to be a legislative enactment that no chimney should be swept by the means of climbing boys, that easy substitutes could be found that would sweep every chimney that now exists? — Necessity is the mother of invention, and we are sure it would be done: I have no doubt of it at all. *I would just suggest whether an enactment could not be devised to prohibit climbing boys being used, excepting to certain chimneys, from which a certificate should be given by one of the surveyors who is appointed under the Building Act, that it could not be swept by the machine.*

Mr. *Thomas Mumford* called in, and examined.

What are you by profession? — A timber merchant.

Are you the inventor of a machine for the purpose of sweeping chimneys? — I am.

What difference is there between your machine and Mr. Smart's? — I conceive that Mr. Smart's is on such a principle at present that it would not act in a flue at right angles.

What means have you invented for that purpose? — I have invented a machine of rods, with joints; it acts as a straight stick, and will turn a square of eight inches.

Have you ever used that machine in sweeping chimneys of the above description? — I erected two temporary chimneys of that description, and I invented near twelve or twenty machines before I got one to act in a square of eight inches.

Have you ever swept real chimneys, not temporary ones, with this machine? — Not with this one; but I have with one upon a principle which, though not so good as this, acts in the same way.

Did it succeed? — It did.

Are you then prepared to state, that in all the chimneys you have seen in London, namely, the difficult ones, that your machine is a complete substitute for the use of climbing boys? — I conceive that the machine is sufficient for any chimney.

Opinion of Surveyors and Builders.

WE, whose names are undersigned, do certify we are of opinion, that the chimneys in houses already built may, with few exceptions, be effectually cleansed by machines worked from below; and that by proper attention being given to the construction of chimneys in future, all in new buildings may be so cleansed with ease.

We hereby declare, that being desirous the practice of employing children to climb and sweep chimneys should be abolished, we are willing to give the aforesaid opinion in evidence before a committee of the House of Commons, if called on for that purpose.

John Wallen, surveyor, Spital-square; Ebenezer Perry, surveyor, Spencer-street, Northampton-square; James Bevans, surveyor, Great Queen-street, Lincoln's-Inn Fields; Thomas Sowter, builder, Golden-lane; William Teanby, builder, Old-street; Henry Lee, builder, Chiswell-street; B. Biles, builder, Devonshire-street, Bishopsgate; William Brooks, architect, Doughty-street; Charles Tuck, builder, Tottenham High Cross; Edward J'Anson, architect, Laurence Pountney-lane; John Walters, architect, Fenchurch Buildings; Thomas Hood, surveyor, Doctors' Commons.

NOTES AND OBSERVATIONS

ON THE

FOREGOING EVIDENCE.

An earlier period than 1788 may be assigned for the first investigation of the Chimney-sweeping trade. It appearing that in 1773 an association existed on behalf of chimney-sweepers' young apprentices, and being the earliest on record, it may be interesting to give the names of its committee; who were, John Thompson, Jonas Hanway, Rev. Mr. Burrows, John Blackburn, Jacob Gonzales, Edmund Boehm, John Anthony Rucker, George Paterson, Thomas Walker, the Rev. Dr. Kaye, John Dorrien, John Levy, and A. Winterbottom. In June 1773, a letter was sent by this committee to master chimney-sweepers, inclosing the form of an indenture (for apprentices), and recommending them to treat the boys under their care with humanity; allusion to which is made by Jonas Hanway in his work published in 1775, entitled "The Defects of Police the Cause of Immorality."

Another association appears to have been formed in 1780, of which Mr. Hanway was the treasurer; by whom nothing however seems to have been done for the children, as the members were advised to receive back their subscriptions and break up the society.

The first allusion to some mechanical substitute for infant climbing occurs in a work published in 1785, by the indefatigable Jonas Hanway, entitled— "A Sentimental History of Chimney-Sweepers in London and Westminster;" from which the following passage is an extract: —

"It is also reasonable to suppose that the work might be done as it is actually performed in Russia, by brush-wood tied to a cord with a weight affixed, which comes down from the top of the chimney, from whence it is pulled up again, and in a short time by this simple method the chimney is swept; .... at the same time I apprehend it to be more than possible, among us, for *men* to perform the whole work of chimney-sweeping, partly by short ladders properly contrived to unite with each other, partly by brushes with long handles to unite in the same manner so as to be rendered portable."

In 1788, the third society, alluded to in the evidence, was formed, chiefly consisting of members of the Marine Society, who began and terminated their labours by promoting and obtaining the existing Act of Parliament (28 Geo. 3. c. 48.) for regulating the trade of chimney-sweeping.

Numerous other instances have been since ascertained of the employment of children of five and six years of age to climb chimneys; among others, Benjamin Brazier, a master chimney-sweeper, residing at Three-Colt Yard, Mile-end Road, began to climb at the age of four years and nine months; and a lively recollection of the misery he then endured induced him to apply for a machine, which has been granted to him, and he has undertaken to use it with care and diligence.

The average number of cases at St. Thomas's Hospital, of the chimney-sweeper's cancer, appears to have been much less, according to Mr. Cline's statement, than at any other of the principal hospitals, from which reports of such cases have been received.

The following account was obtained in 1808 from the medical officers of St. George's Hospital: "No particular account can be given of accidents to chimney-sweepers, as the manner in which an individual receives an injury is not specifically registered; but respecting the cancer of chimney-sweepers, six or eight melancholy cases have occurred at this hospital within the last six years, all of which have proved fatal. These unfortunate patients did not apply for relief before their diseases had gone too far to admit of an operation, or any other mode of cure."

THE

CLIMBING-BOY'S ALBUM.

A WORD WITH MYSELF.

I KNOW they scorn the Climbing-Boy,
  The gay, the selfish, and the proud;
I know his villanous employ
  Is mockery with the thoughtless crowd.

So be it; — brand with every name
  Of burning infamy his art,
But let his *country* bear the shame,
  And feel the iron at her heart.

I cannot coldly pass him by,
  Stript, wounded, left by thieves half-dead;
Nor see an infant Lazarus lie
  At rich men's gates, imploring bread.

A frame as sensitive as mine,
  Limbs moulded in a kindred form,
A soul degraded yet divine,
  Endear to me my brother-worm.

He was my equal at his birth,
  A naked, helpless, weeping child;
— And such are born to thrones on earth,
  On such hath every mother smiled.

My equal he will be again,
  Down in that cold oblivious gloom,
Where all the prostrate ranks of men
  Crowd, without fellowship, the tomb.

My equal in the judgment day,
  He shall stand up before the throne,
When every veil is rent away,
  And good and evil only known.

And is he not mine equal now?
  Am I less fall'n from God and truth,
Though "Wretch" be written on his brow,
  And leprosy consume his youth?

If holy nature yet have laws
  Binding on man, of woman born,
In her own court I'll plead his cause,
  Arrest the doom, or share the scorn.

Yes, let the scorn that haunts his course
  Turn on me like a trodden snake,
And hiss and sting me with remorse,
  If I the fatherless forsake.

J. MONTGOMERY.

Sheffield, Feb. 28, 1824.

THE

CLIMBING-BOY'S ALBUM.

Gentle Reader! if to thee
Mercy's dictates sacred be,
If thy breast with Pity glow
For the meanest sufferer's woe,
Let our Album's humble page
For *their* sake thy heart engage;
For *thine own* despise us not,
While we plead THE OUTCAST's lot;
Mercy's votaries here below,
Shall, hereafter, Mercy know.

In this age of Albums, we
Fain would offer ours to thee:
If it be not fraught with lays
Worthy of a critic's praise;
If no richly tinted flowers
Decorate this tome of ours;
If it fail in rich array,
Splendid clasp or binding gay,

Turn not from our page as one
Which the feeling heart would shun.

Beauty's Album may present
More of tasteful compliment;
Flowers, and shells, and landscapes fair,
May unite to charm thee there;
Here a cheek's vermilion dye,
There the lustre of an eye;
Here a cottage in a grove,
There a fountain or alcove;
All, in truth, that can invite
Passing glance of brief delight.
Toys like these we may not show,
For our theme is fraught with woe:
And the graver's mimic skill
Finds it — leaves it — wretched still:
Never could the painter's art
To the eye its griefs impart;
Nor can artful prose or verse
Half its miseries rehearse; —
Heads that think, and hearts that feel,
Only can our book unseal.

Fathers! unto you we speak;
Mothers! your support we seek;

BRITONS! holding freedom dear,
Abject slavery greets you here;
HOME-BRED SLAVERY! — dire disgrace!
Borne by childhood's helpless race;
Friendless outcasts of our laws,
Having none to plead their cause,
Save the feeble, struggling few
Who solicit aid from you.

CHRISTIANS! of each sect and name,
You, who feel the awful claim
Of our high and holy creed,
Suffer us with you to plead;
May we not, in truth, *command*
Your assistance, heart and hand?
Join, then, in this work of love,
For HIS sake who reigns above,
Nor be sympathy denied
Unto those for whom HE died.

BERNARD BARTON.

Woodbridge, 2 mo. 29, 1824.

THE

SONG OF THE POOR LITTLE SWEEP.

How dark is the morning; the thick clouds how scowling;
How sharp the sleet pierces; the snow drifts how deep;
How frightful to hear the wild storm-spirits' howling
Thus mix'd with the shrill cries of *poor little sweep.*

How dreadful the solitude now that surrounds me,
Whilst, shivering with cold, through the still town I creep;
And the rough broken ice, which both chills me and wounds me,
'Tis stained with the blood-drops of *poor little sweep.*

O see! where the dark clouds are parting, a bright star
Appears through the opening with pity to peep;
It twinkles so lovely as if, in the night far,
It wept for the sufferings of *poor little sweep.*

What art thou, fair mourner, that with such good
nature,
  Thus seem'st for a poor little orphan to weep?
The scorn of all mortals, the dread of each creature,
  A lone friendless outcast, a *poor little sweep*.

The *gentleman* said *I'd a father in heaven*,
  Whose care never slumber'd, whose eye cannot
sleep;
Whose pity to children is constantly given,
  And sees all the sufferings of *poor little sweep*.

O! should yon sweet star be the eye of that father—
  What mean these strange feelings that round my
heart creep?
They are so delightful, than lose them I'd rather
  For ever continue a *poor little sweep*.

It must, O it must be his glories that cheer me,
  Which fill me with gladness, and make my heart
leap;
Then hear me, my Father in heaven! O hear me!
  And take to thy mercy the *poor little sweep*.

S. R.

Sheffield.

CHILDHOOD.

Life is a pilgrimage of care,
Thorny and rough to tread,
And the few flowers that flourish there
Round childhood's path are spread;

For youth, a kindled taper, wastes
In its own blaze away,
And all its glowing splendour hastes
Its passage to decay.

Next manhood, sordid and severe,
The slave of gold and guile,
Dries up each salutary tear,
And checks each heart-born smile;

Then as care chills, or passion burns,
For both alike entice,
Youth's generous tide of feeling turns
To poison or to ice.

Age comes at last, — comes to deride
  The aspiring and the young ;
And life, a dark and troubled tide,
  Flows painfully along ;

Or, like a stream half-stagnant, creeps
  Unruffled by a breath,
Sadly and slowly, till it leaps
  The precipice of death.

But childhood ! 'tis life's balmy spring,
  A happy vernal morn,
When Fancy takes the wild-bee's wing,
  And Joy's sweet buds are born.

When Hope pours forth her matin hymn,
  Poised, like the lark, in air,
And Love, as meaner fires grow dim,
  Lights his own pure torch there.

Yet there are those who, while they look
  On Sorrow's boundless sway,
Would tear from human life's sad book
  Its one bright leaf away :

With Care's stern characters would seam
 That leaf, by Nature blest,
And send it floating down Time's stream
 As shrivell'd as the rest.

Ah ! why round life's sweet morning-light
 Its midnight horrors throw ?
Does bliss too long delay its flight ?
 Is grief's approach too slow ?

Ah no ! the joys yon stripling knows
 Are fleeting as his breath ;
A garland on the victim's brows
 Soon to be led to death.

Then spare, for life's a path of care,
 Thorny and rough to tread ;
And the few flowers that flourish there
 Round childhood's steps are spread.

HENRY NEELE.

London, 28 Jan. 1824.

THE ORPHAN CHILD.

1.

As I went down through London town,
  The sun an hour had shone,
And there I saw a bonnie boy,
  Sit singing on a stone:
But sooty were his shining locks,
  And dark his snowy feet,
And bleeding were his tender hands,
  And O, his voice was sweet!
A lady came and look'd and sigh'd,
  And ceased to pass along,
" My blessings on this comely child,
  He sings a melting song."

2.

"O white, white, lady, is thy neck,
  Where gold and jewels shine;
My arms have clasp'd as white a neck,
  As kind a breast as thine.

A mother's hands have gently nursed
  Me on a gentle knee; —
Oh! oft I weep above her grave,
  Aneath the churchyard tree.
The sea-waves o'er my father roll,
  Full fifty fathom deep."
He ceased his song, that orphan boy,
  And loudly 'gan to weep.

3.

That lady's silken dress was shower'd
  All round with jewels rare,
Ye might have bought a baron's land,
  With diamonds from her hair;
The red gold glitter'd round her waist,
  And sparkled at her feet,
Ten thousand eyes her beauty bless'd
  As she walk'd down the street;
Though like sun-light her beauty shone
  From green earth to the sky,
Curse on the muse who names a name
  That heeds not sorrow's cry.

4.

That lady went, — the orphan child
  Sat still on the cold stone;
He look'd in no one's face, he sung, —
  'Twas less of song than moan.

And lo! another lady came,
Straight to that comely child;
She took his dusky hand, her eyes
More than her ripe lips smiled:
"Come tell me now, my pretty youth,
A tender mother's care,
How could ye leave, all thus to stain
Thy face and shining hair?"

5.

"My father's dead," thus said the child,
"O'er him the salt sea sweeps;
My mother broke her heart; — Oh! come
And see how low she sleeps;
For often I go to her grave,
And lie the cold night long;
I could not do't, but that I keep
My heart up with my song.
O ere the green turf o'er her closed,
Ere her sweet lips were cold
That bless'd me, to this cruel trade
Her only son was sold."

6.

That lady turn'd away, — she turn'd
But went not; like the dew
On lilies, 'tween her fingers white
The shining tears dropt through.

She stroked his sooty locks, and smiled,
  While o'er the dusky boy,
As streams the sun beam through a cloud
  There came a flush of joy.
She took him from his cruel trade,
  And soon the milk-white hue
Came to his neck; he, with the muse,
  Sings bless thee, Montagu.

ALLAN CUNNINGHAM.

London, February 21, 1824.

THE CHIMNEY-SWEEPER'S GRAVE.

Our way was among the lonely hills;
  And the sun had reach'd the west,
When a winding path disclosed a scene
  That allured us there to rest.

The church tower with cottages clustering around,
  From out their shadowing trees,
Like a holy and beautiful mother appear'd,
  With her children round her knees.

And the church and the homes, in the lake beneath,
  Seem'd blended at last in the sky;
As the glorified mother will meet in heaven
  Her assembled family.

I wander'd alone through the silent paths,
  And enter'd the church-yard's bound:
love to muse by the quiet graves
  In consecrated ground.

And surely, throughout the realm of death,
  No lovelier nook might be seen;
For every grave was a garden of flowers,
  Or a bed of the softest green.

And the last light of day through the sycamores glanced,
  And chequer'd their shade on the sod;
Like the hopes and fears that pass over the soul
  Departing to meet her God.

I had paused beside a fairy mound
  —A child might rest below;
And my fancy sketch'd his little lot,
  With its varying joy and woe.

Perhaps, I said, he was one who beheld
  A spirit in the mountain breeze,—
Who would muse by the many-voiced stream,
  Or beneath the twilight trees.

And the flame that burn'd within his soul
  Consumed the enshrining clay:
Before it was blown, ere the world could blight.
  The floweret was pluck'd away.

But one who had come to my side unseen,
  Replied to the utter'd thought,
" Nay, stranger, in other than fancy's loom
  His web of life was wrought.

" His widow'd mother left her child,
A boy of seven years old,
To a friend who would hold the charge, she thought,
More precious than silver or gold.

" But here, where innocence might be found,
If it yet sojourn'd on earth,
We mourn o'er the deep and natural taint
Derived from our mortal birth.

" With the artless unsuspecting child,
Ere long, on some pretence,
The woman set out for an inland town,
Many a long mile from hence.

" She return'd at length, but return'd alone;
And the voice of rumour said
That the wretch had sold her orphan charge,
To learn a dreadful trade.

" She return'd to her home, but its joys were fled;
No neighbour approach'd her door:
She endured their scorn for a little while,
Then departed, and came no more.

" And none hath since cross'd her threshold stone,
Where now the grey lichen grows;
Not a child would set foot in her garden plot
For the gayest flower that blows.

"Months pass'd away, and still we heard
No tidings of the child,
'Till one evening late I wander'd here,
—One summer evening mild;—

"And on this grave, where the widow sleeps,
Where the moonbeams shifting play'd,
I beheld a dark and shapeless mass,
That cast a spectral shade.

"With fluttering heart I nearer drew:
It was a living thing;
A boy in the last appalling state
Of human suffering.

"On a tatter'd soot-bag, motionless,
Was the moaning infant laid;
Through the filthy rags that round him clung
Was his wasted form displayed.

"And they could not hide the festering sores
On each distorted limb:
From the crown of the head to the sole of the foot
There was no whole part in him.*

---

* *Note.*—This was almost literally the case with a poor little wretched being found by a relative of the author's, some years ago, by the highway-side, left there to perish by his master, who came from a distance. Notwithstanding all the care that could be taken of him, the child died in a few days.

"I ask'd his name, and scarce mine ear
Could catch the feeble tone: —
" 'I'm Billy Selby,' he faintly said;
It was the widow's son!

" 'My heart grew sick, for in days gone by
I had known and loved the child;
When he climb'd the unwonted mountain-paths,
In fearless freedom wild.

"Nor ever might those pure mountain-dews
A lighter footstep lave;
Or the winds of heaven on a lovelier brow
The cluster'd ringlets wave.

"The gladness that shone in his deep blue eye
Had scarcely been dimm'd with a tear,
Till the day of grief for his orphan-heart
When they laid his poor mother here.

"One moment this vision of the past
Before me floated — fled: —
I awoke, and stoop'd to raise the boy —
The suffering child was dead.

"And many an eye shed pitying tears
O'er the little *English slave*,
When we laid him quietly to rest
In his mother's quiet grave."

As the mountain-dweller told his tale
  My colour went and came,
With grief for that child and his brethren in woe,
  With shame for my country's shame.

And I sigh'd as the lonely sanctuary
  Disappear'd with the winding road,
That the misery induced by so foul a guilt
  Had polluted that calm abode.

M. A. R.

Sheffield, Jan. 10. 1824.

THE CLIMBING-BOY'S PETITION.

If misery's tale can touch the breast,
  Or check the thoughtless smile of joy,
Then listen to my mournful prayer,
  And save the suppliant climbing boy!

No mother watches o'er my youth,
  No father's cares my wants supply;
My hope is still on strangers cast;
  Where can I look if these deny?

In freedom's clime a wretched slave,
  In mercy's hour remember'd not;
A youth unblest, an early grave—
  Such is your suppliant's hapless lot.

Vainly for me the day-spring cheers
  In infancy, when all is gay;
Before my bud of life can bloom,
  'Tis blighted, crush'd, and cast away.

If misery's tale can touch the breast,
  Or check the thoughtless smile of joy,
O listen to my mournful prayer,
  And save the suppliant climbing-boy!

Doom'd to a vile and loathsome trade,
  Victim of cruelty's controul,
Pain preys upon my feeble limbs,
  And terrors rush upon my soul.

The slave from Afric's burning clime
  Finds multitudes to plead his cause;
Whilst I alone am left, to want
  The shielding power of Britain's laws.

To grief and wretchedness and woe,
  The House of Prayer is open wide;
All but to me! for who would pray
  With me, degraded, by his side!

Instruction's heavenly voice resounds,
  To spread her blessings o'er the land,
But not to chase the mental night
  From me, is shed her influence bland.

Yet I have heard of God above,
  Who pities those whom men despise;
Whose ear is never turn'd away,
  Disdainful, from a wretch's cries.

And I have felt his heavenly love,
  To soothe my bosom's bitterest throes;
And then my humble prayer hath flow'd,
  That He would please to end my woes!

P. M. James.

Birmingham, 1824.

HUMANITY AT HOME.

I HONOR and I love the mind
 Whose warm and generous thoughts embrace
The common interests of our kind,
 Through time's long track and earth's wide space;
And, like the glorious god of day,
Sheds o'er the *world* its living ray.

I watch with throbbing heart the zeal,
 Whose all-incorporating plan
Can teach a million souls to feel
 For all that's man's — for all that's *man*;
And every human title blend
In those of *brother* and of *friend*.

I've travell'd many a country far,
 Thro' Finland's wilds, on Afric's strand;
And there went with me, like a star,
 The glory of my native land:
A star whose light, where'er I trod,
Seem'd blazing with the truths of GOD.

But sometimes sadness came and dwelt
  Within my heart. 'Twas proud to hear
My country's name — but O! I felt
  That misery lived unheeded *there;*
That hearts were sad, — that eyes were wet, —
Forgotten, — how could I forget?

I would not check the nobly good
  Who, joy-diffusing widely roam;
But I would whisper, — if I could, —
  Look round — for there are wrongs *at home,*
And voices — though but feeble — call
On Heaven — on thee — on me — on all!

Dost thou not hear their cry? To thee,
  Who hear'st the lightest plaint of woe
That's borne across the distant sea,
  Can their appeal be vain? O no!
Thou didst but want some tongue to say,
Grief's sons are here — *and these are they!*

JOHN BOWRING.

London, Jan. 6. 1824.

THE

SWEEP-BOY'S LAMENT.

Oh weariness! the world to me
  Is but a world of woe;
So tasked, I cannot help but be
  Forlorn, where'er I go;
The school-boy has his hour of play,
The girl her happy holyday,
  The shepherd-lad his flow
Of spirits, sun-shine, and sweet song,
The whole delightful summer long.

But unto me the seasons bring
  No respite, no relief,
And if sometimes I try to sing,
  The words are checked by grief.
I might as well be doomed to pine,
A slave, within the gloomy mine
  Of some unchristian chief,
As thus with envy or despair
To view the joy I cannot share.

I do not like to be constrained
  Thus all day long to creep,
Like the blind mole, with mirth ill-feigned,
  Up ways so dark and steep;
I do not like to be called down
With brutal curse and savage frown, —
  They haunt me in my sleep;
And scare off scenes that else would be
A very paradise to me.

For in my dreams I oft-times view
  My sister smile, as when
We used to gather violets blue
  In our dear native glen;
I often hear the cuckoo's cry
Between the forest and the sky,
  And shout to it again;
And in the rising breeze rejoice
To catch once more my mother's voice.

But when amidst the leaves I see,
  Or seem to see her face,
And run with all my former glee
  Her image to embrace,
An eye glares on me — the fond dream
Departs, and, waking with a scream,
  I turn, and start to trace

The same fierce glances, come to awe,
Or rouse me from my bed of straw.

Then for imagined groves so green,
  The brooks, the flowers of morn,
Songs of sweet birds, and sounds between
  Of pipe, or huntsman's horn,
Through smoky streets, 'twixt light and dark,
I'm driven along, the common mark
  Of merriment or scorn,
And in the peopled desert pine
For peace that never can be mine.

I would I were the simplest thing,
  So might I but be free,
Some bird to wanton on the wing,
  Or butterfly, or bee!
They know no pain, but are as gay
As the wild squirrel on his spray:—
  I wish 'twas so with me;
But no, oh no! think what I will,
I am the same sad creature still.

The sport of—— it would grieve your heart
  Should I my wrongs tell o'er;
I would not you should feel the smart
  That pierces me so sore:

I am but young — I cannot toil
Like the grown peasant o'er the soil
He ploughs, yet still the more
I slave, the more am I abused;
What have I done to be so used?

I say my prayers! for I have heard
There is a God on high,
Without whose bidding not a bird
Can perish from the sky;
A God that does not love the strong
Who do unhappy children wrong,
But listens to our cry;
He surely does! for when I pray,
My sorrow seems to fly away.

He surely does! for there are those
Who pity what we feel,
And strive, unfrightened by our foes,
The stripes they give, to heal.
O thou good Being, whom I view
In all thy works! let others too
Enforce our weak appeal;
And joy, like angels, when we shed
Tears for past grief and bondage fled!

J. H. Wiffen.

Woburn Abbey, 3d mo. 20. 1824.

AN APPEAL

TO

THE FAIR SEX;

INVITING THEIR ATTENTION TO THE PRESENT SITUATION OF CLIMBING BOYS.

YE BRITISH FAIR! illustrious and far famed
For virtue, beauty, and exalted deeds!
The chiefest treasure of our hearts and homes;
The sweet inspirers of your country's song;
The mothers of her heroes! but most dear,
That title best, and oftenest confer'd:—
On earth, the angels of humanity!
For in your coronet of virtues, shines,
Most heavenly bright, the jewel of benevolence.
I would not idly praise nor flatter here,
And mar the cause which I intend to plead;
But when I speak or sing in MERCY's name,
I *will*,—while there is speech upon my tongue,
Or music in my heart,—I will exalt
The weakest, strongest, loveliest of God's works—
Transcendant WOMAN!

O ye gentle sex!
If ever verse of mine hath pleased your ears,
Or flow'd accordant with your sympathies;
Yet once again, allow a poet's claim;
Not in high phrase, but in familiar words,
I bring a theme of misery to your thoughts,
And ask your pity for a wretched race.

When late, Britannia, roused as from a trance,
By the deep groans of injured Africa,
Bewail'd the blood-stain'd traffic of her sons,
And with a voice, heard through her farthest isles,—
Round hapless Guinea's horror-guarded coast,—
And through the cane-fields of the guilty West,—
Avouch'd the Negro as a brother-man,
Proclaim'd him free whene'er he touch'd her soil;
And call'd upon the world by every claim
Of mercy—justice—and humanity,
T' abjure the horrid merchandise of slaves!

Then while with eloquence the senate rung,
And from the pulpit arguments sublime
Were urged in favour of the race of Ham;
While poesy, with bland enchantment, led
The sister-spirit of sweet harmony,—
'Twas then, that WOMAN's smile, and WOMAN's voice,
Pleaded for injured Africa,—with *him*

Whom she had borne and suckled, nursed and taught;
With *him* who sought her love; — with *him* who bless'd
Her with the dearest, holiest name of wife;
With *him* who sought her husband's social hearth:
With *each*, — with *all* within her little sphere, —
Far as her influence or her virtues reach'd.

The triumphs of *that* cause, hath crown'd our isle
With prouder glories than her diadem;
And it hath written woman's tender name,
In everlasting characters of love.

But O ye fair! though Africa be free,
And negro blessings come upon our land;
Yet we have slaves at home! an infant race,
Doom'd in their tender, unresisting years
To cruelty's sad heritage of woes:
To stripes and misery; and a harder lot
Than even imagination can conceive.

The chimney-sweeper is a little slave,
Whose presence and whose horrible employ
Are so familiar with our earliest thoughts
That we forget to question their humanity;
As if the lash of cruelty became
Less dreaded as most regularly plied;

As if atrocities of deepest dye
By sheer long sufferance into virtues changed.

O there is *comfort* in an English home;
And there is *comfort* in an English fire;
Yea, like a magic spell, this very word
Binds to a British heart, where'er it roves,
The precious picture of its own dear hearth.
Yet, ah! while sitting in the social group,
With every comfort, — every blessing blest,
How often we forget to pity them,
Who have no comfort! day by day we read
Of sufferings, perils, deaths, devolved on those
Who to the murky dungeons of our flues
Condemn'd, than felons bear a harsher lot!
O with what apathy we oft peruse
The annals of their woe, and flippant say, —
" 'Tis *but* the common story of a sweep
" Beat by his master: — O, 'tis *but* a boy
" By chance was suffocated in a flue:
" Tis *but a chimney-sweeper* burnt to death,
" In an ignited funnel!"

Think, ye fair, —
Think with what foul injustice he is doom'd
To stern neglect and hatred! an offence,
Deem'd shocking and obscene to dainty thought.

Oft as you meet him in the public street,
You pass him quickly as a noisome thing,—
Society's most rank detested weed;
And sooner would you pluck the aconite,
Or wear the deadly nightshade in your bosom,
Then you would grasp the little *sweep-boy*'s hand,
Or press him in his misery to your breast.

O turn not from him thus; he *is* a blot
On the fair scroll of our humanity:
But, shut not then your ears against his plea;
Nor let your tongue be silent in his cause;
Yea, give your tears,—let them wash out this stain,
This long, deep-written scandal of our isle.

O would you call the little plaintiff up,
And smile him into frankness in your presence;
Then could the *sweep-boy* tell his own sad tale!
All that he saw, and thought, and felt, and fear'd,
When sold to slavery, cruelty, and want,
And doom'd himself, in sad distress, *to be*
That very bugbear, which, but named erewhile,
Could scare his crying childhood into peace!
Your ears would tingle, and your eyes would weep,
Could he but tell what horror he endured
In his first passage up a noisome flue,
Through sulphur, soot, and darkness! could he tell

What tremors shook him, as he forced his way
Up the foul vent; with lacerated feet,
Now scrambling hard, a footing to ensure;
Now writhing like a serpent, to intrude
His agonizing frame through some dread pass!
His eyes, meanwhile, blind with the falling filth,
Nor from his ears, his nostrils, nor his mouth,
Can he exclude the particles obscene.
And worst of all in this revolting task,
That climax of all horrors to a child, —
The dread of suffocation which he *feels*.
But what avail his terrors or his tears;
His knees excoriate, and his sinews cramp'd?
Sold into slavery, doom'd to be a wretch,
His flexile form, so exquisitely nerved,
Goaded with curses, or at the rope's end,
Must henceforth, as an animate machine,
Be used, and treated vilely, day by day.

'Twas winter, and the air was frosty-keen,
White, deep, untrodden, lay the level snow,
When through the streets, in sooty blankets wrapp'd,
This way and that, the *chimney-sweepers* went,
Hirpling and shuddering to their wonted tasks.
Day had not dawn'd; the clear blue firmament
Yet shone with starry glory unextinct.
The ban-dogs, and the menials were abroad,

And houseless wretches slowly skulk'd away
From kennel, bulk, and penthouse, where they lodged:
But most were wrapp'd in comfortable sleep!
Unwedded beauty, her soft pillow press'd,
Lapt in a paradise of golden dreams:
While, with her children round her, safe at rest,
The mother slumber'd on her husband's bosom:
And if, or wife or maiden, was disturb'd,
By an unwonted rattling in the wall,
" 'Twas *but* the *chimney-sweeper* in the flue,"
Said they, — and dozed into delight again.

One little boy, along the new-fall'n snow,
Past slowly on, leaving a sooty track:
He ambled sadly with unequal gait,
Musing, and mourning his sad destiny.
He seem'd a novice in the horrid school,
But just apprenticed to that wretchedness:
Few were his words, with many tears between,
And they who caught imperfectly the sounds,
This hope-abandon'd colloquy o'erheard:

" O, I would quit this vile employ,
But father's gone to sea;
And mother died, and left her boy;
Now nobody loves me.

"But I am forced to work and weep,
Though cold and cramp'd I be;
Because I am a little sweep
There's nobody loves me.

"My playmates, once who loved me well,
Now from my presence flee;
They say I have a sooty smell;
So nobody loves me.

"I'm weak, and young, and frighten'd oft,
When the dark flue I see;
By blows and threats forced up aloft,
Where nobody loves me.

"My master beats me with a rope,
—A cruel master he:
But I have neither friends nor hope;
For nobody loves me.

"Would Christian men, and ladies fair,
In kindness but agree,
To think upon the ills I bear!
But nobody loves me.

" They loved the Negro o'er the wave,
They strove to set *him* free ;
But though *I* am a little slave,
There's nobody loves *me !*"

Poor Henry's master now appear'd in sight,
Scaring the boy into a quicker pace,
As if his presence was a thousand stripes.
Anon they enter'd an adjacent dwelling,
Whose tall and zigzag chimney, crept aloft
By the next gable, like a tortuous snake ;
Up the strait aperture of this foul flue
Was Henry sent ; awhile he made his way,
And nought was heard, save now and then a sob
At intervals, when paused his rattling scraper,
A sigh suppress'd : but soon his wheezing lungs
Inhaled the stifling damp, and the close pass
Forbade his progress ; there he lay, close wedged,
Panting in agony and weeping loud ;
Darkness above, — below, his master's curse,
Threatening with fire and stripes the shuddering boy.
His cries sunk down to moans, his moans grew weak,
Anon, and all was still : — the master now
Betray'd one vague emotion — bit his lip —
And seem'd to quell some struggling agony.
He scaled the wall, and broke an aperture
Into the fatal vent : there lay the boy,

Smother'd beneath an avalanche of soot!
He brought him down, unstiffen'd yet, and warm,
His eye-balls started and inflamed — his cheeks
Still moist, and mark'd where the hot tears had flow'd.
O, had you seen poor Henry on the hearth,
Stretch'd out, a little, black, unlovely corse,
While o'er him stood his master, not to weep,
But to upbraid his luck, thus foil'd by death,
Of the possession of his living frame,
Surely your hearts had overflow'd your eyes;
And while a prayer ascended for *your* children,
Ah! sure your lips had vow'd, that never more
Up your foul chimney should a child be sent.

This is no tale of misery, feign'd and colour'd
From the creations of a poet's brain;
'Tis but a specimen of common woes;
A tragedy, too frequently perform'd,
But, like a deed of darkness, hush'd and hid;
Or, register'd with common accidents,
It speaks not always as it ought to speak —
With guilt's deep tongue in murder's voice of blood.

" But *how* shall we," I hear a fair one ask,
" Say, how shall *we* assist your great design;
" Abridge this sum of needless misery,
" And from our isle erase this sable stain,

"This blot on our humanity?" — O *feel!*
For 'tis your happy privilege to feel,
And make your feelings known; — 'tis yours
To rouse the dormant sympathies of man,
And league them in humanity's best cause; —
O then, *become* the *chimney-sweeper's friends,*
Peruse the annals of his horrid trade,
Weep o'er his sufferings, advocate his rights,
And tell his tale of woe in gentle ears.
Amidst your elegant pastimes, speak his name,
Write with your pens, embroider with your needles,
Sing to your music, "*Pity the poor sweep!*"
O let your pencils picture his deep miseries,
Sketch in your *Albums* his dejected state;
And on your winter screens, and summer fans,
O let his likeness greet you, till no more
This infant slavery in our isle be found:
So shall the smile of Heaven approve your work,
And thousands, rescued from this labour vile,
Pour blessings on your heads; so shall you still,
With fairest charms and noblest virtues, be
On earth the angels of humanity.

JOHN HOLLAND.

Sheffield, Feb. 3. 1824.

THE STOLEN CHILD.

ADDRESSED TO LADY STRICKLAND.

The liberty taken by the writer of the following lines with the name of Lady Strickland, in thus giving it to the public, requires apology; and the deep interest excited by the affecting narrative below, together with a slender hope that some clue may yet be found to the bereaved family, must form that apology. The circumstances will be well remembered by some, and to others, they cannot fail of being painfully interesting.

About the month of August, 1804, a chimney-sweeper at Bridlington, Yorkshire, bought a little boy, for the sum of eight guineas, of a beggar woman. This child, who appeared to be about four years old, was employed to sweep a chimney in that town; he was taken up it by an elder boy, who left him there, when he fell down, and was terribly bruised against the grate. His air and manner appeared so different from those of the children usually employed for that purpose, that the inhabitants of Bridlington became very generally interested for him. The lower people said it was a shame to keep such a child to so mean an employment, and that, poor as they were, he should be welcome to share with their own children. Lady Strickland, hearing of the child, went to see him. She was much interested in his appearance, and so persuaded that he had been stolen, that she took him home with her, the chimney-sweeper being glad to part with him. Soon after he got to Boynton, the seat of Sir George Strickland, a plate, with something to eat, was brought him; on seeing a silver fork, he was quite delighted, and said, *Papa had such forks as those.* He also said the carpet in the drawing-room was like papa's. The housekeeper showed him a silver watch; he asked what sort it was,—*Papa's was a gold watch.* He then pressed the handle, and said, *Papa's watch rings, why does not your's?* Sir George Strickland being told this circumstance, showed him a gold repeater; the little boy pressed the spring, and when it struck, he jumped about the room, saying, *Papa's watch rings so.* Seeing one of the young ladies employed at her pencil, he said, *Are you drawing, Ma'am?* and when surprise was expressed at this, he replied, *My mamma used to draw.*

At night, when he was going to bed, he said he could not go to bed *without saying his prayers;* he then repeated the Lord's prayer almost perfectly.

The account he gave of himself was, that he was gathering flowers in his mamma's garden, when a woman came in, and asked if he liked riding; he said, *Yes*; and she told him he should ride with her. She then put him on a horse, after which they got into a vessel, and *away we went!* He had no recollection of his name, and was too young to think his father could have any other name than that of *papa*. He started whenever he heard a servant in the family at Boynton, called *George*, and looked as if he expected to see somebody he knew; on inquiry, he said he had *an uncle George, whom he loved dearly.* From many things he said, he appeared to have lived, at least some time, with an uncle and aunt, whom he invariably said were called Mr. and Mrs. *Flembrough*. His dialect was good, and that of the south of England. He was described as having beautiful black eyes and eyelashes, a high nose, and a delicate soft skin. He had had, he said, *many mothers, but only one mamma;* and when told that his mother had been sent for, he expressed the greatest terror, till assured that he should not go to her again. This woman, on being interrogated, positively affirmed him to be her own child.

Many endeavours were made, at the time, to discover his relatives, but without success; and it is understood that he continued, and received his education, in the family of Lady Strickland.

The above particulars have been partly extracted from an account communicated to the Committee of the Society for superseding the necessity of Climbing Boys; printed also in the Gentleman's Magazine for September, 1805; and collected, partly, from the testimony of a person then residing at Bridlington.

MADAM, a stranger, unpermitted, weaves
Your name, a flower, among these votive leaves;
She claims your ear by one warm plea alone,
One name she bears in common with your own;
On that presumes, and fancies, in her pride,
That *mothers* meeting *mothers*, feel allied.—
Theirs the same pangs have been, and theirs the dart
Of trembling joy that quivers at her heart,
In that strange hour of mingled pain and fear,
When first her infant wakes a mother's ear!

Theirs too the thrill (unknown to all beside,)
The feast of early nectar to provide,
And yield, with cheerful bounty, all the wealth
Of the warm bosom, of the failing health,
To feed the unmindful suckling, as it clings
To the pure well, whence all its pleasure springs.
To them, the cry that wearies other ears,
The tender, speechless sufferer, endears,
And wakeful energies, before unknown,
Start into being with that piteous moan.
Theirs, from that anxious season, must have been
Those quick solicitudes that move unseen,
And stir the watchful spirit, blending there
Fears full of pleasure, pleasures full of care!
Theirs, with a glow of nameless joy, to see
The rosy climber to its father's knee;
To mark the early gleam, by which to scan
The powers and virtues of the future man;
The heart's first flower, in the young blush to spy,
The mind's first day-light, dawning in the eye.

And thus, when Sabbath eve, with holy spell,
On the worn breast with soothing influence fell,
When the dear, sleeping babe unconscious lay,
And left the mother's thoughts their tranquil way,
With fear, and faith and hope, and joy to trace,
The gladdening promise of a *Christian race*;—

Then to her tearful eye what scenes have sprung !
What fervent prayers have trembled on her tongue !
What dear anxieties, her child to shield
From the barb'd arrows of this battle-field !
From thousand deaths to screen him, and provide
Peace, safety, conquest, at the Saviour's side !
O ! 'tis not health, or gold, or life he needs,
One thing is needful, — and for that she pleads.

Yes, from a mother's heart a fountain springs,
Warm as the purple wave that round it clings ;
And all of dear or tender there combined,
Beats in that pulse, — the life-blood of her mind.
Whether she sits beside her cottage door,
Spins as she thinks, and, thinking, spins the more ;
Or, restless on a throne, her infant hears,
And drops her diadem to hush its tears ;
'Tis the same glow that, kindled from above,
Gilds the mild current of a mother's love.

Then to a mother let a mother pay
Spontaneous tribute in this humble lay.

And must it be that feeling thus intense,
Twined with the very heart, — a nerve, — a sense,
Alive to every touch, to every breath,
Shall writhe and pine in anguish worse than death ?

Not on the ivory corse its griefs to pour,
Not on the little grave to tend the flower,
Not on the frozen smile to vent its sigh,
Then trace the parted spirit to the sky:
No, this, — 'twere happiness, 'twere joy, 'twere bliss;
Compared with other grief, what rapture this!
Compared with that worst woe a mother knows,
To lose her babe and trace not where it goes!
O, if there be a pang whose depth might claim
All undisputed sorrow's keenest name,
'Twere that a mother feels when, weak and wild,
She seeks, and seeks in vain, her stolen child.

Mother, thy nursery enter, is there one
Thy heart hath fix'd its very life upon?
One whose bright eye, whose pale or hectic cheek
Seems nought of body, all of mind to speak?
A flower for future manhood but too fair,
Too frail to bloom but 'neath a mother's care;
One whose sweet look of love, when glanced on thee,
Seems its whole world of happiness to see;
Whose little arms (for other service weak)
Are strong to climb, and cling, and kiss thy cheek?
Whose gleaming intellect, so bright, so clear,
Awakes thy liveliest hope, thy tenderest fear;
One whom to own seems more than mother's pride;
One whom thou lovest more than all beside?

And fancy then (if Fancy dares the smart)
The throbs of grief that rent that mother's heart
Whose dear, fair boy, from his paternal door
By vagrant fiends decoy'd, returns no more.

Madam, 'twas thine that tender child to trace,
To read its story in its withering face;
To mark the look of culture, that express'd
More than the offspring of a gipsy breast:
The air, the tone, the accent, that betray'd
Far other habits 'neath that sooty shade.
'Twas thine the hapless wanderer to see,
'Twas his to find a mother's heart in thee.
No; not a *mother's*, – to his frighted ear
That soothing name convey'd but pain and fear;
The scanty crust by grudging avarice thrown,
The cold dark chimney, the unpitied groan,
The piercing blast of winter's snowy morn,
At night, the feeling hopeless and forlorn
Of one, an outcast from that tender fold
That screen'd him once from sorrow, pain, and cold.
These, and all worse than these, with terror came
To that poor foundling in a *mother's* name.
No; it was thine, most blessed, to supply
His lost *mamma's* soft arm, and tender eye.

The music of that name, though long unheard,
The world of comfort in that pleasant word
Recall'd the memory of vanish'd years,
That, swelling in his bosom, burst in tears;
Strange recollections on his spirit fell,
He knew they had been — where, he could not tell;
Nor who was she, whose long-lamenting eye
Had wept in anguish till the fount was dry;
All, all he could remember was, — that he
Had *once* a kind mamma, — kind once like thee.

O! if that mother on the dusty bed
Has not in sorrow laid her sinking head;
If those wild throbbings have not long been still,
Calm'd in that rest reserved for heaviest ill,
What chain could bind her, if the name she knew
Of her to whom her cherish'd nursling flew,
And found a second mother? — One who tore
The tatters from his limbs, who wiped the gore
That trickled from his feet with tenderest care,
Wash'd his wan cheek, and smooth'd his tangled hair,
Then to the heavings of her bosom press'd
The pale, thin child, and housed him in her breast.

In that dread day when Mercy's humblest deed,
From Mercy's record gather'd worlds shall read;

And He, the houseless Saviour, shall begin,
"I was a stranger and ye took me in,"
Then may this deed of thine his favouring eye
Fair 'mid the fruits of living faith descry,
And when, indebted to His love alone,
Thy wondering spirit shall the claim disown,
May this the answer of thy Saviour be,
"Thou didst it not to him, but unto Me."

But is there yet a traffic that can lure
The dark-eyed vagrant (hardy to endure
The cry of infant anguish) to decoy
Far from some other home some other boy?
Is there a babe, now watch'd and sooth'd to rest,
Cradled in comfort on a mother's breast,
Screen'd from the winter's blast, the summer's ray,
Star of her night, and sunshine of her day;
Whose tender bosom, in its prime of bliss,
Is doom'd to wither in a woe like this?
And whom no fostering eye or arm shall save
From pain, and cold, and hunger, and the grave?
And shall the matrons of a Christian land
Unmoved spectators of this traffic stand?
No! rise in virtue's strength, in feeling's glow,
Mothers of England! say, indignant, — No!

High as the horror let the passion swell,
Surround the throne your tale of woe to tell;
And wait and weep there, till a princely smile
Chase the foul trade from Britain's happy isle.

ANN GILBERT.

Hull, Feb. 1824.

FRANK AND WILL,

THE LITTLE CHIMNEY-SWEEPS.

One windy disagreeable day in January, 1803, the inhabitants of a small house, situate in the outskirts of a village, in the West Riding of Yorkshire, were disturbed by an altercation between their maid-servant and a party of chimney-sweeps, who almost clamorously entreated for a job, observing truly "that the hurricane of the preceding day had made many houses smoky, and this appeared to be of the number."

"The poor creatures could never have come at a better time," observed the elder of two ladies, then retreating from the puffs of smoke given by the parlour fire, "Tell them to come in, Sally, and get the fire out of this grate as quickly as possible." Her companion expressed fear that it could not be safe for some hours; — "she had never heard of such a thing as a chimney swept in the day-time." — "But I am a much older housekeeper than you, my dear, and have always adopted the plan of using sweeps only in the day-time; in consequence of which the work is better done, I escape the pain of contrasting the feelings of a little wretch freezing with cold at my chimney-tops, whilst I am warm in bed; and I have the satisfaction of seeing him fed, which I consider the best way of rewarding his exertions." "Let us go up stairs, the fire is now out, and a few minutes of this cold weather will render the chimney ready for the boys."

The ladies departed, and the younger carried in her arms her only child, a boy about two years old, the sole comfort of his widowed mother, who wishing him to dispel some little dread of the black boys (contracted from his nurse) went out to them, and desired them not to be in a hurry, as the fire was newly removed. She found the party consisted of a tall lad about fourteen, and two little boys of about five or six years, one of which was considerably smaller than the other; they had scanty clothing, were barefooted, and shaking with cold; their faces were covered and disfigured, or the young widow would have seen that the child she pressed instinctively still closer to her breast, as pity for these helpless little castaway boys was excited, had received from Nature far fewer advantages than they. Frank, who was a few months the older, had once an open, brave, and intelligent countenance, a clear and ruddy skin, with dark sparkling eyes. Will was fair as a lily, with soft features, meek expression, curling flaxen locks, and eyes like the deep blue vault of heaven.

Mrs. Sutherland was a woman of acute feeling, and many sorrows of her own had not quenched compassion for those of others, but this peculiar case, the hardships of children so situated (though the most evident and deplorable ever offered to the public eye) had never engaged her attention, beyond a momentary shudder as the shrill cry of "*sweep*" disturbed her sleepless hours, or the sight of some very young creature dragged prematurely to this loathsome toil caught her sight. This day-light operation in the house, by bringing the evil immediately before her, awoke anxiety as well as humanity; and fearful lest the evident hurry and solicitude evinced by the eldest and governing boy, should induce him to enter the chimney too soon, she could not forbear to return to the parlour, and caution him against injuring himself or the children.

On entering the room she found the lad standing with a large cloth which entirely covered the aperture of the chimney, and which the youngest assisted to keep down. She remonstrated on the impropriety of keeping out all light and air, but was told it was necessary in order to guard the furniture; "he has light enough from the top," said the lad, "and as to air, why it's what we're used to doing without." — "But," said little Frank, "it was want of it as smothered me last week, when I fell down and hurt my leg." Mrs. Sutherland perceived then that his ancle was red and terribly swollen, and that a filthy rag which had been its only bandage was too much torn for use. She determined to apply relief to this grievance immediately.

A faint cry in the chimney was now heard, and with a rumbling sound the poor child descended as if falling, and the youth who held the cloth putting forward his arms caught him, rolled him in the cloth, and carried him out of the house; it was but the work of a moment, yet never will the eye that witnessed it forget the agonizing sensation it inflicted. The child was perfectly naked, and in that situation he was carried out into the yard, in the depth of winter, to be swept, and have his few ragged clothes replaced. What mother's eye could glance over that young and tender form (bruised and defiled as it was) without trembling for its safety, and feeling for its pains? What Christian could see the image of God, a creature born to the inheritance of eternal life,—one for whom the Redeemer had shed his blood, and whom the Lord of Providence had placed in the land of liberty and of plenty, so degraded, so injured? Bitter tears, gushed from her eyes; she sunk almost fainting on a seat, and felt as if not only overwhelmed with sorrow, but even with guilt, against one whom she regarded as a victim.

The voice of her mother roused her from the indulgence of fruitless regret, and she entered the kitchen where the sweeps were again assembled, waiting for the hard-earned shilling, and the old lady was according to her wise usage feeding them herself. Here was a near claim upon the sensibility of a humane heart. The children, hitherto extremely modest in their demeanour, seized on the victuals almost with the voracity of birds of prey, and devoured them for some moments at least with an avidity that could only be produced by terrible and insatiate hunger, the pains of which can only be comprehended by those unhappy beings who have thus experienced them. The elder boy stood a little aloof, though he also accepted thankfully what was given, yet was desirous of apologising for the children, by saying, "They are worse off than me, for I got something to eat last night, and they have had nought at all since we left home yesterday morning, poor creatures."

"Nothing since yesterday? Is it possible? Have you then run away from your master? Tell the truth. I fear you have done wrong."

"Oh! no, ma'am; master sent us out yesterday-morning to seek work, and if we'd had luck to get a job then we should ha' got some bread; but we had no luck, and we were ordered to stay out till to night; so we've had nothing, only that I being strong, helped a man with his cart, who give me a piece o' bread and a drink o' beer, last night, when they were asleep."

"And where did they sleep?"

"We had leave to lie in a smithy, down the lane yonder; if we had not been there, we should have been perished wi' cold, most like."

"Does your master often send you out on such chances of starving?"

"No, very seldom; he is badly, and work have fallen off lately, or he would not have done it."

"No, he would'nt," said Frank, "becase, lady, he's not a bad man; its Dick that's bad, an' beats us, an' drives us about."

"Hush!" said Will, casting his eyes about with an air of terror, as if he feared they should be overheard by the tyrant in question; "hush, Frank, say nothing, for fear he should hear you;" and he nestled a little nearer to his interrogator, as if for protection; then suddenly sprung back, as if recalled to a sense of his situation, — a sense that a "great gulf" was placed between poor desolate despised sweeps and the rest of the world; which even the bounty and pity of the moment did not authorise him to pass.

The action was affecting in itself, and rendered still more so from the deprecating countenance, and the extreme youth and simplicity of the child; but he became still more interesting when Mrs. Sutherland applied salve, and put bandages and a stocking upon Frank's leg, for his eyes one moment gazed with sparkling surprise, the next were suffused with tears; but he remained in perfect silence, as if almost oppressed with wonder and gratitude; whilst Frank, on his part, poured out, as well as he knew how, a thousand thanks; and what was better, an assurance that "he should be well again presently."

The address to their master was taken, in order to remonstrate with him on the cruel abuse of power, and neglect of duty, thus displayed; and the children were dismissed with plenty of food for present use, aid in clothing, and money; and told "that they must always call when they came near the neighbourhood;" as they lived at the distance of seven miles, it was not likely that would be soon.

Yet on the very following Sunday, two little boys made their appearance at the kitchen door, who announced themselves as the sweeps. Frank said "they were in a great hurry, but they wanted to see madam's little lad."

Mrs. Sutherland heard the voices, and entered just as Will drew from his pocket two pieces of polished bone, which they had jointly prepared as a pair of knick-a-knacks, the only present their humble means, and grateful hearts, could devise for one, who had awakened all the thankfulness, and even veneration, of which they were capable.

The children had begged the day, in order to present the offering, and to assure Mrs. Sutherland that Frank's ancle was cured, and their master had promised the squire he would not send them such wide errands again. The moment their little offering was accepted, both children darted out of the house, as if fearful of receiving further boon, and having the purity of their intention frustrated. This was, however, not Mrs. Sutherland's wish ; she merely sent the maid after them with the bread and butter then preparing for tea, and an exhortation to them not to loiter on the way, and left them to the quiet enjoyment of self-satisfaction, in having pleased the child of her whom they deemed a friend and benefactress.

Often were the knick-a knacks shown and descanted upon, and many a scheme for the present relief and future advantage of the donors was contemplated by those, whose powers were, alas ! extremely bounded, and whose difficulties were increasing at this period.

Some months having passed without seeing any more of the children, they again troubled that friend in their neighbourhood who had interfered in their behalf, intreating him to inquire after them. In reply he said, " that during his absence from home the master of the boys had died, his widow had married his assistant, and the whole family were removed either to Manchester or Liverpool."

From this time the poor children were, therefore, unavoidably lost sight of to these their first, and perhaps only friends. Their manifold sufferings, their opening dispositions, good propensities, or evil passions; — the peculiar temptations which might assail them, the abilities which might distinguish them, their capabilities for good or evil, happiness or misery, eternal blessedness or unalterable wretchedness, excited probably no further attention; they were absorbed in the great mass who *then* escaped the eye of humanity, and were unrecognized in her family, save as " beasts that perish."

But to those who can read " the short and simple annals of the poor," the development of those feelings, the movements of " that spirit which striveth" in the heart of man, whether high or low, in solitude or society, — to such we will offer the history of these children, which, in the principal features, doubtless resembles that of numbers similarly situated.

Alice Banks had the irreparable misfortune of losing an excellent husband, and being compelled, with five small children, to seek aid from the parish, at the very time when the husband of her neighbour Sarah Green, deserted his family, by enlisting for a soldier, and thereby reduced them to the same situation.

The charge thus suddenly brought on a small parish, induced the overseers to look out very quickly for some method, by which the families so cast upon them might assist themselves, and were glad when a chimney-sweeper offered to take a couple of boys from the workhouse. A number of children were presented for his choice, which soon fell upon the eldest son of the deserted wife, our little Frank, who was a fine, healthy, robust child, evidently capable already of exertion: he hesitated how to fix on a second, but was directed to the widow's only boy, a child of singular beauty and of delicate limbs, recommended as possessing a small and flexible form, which could creep into the narrowest flue possible.

The chimney-sweeper accepted the recommendation, observing "that he looked a sickly sort of a thing, but yet might be put to some use;" and proceeded to pack up the few cloaths which belonged to the animals he had bargained for with the utmost *sang-froid*.

But a great cry was heard in the house; the two

bereaved mothers deprecated the sentence, and clung around their children with sorrow that "would not be comforted." It is true, their grief was differently expressed; for Sarah was a violent woman, terrible in her passions, and sinful in the expression of her resentment; whilst Alice was meek in her manners, even when overwhelmed with bitter grief, and conceiving herself injured irreparably in the loss of that child who was more especially dear as the representative of his lamented father. Their sorrow or their blame was alike disregarded beyond the disturbance it made, and the poor children were torn from the necks round which they clung, and consigned to their new owner's mercy, with much the same feeling which belongs to the purchase of a calf; — provided that there were no children to witness the removal of their quadruped playmates, as in that case the bleatings of the calf would have excited far more compassion than the tears of the children.

Frank, it is true, did not cry long; — he loved his mother, for he had a warm and affectionate heart, but he had no remembrance which bound him strongly to home: his father had been idle and profligate; his mother alternately kind or severe, as the temper of the moment prevailed; and of duty to either he had never heard, save where obedience was impelled by blows or threats. He had, therefore, in his new destination, something to stimulate courage and curiosity, and nothing greatly to lament, when the shock of parting with his mammy and brothers was over; and in a short time he trudged along with a calm and confiding air, sometimes looking up in his master's face with good-humoured contentedness, at others, with pity on his companion, whose hand at length he took, and thereby assisted his lingering steps, whilst in the action he soothed his spirits.

Yet long and terribly did poor William sob and weep, although he endeavoured to suppress his anguish, and not only imitate the manliness of his companion, but obey the injunction of his mother, who, as she printed the last trembling kiss, on the soft cheek that was deluged by her tears, exhorted him "to be a good boy, obey his master, and try to be cheerful." Alas! with her words arose also the memory of her love to *him*, her sorrow for his father, the kindness of his little sisters, all the late lost comforts of his humble, but happy home; and then he wept again.

The master to whom these children were consigned was not an ill-natured man, or given to that undue severity often practised by men in his situation; he was the father of a family of children, whom he loved tenderly, and his feeling for them taught him some regard for those committed to his care. His eldest son was about two years older than Frank, whom he had never yet initiated into the painful duties of his profession; and his next child being a girl, the same age as Will, was alike exempted; but as they, with three younger, were all to be maintained by its very slender profits, (for in the country, such profits are, indeed, scanty,) it was evident that great care was necessary in providing for such a numerous family, and but too likely that an indulgent father might prove a pinching master.

Another cause likewise contributed to this end; the poor man's health was irreparably ruined by his business, and his appetite so delicate, as to compel him to seek food he was ill able to purchase, and medicine, for which he could ill afford to pay, and which it was the care of his wife to provide, so far as she could, by abridging in quantity the coarse food allotted to the apprentices. Our poor children, therefore, soon entered upon a state of suffering and trial, for which the plain plenty of their former homes had utterly unfitted them, at a period of life when all who have children well know how keenly hunger is felt, and how severe are its inflictions.

This evil was experienced much more acutely by Frank than Will, as being the more robust and active child; his natural courage, his love of praise, and the good-humour with which he entered into every exertion required by those around him, operated to make Frank a willing, and dexterous as fearless, climbing-boy. The horror of poor Will, at encountering the suffocating passages, the rough walls, the impervious labyrinths, and the giddy heights, was, on the other hand, dreadful. No exhortation could string up his spirits, no praise reward his exertion, so far as to conquer his timidity, until he had been compelled by blows and cruel goadings, to ascend so often, that at length he became to a certain degree habituated to the danger, and inured to the sensation.

During this period the two boys mutually aided each other. Frank frequently received a part of poor Will's already scanty breakfast for performing his work, for which, in his gratitude, he frequently offered all; hence he continued still little, and, therefore, unhappily fitted for the most difficult undertakings, from which, at times, the friendship of even Frank could not rescue him. That friendship was, however, invaluable to both; it enabled them to fulfil between them many tasks that could not be performed singly, — to please their master's son in play hours, nurse the little ones, when they were in the house, to propitiate the mistress, do jobs for the neighbours, such as getting in coals, &c. by which a few pence, or a good meal, might be earned; and above all, it kept them from associating with those who would have led them into wicked and profane habits, to which, from the total absence of instruction, they were liable even now.

The second winter of their apprenticeship the master became seriously ill, and utterly unable to attend to his business, and he was, therefore, induced to hire an assistant, who had formerly been his apprentice, and whom he knew to be clever, active, and honest, in his business, though sullen in his manners, and severe in his temper. This was Dick, the person alluded to in the opening of our narrative, whose entrance into the family had just taken place at the time when the three apprentices were sent out, as we have seen, to work, beg, steal, or starve, as their necessities might prompt them, at a time when the severities of the season exposed them to every description of suffering.

Our poor children had long felt as if they were in some sort cut off from a right to the ordinary enjoyments, and the common suffrage of mankind. Little babes cried as they approached, and boys like themselves (sons of the smith or the labourer) shrunk from their contaminating touch, which so far operated as to deny them the power of asserting valour, or repelling insult; for even the beggar's brat would not fight with a sweep. Yet still they had a portion of those enjoyments which belong to infancy; — that spring of heart which repels care; that love of play which in catching a fugitive enjoyment is rewarded for toil; and that pride of power which is inevitably the reward of exertion, however branded or disagreeable its field of action. But from the time that Dick became their guide, and in fact their master, all the little of good which had sweetened their hard lot quickly vanished, and every hardship was doubled. To propitiate his tyrannical temper they gave *him* the money which Mrs. Sutherland had given *them*, and on their visit there, on taking the knick-a-knacks, permission had been only granted in the expectation that they would be liberally rewarded; and, on finding this was not the case, they were accused of having spent the money, beaten, and sent supperless to bed; and thus a practical lesson given them to be ungrateful for the future, and to practise, henceforward, that cunning of which they had been wrongfully accused.

Contrasted with the dominion of Dick, the conduct of their master appeared to have been all kindness, and the children therefore lamented his sufferings and sincerely mourned his death. They sympathised also with their mistress, concluding that she had been compelled to starve them, in order to assist her husband, and resolved to be useful and active in her service; and as even Dick appeared to be affected by this awful though long-expected event, even he was included in their good wishes.

For a few weeks (but it was only a few) the hateful tyranny of Dick was softened, and the poor widow was sensible, that to his care in the management of her affairs she was deeply indebted. He used the opportunity her thanks for this care afforded, to inform her, "that unless she married him he should immediately quit her service, and use the connection he had now gained in the country, to begin business in opposition to her."

What could a woman with five children, and whose eldest apprentice was just quitting her, do in a business which precluded personal exertion? She consented; and, in doing so, sealed her own misery and that of all beneath her roof.

From the day of his marriage, Dick protested, "that he should turn over a new leaf in the house;" and he began by compelling not only his step-son, but even the little girl to go out with the apprentices, and begin to climb chimneys. The distress of the mother, the clamour of the children, and the violent methods used to enforce their obedience, formed the conversation, and, in many cases, drew down the reproaches of the neighbourhood; and when the new master found that the magistrate, who had formerly interfered on behalf of the little boys, was about to return home, he suddenly resolved to remove, being aware that he was hated by all around him, liable to punishment, and, at the same time that his knowledge of his business, and his possession of a set of clever children, could hardly fail to procure employment wherever he should fix himself.

A hasty (and of course disadvantageous) sale of his predecessor's effects, enabled the man to quit the country, and plunge at once into that best hiding-place, a large, populous, and busy town. As, however, he found that there was a tolerably vigilant police, and a new system of district overseers then about to be established, he became aware that he must control his temper, and at least confine his cruelties to home exercise.

The alarm given by a fire breaking out in a large manufactory, first called Richard and his young train into notice; and here the exertions of Frank, under his directions, were so beneficial, as to pave the way for him to excellent and constant employment, for which he received more than double of his former wages, besides the power of good and ready sale for the soot; and his wife perceived that he had really obtained the power of maintaining her and her family in a much better manner than her former husband ever possessed. The children had, however, no reason to rejoice in the change, though they were well disposed to do it, and would have thought little of increased labour if their comforts had been increased in proportion, or even if kindness of manner had been offered in compensation of hardships. This was so far from being the case, that the master, on finding of course that their food cost more in the town than in the country, abridged it in quantity and reduced it in quality. Milk, which had hitherto been the most nourishing substance which passed their lips, was now entirely denied them; the refreshing effect of pure air, even the benefit of clean dry straw, was no longer theirs; the common gift of buttered oaten cake offered to the poor sweep by the farmer's wife or daughter, in reward of trivial services, now never reached them. Huddled up in a miserable garret, half starved, yet half suffocated by the atmosphere which inevitably surrounded them, their inflamed eyes, heaving lungs, shrinking muscles, and withered flesh, denoted constant disease, independent of many a festering wound, hidden by their ragged garments, many a bruise concealed by the still blacker soot.

The compassion they had excited in their own country failed here also, not less than the other reliefs formerly experienced; for although there were perhaps a greater proportion of wealthy and charitable people, really concerned for the poor and helpless, around them, than in any circle they had ever moved in, yet that class with whom they more immediately were connected, and on whom they depended for much amelioration of their hard lot, were proud, ignorant, thoughtless, and unfeeling, beyond what they had ever met with. The conceited housemaid, whose light labours and heavy wages had taught her to forget the privations of infancy, could allow them to sue for admittance many a cold hour in vain; and the fierce cook laughed to see blows inflicted on the little wretch, who hesitated to encounter certain pain, and threatened death, in cleansing the foul flue which yesterday spoiled her dinner. To drive the cold, hungry, beaten child out of the house, and far from the sight, the instant he had performed a loathsome but most necessary task; to consider him a machine made for drudgery, born to suffering, distinct from themselves in his rights as a human being, and in his perceptions and capabilities of endurance, appeared to influence the feelings and conduct of all whom they approached. He was no longer remembered as "man born of a woman" (welcomed to life with tender joy, sustained in it by Nature's purest current) save as he was "born to misery."

It is certain, that Tom (the step son) was yet for a long period more to be pitied than the poor children of whom we speak. He had been nurtured with kindness, exempted from early labour, was old enough to remember and regret his father, yet far too young to emancipate himself from the worse than Egyptian bondage in which he was held, and he loved his sister so fondly, that to see her share his own toil, and partake his privations, added to his sorrow, and inflamed his useless anger to phrenzy. Every effort the poor boy made only bound him stronger in the toils, and it soon became evident to the apprentices, that he had more difficult tasks given to him than they had, and although considerably bigger, was forced into places of more difficult entrance. Of this he naturally complained to his mother, who in consequence revenged the evil upon them, innocent as they were of it; in fact, the woman's misery hardened her heart, she was herself treated with barbarity, and she dealt to others that which she received from a husband, who was yet industrious, prosperous, and therefore apparently respectable.

A spirit like Tom's, incessantly nursing the memory of injury, became soon ferocious, as well as rebellious, and desirous of exercising on others similar cruelty with that under which he smarted, and towards poor gentle Will, as the youngest and most helpless, he daily displayed malignity of every kind in his power. From this Frank protected him as far as he was able; and for some time the sense of his kindness operated as the cordial drop, which cherished his sinking heart, and roused his energies; but the time came when this failed to operate. The bright blue eye no longer beamed with intelligence; the mild voice no longer promised obedience. Weakness of body and stupor of mind; benumbed faculties; confused recollections; the listlessness of despair; the apathy of disease succeeded.

The stronger constitution of Frank enabled him better to stem the current, but his faculties quickened by torture, alive to revenge, stimulated by hunger, and untaught, save by punishment indiscriminately given alike for misfortune or error, might be said to hold himself ready for any species of crime which promised temporary pleasure or permanent relief. Tom already was associated with a gang of wicked children, whose depredations he sought to share for the purpose of gaining the means of escape from his step-father, a scheme in which Frank readily concurred, but his remaining tenderness to his weak companion induced him to let the favourable time slip by, in consequence of which the plot was discovered, and the delinquents punished with such horrible severity that for many days they lay in agonies, and the half-murdering master in his turn suffered the terrors of the guilty, and became the croaking attendant, the flattering soother, and the liberal feeder of the wretched invalids.

Will shook off the languor which had so long affected him to wait on Frank, to talk to him about God and good things, now he believed him dying, and earnestly to intreat him, when he got to heaven, to seek out his father, and inform him how much he also desired to go thither. These conversations, together with the apparent penitence and actual kindness of his master, touched the heart of Frank, and he freely confessed and sincerely repented the sins and the schemes into which he had been led. As Tom stretched his bruised limbs on the bed of pain, far different thoughts affected him, and the desire of vengeance, or of everlasting flight, alone possessed him. Contempt for his present humility alone varied the character of that bitter hatred with which he regarded that detestable tyrant, whose every action in this season of solitude rose to his mind's eye in all its reiterated and horrible atrocity, more especially the death of a little brother whom he believed to have been the victim of an experiment in their own chimney.

It was summer when this trouble occurred, and therefore the labours of the invalids had been little required, but yet those of poor Will, who was nearly as ill able to move as they had been, were in pretty constant requisition; and it so happened that the first day they had ventured to crawl out, he was absent with his master at a time when their services were hastily demanded by a most generous and regular customer.

The unhappy mother knew not what she ought to do; the servant who brought the message had seen two sweeps in the house, and if they did not go his master would be offended and her husband angry.

"I am willing to go," said Tom, secretly resolving that he never would return; and, fearing that Frank might inadvertently betray him, he determined to go alone; but the mother would not suffer this, as she thought he might require assistance, and she also, in her anxiety to help him, imprudently gave him a glass of strong liquor. On arriving, they were informed that the chimney they were required to sweep was difficult from its construction, many directions were given, and a liberal reward was promised, on which Tom, anxious to gain the money which might forward his views, prepared immediately to ascend.

He found that the soreness of his body, as well as the form of the chimney, for a considerable time presented great difficulties, but the resolution he had formed, and the intoxication produced by the liquor, gave him a temporary strength. On arriving at the top he rested upon his arms, and sought to regain breath by inspiring a purer air, and to arrange his plans for flight, which he knew must be immediately adopted, or resigned; and in the heat and perturbation of the moment he hesitated on the subject from that burning desire of revenge which unceasingly pursued him.

In the meantime Richard had returned home, and on learning the destination of the boys he became extremely alarmed lest any part of his past conduct should transpire, and followed them immediately. His presence was hailed with joy, as the persons present were extremely anxious respecting the poor boy in the chimney.

Richard followed with celerity, and being both slight and strong was soon nearly at the top. Tom was then aware that his scheme was frustrated, and his rage became even greater than his terror; he was first sensible of the close approach of Richard from finding that his feet, which were now dangling in the chimney, touched the chin of Richard as he ascended, and he well remembered that the winter before a similar occurrence had induced the brutal master, in mere sport of cruelty, to seize his toe and bite it to the bone; — "perhaps he had now followed him in anger, and would do it again?"

The hellish passion of revenge so long nurtured; the heated and perturbed state of his mind; the sudden recollection, that at that part of the chimney where Richard now stood, he had no footing, but was necessarily supporting himself on joists by his arms, contributed to inspire him with diabolical fury and resolution, — in a moment he wound his feet round the naked throat of the helpless man, with a closeness of adaptation and power of compression which the practised clinging feet of a climbing-boy alone could use. Richard shook his head, and endeavoured to groan, but no sound issued from his gasping lips; at length, in the agony of departing life, he forgot all other danger, and put up his hands to assist his liberation, and at the same moment was precipitated down a considerable part of the chimney, but not to the bottom. The sound of his fall alarmed the family. Firemen and bricklayers were procured, but nearly an hour passed before the mangled body, then completely lifeless, was drawn out. That of Tom was sought for in vain; and it was at length concluded that he had contrived to get out of the top, and make his way over the roofs of the adjoining houses, in his dread of descending a chimney which had proved fatal to his master.

When Frank beheld the dreadful spectacle presented by the body of his master, and found that Tom was lost, he could not forbear concluding that he had been accessary to his death; and he experienced a degree of terror which overcame every other sensation, and combined with his late sufferings to render him extremely ill. He crawled home as well as he was able, and finding Will alone, he told him what had happened, and so strongly protested against remaining near the body, that Will accompanied him into the fields; and when there, they consulted together, and conceiving that Tom would now be their master, resolved to brave every danger, rather than return to a scene of so much horror and misery.

Without money or food, save what scanty alms, or the boon of nature in summer supplies, the poor boys at length reached the village where they were born; but recollection had so far failed them, that when arrived there (in consequence of that inquiry which was ever on their lips) they knew not whom to ask for, or where to drag their feeble steps. The circumstance of two strange sweeps standing near the village well, and afterwards sitting down by it, as if they could not move, at length induced a decent charwoman to steal a few minutes from her day's toil to speak to them, and help them, for she had a sympathy for all children devoted to this employment.

The poor woman soon perceived that the elder, and stouter, was in a state of high fever, and her compassion induced her to take him to her own cottage; and meeting with a neighbour who had been labouring in the fields, she earnestly entreated her "to go in with him, wash him, and take care of him:" —the woman said "she was already tired enough; she had been up ever since daylight."

"That is true, I doubt not, Sally, and the very moment I have done scouring I will relieve you; but pray do it for the sake of your own poor Frank."

"*That* is Frank," said Will, with that feeble voice which bespeaks utter exhaustion.

"That Frank! then who art thou?" cried poor Alice Banks, in agonizing expectation.

"I am little Will — I want to find my mother." The mother was found; — her arms were around him; she carried him into her cottage; — her gushing tears fell on his face, and she eagerly called her girls to welcome their brother, "her pretty, fair-faced, gentle Willy." Alas! she looked in vain for the gladsome eye, the grateful smile; and as her cares proceeded, she found that she held to her heart the wasted remnant of a creature destroyed alike in body and mind; willing, but unable, even to rejoice in her love, and be thankful for her kindness.

The days of both were numbered; but Frank was the first victim; and the frantic grief of his mother, as she wept over the unhealed wounds that disfigured his corpse, awakened the attention of those overseers who had bound the boys to this service, and excited their sincere compassion, which flowed with still warmer pity as they gazed on the pale shadowy form of little Will, and heard him whisper, "dear mammy, bury me beside Frank."

In that grave he was soon laid, and by some his hard fate was soon forgotten; but there were others on whose minds it rested, and whose conduct it influenced; and never has the village since then destined another of its children to this worse than Egyptian bondage. It is true that a few years after this time, a young man came thither, whose appearance proved him comfortable and thriving, and whose inquiries after the poor children bespoke his affection and humanity. He was the elder apprentice of whom we spoke, now returned, after long absence, to visit his native country; and he said that he had long been happily situated as the servant of a mistress at Hampstead, whose whole family were rendered so comfortable by her kindness and wisdom, that even chimney-sweeping was divested of nearly all its horror. Her children were well fed; perfectly clean, except in the hours of employment; regularly instructed in their duty to God and man; and in actual possession of more comforts than the working classes often secure. In summer they cultivated her garden; in winter they learned to read and write, during the afternoon hours. She took them constantly to church, where their healthy and happy looks, and the propriety of their manners, had excited so much approbation as to induce others to follow her example.

To this pleasant account, the stranger added the

sad news, that Tom, his late master's darling child, had lately died on the gallows; and the shuddering circle were again led to recollect the poor children with whom once he had been connected, and to protest, "that whilst they could rely on the truth of his statement, and honour the virtuous conduct of his mistress, yet never, *never* could they forget the hard fate of Frank and Will."

B. Hofland.

London, February 26. 1824.

THE CHIMNEY-SWEEPER.

A SKETCH.

SCENE I. *A Garret in ——.*

STRONG, PHILIP, *and other Boys and Children, are seen lying on the floor.*

Voice. (*Without.*) You, Sirs, within, awake! what cursed drugs
Have ye been stealing that ye lie so long?
Awake, ye sleep-fed villains! are ye dumb?
Strong. Master, 'tis scarce past four.
Voice. Must I get up,
And hunt ye to your work?
Strong. Philip! Poor child,
He sleeps as soundly as in his mother's arms.
Hunger and blows but drive him to his dreams,
As music, I have heard, will sometimes do.
Voice. I hear no feet yet stirring on the floor.

Strong. We come, Sir. Philip! Is your rest so sweet
That you dare loiter? Rub the heavy sleep
From off your eye-lids, man: 'tis time to rise.

Philip. Oh! — 'tis not day. My limbs are chain'd with cold;
And that sharp hunger, which so pierced my stomach
Last night, is come again. Is there no bread?
Not a poor morsel?

Strong. Not a crumb, my boy.

Voice. Where is my whip? These rogues are fed so high,
They will not work until their skins be scored.
Now, let the devil sit upon the thong;
We'll try what backs are made of.

The MASTER *enters: the Boys rise.*

Philip. Pray, Sir! pray!

Master. What puny noise is this? Beggarly thing!
You, who have nothing left but bones to lift,
Are *you* a-bed still? [*Strikes him.*

Philip. Pray, dear master! pray!
I am so hungry, and so stiff with cold.

Master. Hungry! — I'll spoil your appetite, puling imp!
Whom a good blast o' the north wind would blow through: —

Gather your crazy limbs up, dog, or else
I'll whip new life into you. [*Striking.*
Strong. (*Aside.*) Or the old out.
Oh! master, do not beat him, lest he die.
Master. "Die," villain? — Well, and if he *does*, I hope
I've paid my money for him; three good pounds.
Who suffers, fool, but I? — These weakly imps
Are always chargeable. I'll no more of them;
But lay my money out in lusty limbs,
Strong, thick-set rascals, who will work and starve.
You, Clement, see you fill your bag to-day
At the old widow's. You, Sir, take good care
You cram the bottom of your sack with coals:
Our parson suspects no one. Harry, mark,
You'll mount the doctor's chimney: — In his room
He scatters copper, and his cupboard's rich
With dainties: hide this cloth beneath your jacket,
And catch whate'er ye can: you shall have half:
If you bring nought, — look! here's the whip for dinner.
(*Aside.*) If men *will* let these hungry shivering imps
Mount their black tunnels, and turn boys to brooms,
Why, they should suffer. *They* are in fault, not I.
Away; ye ragged knaves. [*Boys, &c. exeunt.*
Now, then, to sleep.
These rogues are useful, too: — they sweep and earn,

Fetch, carry, and sometimes — steal, and sometimes
— die;
And then the parish hides 'em:— Six plain boards,
A good deep hole, a prayer, and plenty of dust,
And there's an end of a sweeper. Ah! — 'tis cold:
I'll in, and sleep 'till day. [*Exit.*

SCENE II. *A Street in* ——.

STRONG *and* PHILIP *enter:* STRONG *is singing.*

Philip. Strong, you've a merry heart.

Strong. A stout one, at least.

Philip. And *very* tender; as *my* heart oft tells me.

Strong. Tush! do not cry; this life is bad, 'tis
true,
But there are as hard, boy. *I* have been to sea;
I ran away from my old mother.—Pshaw!

Philip. Your voice shakes.

Strong. No, no; well, I ran to sea.
I had been cheated by some lying tales
Of an old sailor, with a wooden leg.
He swore he had trod on gold, (he brought none
home,)
Had rid upon the huge cloud-kissing waves,
Had touch'd the moon, talk'd with an elephant,
Got prize-money and honour.

Philip. What is that?

Strong. 'Faith, I can't tell; some salve, he said, which cured
Gashes, and staunch'd black blood. It made him stand
Upright upon his stump, proud as a lord;
Yet was he but a cripple, and would drink
The puddle, for lack of two-pence to buy beer.

Philip. What! was he straight and proud?

Strong. Straight as a stick,
Proud as the devil.

Philip. Hush!

Strong. Ah! I forget
Thy pretty lessons, Philip. A sea-liver,
My fate has been hard words, hard fare, hard blows,
What wonder if a little sticks by me;
Yet, child, I do my best. E'er since you heard me
Swearing in my dark dreams, I've fought with sin,
Struggled with curses, as a madman flings
Wild thoughts from off his brain. Oh! *you* can't guess
How I've been tempted. Once, in a mutiny,
Grey villains forced a knife in my small hands,
And bade me strike it through a good man's throat.
I did not do it; thank God! I did not do it.

Philip. Where are those villains?

Strong. Rattling in the wind;
Kicking their heels in iron stirrups, boy,
On the sea-shore; hang'd by the neck,—dead,—dead.

Philip. You frighten me.

Strong. Then let us talk no more.
Stay, you must enter here; 'tis a kind man
Who lives here; do not steal a morsel from him;
I'll call as I return, and bring you bread.
[*Philip goes in.*

SCENE III. *A large Library.*

MR. AUBREY *is pacing up and down; he looks out.*

Aubrey. The sullen morning lags in the dark east.
Is he so happy on his boisterous bed
That he still sleeps? Hark! the clock speaks: 'tis four.
I had mistaken, and, in my restless grief,
Have risen an hour too early. My friend's house
Is still as death. [*Goes to the books.*
Come forth, ye silent spirits!
Men of a thousand years, whose golden tongues
Still talk rare music, though your flesh be cold;
Xenophon, Plato, death-drinking Socrates,
Theocritus, and Bion, that sad singer,
(Απολετο καλος Αδωνις, thus he mourns,)
And Homer, like Jove's brother, who once rode
Upon the stormy billows of fine sound,
And, in his prodigal strength, cast forth huge shapes,
Which dwarf the pigmies of this meaner world.
Alas! I cannot relish war, nor love;
Sorrow befits me only, who have lost

My "poor Marcellus;" so, — sweet Virgil, come,
With Mantuan laurel crown'd, or Mincian reeds,
And sooth me to sleep with mournful melodies.—
I cannot read; the letters yawn, and Death
Looks busy in every line. [*A sound is heard*
What noise is there?
It was as though some strangling babe had spoke;
And the sound struck upon my brain and heart
Like stunning music. I have dreamt such things
In extreme pain; but when I stretch'd my arms
(Which loved to circle children once, and pay
That sweet mute homage which man's nature yields
To infancy) the little phantoms fled.
Oh, nought is real in this blind, bitter world,
Save Hope, or strong possession, and *I* have neither,
But am a childless man, grown early grey,
Merely from sorrow. [*A low cry is heard.*
Ha! this is no dream.
Who cries?

A SERVANT *enters.*

Serv. A child has fallen, Sir, from a great height,
And lies here senseless, cover'd with soot and blood.
Aubrey. Quick, bring him in. (*Serv. exit.*) Where are my instruments?
Quick, Sir, you loiter.

PHILIP *is brought in.*

Ah, poor infant! dead?
No, no, thank Heaven! Now, cleanse this mire away,
The wound is hidden: Ah, 'tis a terrible gash;
But we will heal it. What a poor, thin child;
And pale, no doubt, but that his face is mask'd
In the black dust. He breathes: hush! and his pulse
Ebbs faintly with returning life. His eyes
Are seal'd still; but no matter, he will live;
And Fortune, who has thrown him at my feet,
Shall raise him to my bosom. Cleanse his brow,
And pour the water gently on his cheek,
And o'er his lips, which part, and seem to smile
(Poor wretch!) for life, though bitter. Ha! great God!
Who's this? — Thou brute, why hast thou rack'd me thus?
So, you'll bring ghosts i' the chamber? Raise the house!
I will not sleep alone, nor sit, nor be—

Serv. Sir,—I,—

Aubrey. By heaven, it *will* not vanish, though I pray;
Though I pray strongly, dumbly; though the cold sweat
Runs like a river down my quivering forehead.
Speak to it. — Child!

Philip. Ah, father! my *dear* father!

Serv. Look up, Sir. Is *he* gone too? 'Sdeath! my flesh
Creeps and grows cold all over. Ho! youngster, speak.
You'll kill this gentleman, my master's friend.

Philip. Ah, father! father!

Serv. Sir, you'll press the child
Into a shadow. Sir, be wise, and speak.

Aubrey. Am I alive? Art *thou* alive? My child!
My only one! My lost one! My lost — found!
Oh, let me *feel* thee! — nearer, — so. I fear
Lest thou shouldst 'scape me, like a faithless dream.
Speak to me.

Philip. Father, my dear father!

Aubrey. Dear!
Dearest and most beloved! My poor waif,
Cast on the rough wild shore, art come *again?*
What will thy mother say? Thou'lt be the spring
To breathe new life into her desert heart;
Thou'lt raise her, sweet one, as the broken flower
Is raised up by the gentle sun, returned
After a tempest. Once more, come to me!
There, — there: lie there for ever. Tears? — sweet thanks!
Weep, Philip, weep; let all thy sadness flow;
We will be happy soon; I have no tears,
Though now they are a balm. Thy foes, thy friends,

To both we'll give great dues. Misused child!
Did I not say that Fortune cast thee down?
She did; but we will chain her to our lives,
And make her smile hereafter.

B. C.

London, February, 1824.

FROM

PHILANTHROPY,

A POEM.

COMMUNICATED BY THE AUTHOR.

Poor little swarthy boy, why dost thou weep,
And mingle bursting sobs with cries of "Sweep?"
Did some base wretch thine innocence betray,
And from thy cradle drag thee far away?
Or did thy parents, worse than savage wild,
With brutish cruelty desert their child?
Poor babe! the sun of life had scarcely shone,
Ere sorrow seem'd to mark thee as her own.
The little lambkins, destined for the knife,
May sport away the brittle hour of life;
Nursed by their tender dams, no pangs they feel,
Till call'd to perish by the murd'rous steel:
But thou art doom'd the toils of life to share;
Thine infant brow is mark'd with hoary care,

And groaning deep beneath the dusty load,
Thy steps are moisten'd with thy sweat and blood.
Perhaps, poor boy, thy mother doth deplore
Her long-lost darling she can see no more;
Perhaps the wretch that tore thee from thy home
Seal'd her death-warrant, sent her to the tomb.
O! it had fill'd her yearning soul with joy,
But once again to gaze upon her boy;
O! it had made her dying moments bliss,
Could she have press'd his lips with parting kiss.
But, ah! thy rose-bud cheek no more doth glow
With charms that made thy mother love thee so;
The coral hue nor paints thy pouting lip,
Whence virgin love might sweetest honey sip:
Dimm'd is the splendour of thy sparkling eye,
Thy lively prattle lost in swelling sigh;
While the loved form that did the heart engage,
By labour bow'd, resembles drooping age.
Poor boy! thou smilest in the month of May,
For then thy master bids thee to be gay;
And, deck'd with tinsel garlands, to appear
Light-hearted and light-footed once a year.
Now, to dispel thy melancholy gloom,
Thou dancest to the shovel and the broom,
Or tread'st the limping step along the green,
With labour, more than grace, in all thy mien.

Ah! drop a tear, for MONTAGUE's no more,
To spread for craving sweeps the May-day store; *
A few poor pence reward thee for thy toil,
And hungry comrades share thy scanty spoil.
Short is the pleasure, mingled with thy pain; —
Long lag the months, till May-day smile again;
But keen as eagle's glances Mercy's eye,
The little sufferer nor passes by
Without regard — and art her aid doth lend,
The most despised and helpless to befriend.
Ye ladies fair, when seated round the urn,
Ye view the winter's fire so cheerly burn,
Think how the poor neglected sweeper-boy
Contributes to the comforts you enjoy;
Without whose aids, your robes of snowy white
With smirched tints had vex'd your tender sight;
And noxious smoke had spoil'd your rich perfume,
Tainted your toast, and fill'd the sweeten'd room.
When rising from the downy arms of sleep,
Ye to the breakfast-parlour shivering creep,
And catch the warming beams of blazing grate;
O! think how hard the little starveling's fate,

---

* Mrs. Montague, of Portman-Square, used to have all the chimney-sweepers dine on the lawn, before her elegant mansion, every May-day, till the time of her decease. As a reason for this kindness, it is said that a member of her family, when a child, was once stolen, and exposed among the little sufferers, and rescued by an accidental discovery.

To trudge, bare-footed, through the wintry snows,
While ye enjoy the hour of calm repose;
And often urged, by cruel master's ire,
To clear the channel for your glowing fire.
Pity the drudging boy, ye feeling fair,
Relieve his sorrows by your watchful care;
And when you wish your chimneys to be clean,
O, spare his toils, — employ the kind machine!

J. COBBIN.

March 22. 1824.

THE CHIMNEY-SWEEPER.

COMMUNICATED BY MR. CHARLES LAMB, FROM A VERY RARE AND CURIOUS LITTLE WORK.

When my mother died I was very young,
And my father sold me, while yet my tongue
Could scarcely cry, " Weep! weep! weep!"
So your chimneys I sweep, and in soot I sleep.

There's little Tom Toddy, who cried when his head,
That curl'd like a lamb's back, was shaved, so I said,
" Hush, Tom, never mind it, for when your head's bare,
You know that the soot cannot spoil your white hair."

And so he was quiet, and that very night
As Tom was a sleeping, he had such a sight,
That thousands of sweepers, Dick, Joe, Ned, and Jack,
Were all of them lock'd up in coffins of black.

And by came an angel, who had a bright key,
And he open'd the coffins, and set them all free;
Then down a green plain, leaping, laughing, they run,
And wash in a river, and shine in the sun.

Then naked and white, all their bags left behind,
They rise upon clouds, and sport in the wind;
And the angel told Tom, if he'd be a good boy,
He'd have God for his father, and never want joy.

And so Tom awoke, and we rose in the dark,
And got with our bags and our brushes to work;
Though the morning was cold, Tom was happy and warm,
So if all do their duty they need not fear harm.

From BLAKE's *Songs of Innocence.*

THE LITTLE SWEEP.

TO BRITISH SENATORS.

1.

THEY sing of the poor sailor-boy, who wanders o'er the deep,
But few are they who think upon the friendless LITTLE SWEEP!
In darkness to his dreary toil, thro' winter's frost and snows,
When the keen north is piping shrill, the shivering urchin goes.

2.

He has no father, and from grief his mother's eyes are dim,
And none besides, in all the world, awakes to pray for HIM:

For him no summer Sundays smile, no health is in the breeze;
His mind dark as his fate, his frame a prey to dire disease.*

3.

Oh, English gentlemen! your hearts have bled for the black slave,
You heard his melancholy moan from the Atlantic wave;
He thought upon his fathers' land, and cried, "A LONG farewell,"
But bless'd you, gazing at the sun, when first his fetters fell.

4.

And if ye plead for creatures dumb†, and deem their fate severe,
Shall *human* wrongs, in *your own* land, call forth no generous tear?
Humanity implores! Awake from apathy's cold sleep!
And, when you plead for others' wrongs, forget not the POOR SWEEP.

---

* The terrible "soot cancer" to which all climbing-boys are subject.

† See Mr. Martyn's bill.

5.

When summer comes the bells shall ring, and flowers
and hawthorns blow,
The village lasses and the lads shall all "a-Maying"
go:
Kind-hearted lady*, may thy soul in heaven a blessing
reap,
Whose bounty at that season flows, to cheer the
LITTLE SWEEP!

6.

'Tis yours, ye English gentlemen, such comforts to
prolong;
'Tis yours the friendless to protect, and all who suffer
wrong.
But *one* day in the toiling year the friendless sweep
is gay,
Protect,—and smiling industry shall make his long
year MAY!

WILLAM LISLE BOWLES.

January 24. 1824.

---

* The late Mrs. Montague, whose bounty, on May-day, to these children is well known.

THE MOTHER'S GRAVE,

AND

THE ORPHAN'S PURGATORY.

I.

ONCE I saw thee in thy dwelling,
  Widow'd, young, but angel-fair;
All around the storm was swelling,
  O'er thee clouds of dark despair:
Every hope with *him* was buried,
  Him whom thou didst fondly love,
Who from hence in prime was hurried,
  Hurried to the realms above.

While the storm was thus assailing,
  Slumbering lay thy baby dear,
All unconscious thou wert wailing,
  Till he felt thy cold-dropt tear,
Where it stood on cheeks of roses
  Like the dew-drop on the flower,
Oped the eye which slumber closes,
  Oped to cheer a joyless hour.

Starting on the knee that bore him,
  From a trance of golden dreams,
Soon thy looks, while bending o'er him,
  Lit his face with morning beams:
Then his eyes, like stars so sparkling,
  Then his face, like smiling spring,
Chased away the clouds so darkling,
  Brought back Hope upon the wing.

Yes, in him, thine only treasure,
  Thou didst see the dead arise,
He could yield thee light and pleasure,
  When the clouds o'erhung the skies:
Shining forth with every blessing,
  Thine, in him, were joys to come,
Thou couldst hail his kind caressing,
  View his cot thy future home.

On he grew, and prattled by thee,
  Mimic of thy words and deeds;
Ever pleased when he was nigh thee,
  In the house or o'er the meads;
Till,—Oh shame to Christian Britain!—
  Kidnapp'd on an evil day,
When again Despair was written
  On the couch thy body lay.

Never more didst thou, — Oh never! —
  See him in thy sojourn here;
Soon thy woes were closed for ever,
  Wafted to a higher sphere;
When, perchance thy spirit hovering,
  Glancing earthward, saw thine own;
But to thee, then past recovering,
  Left to meet the storm alone.

O, that now a Pharaoh's daughter
  Would but stretch the royal hand!
Save, like Moses, from the water,
  Gently draw the ark to land;
Rescue from impending danger,
  Prove, to fill the cup of joy,
Guardian to the little stranger,
  Mother to the orphan boy.

II.

Off, — away, — away they bear him,
  "MOTHER!" is his only cry;
From *her* bleeding heart they tear him,
  His is rent with every sigh:
But the monster's grasp tenacious,
  Like the miser's with his gold,
Is as cruel, as ungracious,
  As the fierce hyena's hold.

Yes, — away, — away to slavery,
  Worse than that which negroes know;
Man with man to cope is bravery,
  Here an infant's miseries flow:
Still in blood the vulture revels,
  Heedless of the clay-cold dam;
With that vulture — MAN, he levels,
  Preys upon the harmless lamb.

Nay, below the feather'd creature;
  In his voice the tiger's growl;
Herod burns in every feature;
  Demons rage within his soul, —
Rage the more while boys are turning
  Round his hell of fire and smoke,
Where they barely 'scape from burning,
  Where the soot their breath would choke.

Ah, poor boy! how changed thy figure
  Since thou hadst a mother's care!
Dealt, with cruelty and rigour,
  Sleepless nights and scanty fare;
Limbs beneath thee weakly bending,
  Lacerated to the bone;
Every step is grave-ward tending,
  Every breath becomes a groan.

All thy members, through oppression,
  Shrink from rising up to man;
Powers precocious, through transgression,
  Never stretch beyond a span;
Settling down from cherub beauty
  To the imp of fiendish make;
Lost to all religious duty,
  Air is breathed for slavery's sake.

Underneath that garb so tatter'd,
  Deep as is thy ebon hue,
From a frame so weak and shatter'd,
  Where but misery meets the view,
Low is laid a germ for rising,
  Rosy tints to blush again;
Limbs for actions enterprising,
  Mind to triumph over pain.

III.

Say, did kindly HEAVEN intend it?
  Say, does stern NECESSITY?
Will HUMANITY defend it?
  REASON dare to urge her plea?
Will they singly, — all united,
  Give their voice for chimney-slaves?
See the bud of man, thus blighted,
  Raise a mound of early graves?

No, they cannot, — will not favour
  Such as with the lightning scathe,—
Blast the flowers of sweetest savour,
  Thickly o'er Destruction's path:
Sooner would annihilation
  Fill with joy the feeling heart;
Sooner than reverse creation
  Reason from her throne would start.

Who can tell, by care and training,
  But the kidnapp'd orphan boy
Might have gain'd,—been still maintaining
  Summits in the first employ?
Shining in the field of glory,
  Senates hanging on his tongue,
Mitred, in the church, and hoary,
  High in arts or sweet in song?

Lo! the mount of fairest science,
  Lo! the path to purest fame,
Court from all unmix'd affiance,
  Stand aloof to birth and name;
Where — let England be exalted!
  Oft the proud have been debased;
Humble worth has never halted
  Till the wreath the brow has graced.

What is Britain now foregoing?
  Genius strangled in the birth!
Slender toil on gems bestowing,
  Gems embedded deep in earth,
Soon will pay in worth and splendour
  Every *chimney sacrifice*,
Nobly raise the child's defender,
  Smoke still rolling to the skies.

Let the nation's voice be sounded,
  Like a clarion shrill and strong,
With the blast the senate 'stounded
  Soon will mingle with the throng:
Then, so soon shall fiends in manners
  Start to cherub forms in sight,
Human nature wave her banners,
  Men, with angels, spring to light.

JAMES EVERETT.

Sheffield, Jan. 22. 1824.

A BALLAD OF THE HOUSE-TOPS.

The village bells ring merrily, and brightly shines the sun,
And shouting through the woods and fields the task-less children run;
Whilst some gaze down, with peaceful looks, upon the river's flow,
And some are sporting with the flowers that on its margin grow.

The ball, the hoop, the soaring kite, and every implement
Of youthful pleasure, have their aid to swell their frolics lent;
And all seem lost in innocent and undissembled joy,
And all seem welcome there but one, the ragged climbing-boy.

Yet there are motions in his lip and in his mournful
eye,
That tell his heart with those wild sports still keeps
its sympathy ; [he tells,
Whilst to a stranger's willing ear his plaintive tale
As merrily upon the breeze ring out the village bells.

" Once was I like the mountain kid, that climbs the
rocky steeps, [der sleeps ;
Where danger ambush'd in their wilds in silent won-
But now my limbs are paralyzed, my feet have lost
their spring,
And I amid this world of life am a forgotten thing.

" Once I could breast the strongest wave upon my
native lake ;
The eyrie on the pathless cliff this nerveless hand
could take ;
The pinion of the forest-dove was scarce more swift
than I,
When strong of foot and light of heart in days of
infancy.

" My father dwelt among the hills, a pastoral shep-
herd's cot,
With wood-bine shaded in a glen, was our unenvied
lot ;

And by our door a mountain-stream with murmuring lapses strayed,
And music welcome to our ears in that seclusion made.

" My mother was a gentle soul, and oft upon her knee
She sang maternal songs of love in fondness unto me ;
And nurst me with the kindest care, and blest me in her joy,
And call'd me, with a tender smile, her own dear [mountain-boy.

" And oft I roved, with vagrant feet, among the eternal hills,
Or laid me down beneath the woods beside their [sparkling rills ;
And when the voice of spring was loud amid the groves I'd stray,
And listen with a gladsome heart the blackbird's earliest lay.

" No prince was happier in his halls than I in that dear glen,
Which was my hope, my home, my pride, my world, my wonder, then ;
For I had health and spirits pure, and friends to call my own,
And never had my infant cheek the touch of sorrow known.

"But ruin like a whirlwind came, and whelm'd us
with its might,
And o'er my sinless pleasures came an unexpected
blight:
My father died; my mother's hands could not our
living gain;
And I was sent afar, my life by labour to maintain.

"At first my master seem'd to be a kind and tender
man, [trepan;
But this was but the hunter's snare, his victim to
For when, by deeds of law, for years of misery I was
bound
To serve him for a scanty meal, his tyranny I found.

"This kindness soon was changed to wrath, his smiles
to bitterest frowns;
And trembling 'neath a cruel lash, I march'd to distant
towns,
Where, 'mid the thousand faces there, no friendly
stranger smiled,
Or looked with eye of tenderness upon the captive
child.

"My curling locks that floated oft upon the mountain
air, [sever'd there;
With filthy dust all clotted thick, were shorn and

And tatter'd rags, that shock'd the sight, was the unseemly dress
That robed those limbs which oft had shared a mother's fond caress.

" And soon my infant back was bow'd beneath a sickly weight, [fate;
And I became, beyond my years, the victim of my
For faintness stole along my veins, and sorrow struck my frame,
And weakness in my youth, instead of strength and vigour came.

" The morning, which I worshipp'd once, is now a time of dread, [bed;
And evening brings no rest to me, upon my sleepless
I wake in pain and misery before the dim twilight;
And lay me down to dream of peace, that cometh not with night.

" And oft, when from some chimney-top, I scent the breath of morn,
My spirit flies to that sweet spot from which I first was torn;
And mem'ry brings before my sight, at Fancy's magic call, [water-fall.
The brook, the glen, the garden-seat, the wood and

" And then I seem to hear the sounds that oft in days gone by
Could cheer my heart, or check the tear that gather'd in mine eye:
The whisper of the summer winds, the wild bee's sportive hum,
And melody of happy birds that to our bowers would come.

" The swallow that with rude assault I frighten from its nest,
Reminds me of the hours when she had been a welcome guest;
When on the surface of our lake I watch'd its rapid flight,
Or track'd its wheeling wing on high, with superstitious sight.

" When too, upon the village green, among the lads I stand,
No friendly voice my presence hails, I press no friendly hand;
I fain would mingle in their sports, but, ah! my brow doth wear
A mark that bids that noisy crew my converse to beware.

"I was not unto foreign lands by foreign foes convey'd,
But in this land of liberty a free-born slave was made,
Condemn'd to toil, whilst others rest, for bread which God hath given
To all who earn by innocence the bounteousness of heaven.

"God never gave us pliant limbs for labours such as these;
He never doom'd his chosen race t' uncleanness and disease;
He blest the infant, and his Son invited them to Him,
Nor doom'd to premature decay the young and healthy limb.

"Oh little know the great, the gay, the happy, the secure,
By what a train of noxious ills their comforts they ensure;
They little deem that when around the cheerful hearth they press,
That comfort was for them procured by others' wretchedness.

"Alas! and why to distant climes shall Freedom's chosen go,
Whilst slaves to serve us in our homes we blindly can allow;
Say, should not they who to the world exalt themselves as free,
Shake off the tightest shackle first, — Domestic Slavery?"

WM. B. CLARKE.

East-Bergholt, Suffolk;
March 17, 1824.

To face page 363.

THE

PETITION OF A CLIMBING-BOY

TO A NOBLE LEGISLATOR.

(WITH A PRINT.)

"Oh! pray, my Lord, regard an infant sweep,
Whose trembling limbs have fail'd him at your door;
Exhausted now he can no farther creep,
Oh! give an ear at least, if nothing more.

"These tatter'd rags my wretchedness bespeak,
This tiny frame proclaims how few my years;
While every white streak on my sooty cheek
Hath been the channel of unnumber'd tears.

"Pity the sorrows of an infant sweep!
Keen was the driving sleet and cold the wind;
From earliest morn to this late hour I keep
My destin'd course, yet little work I find.

" I cannot, dare not, to my home return ;
  My strength is gone, and master cruel hard :
Deep are the wounds which seem my frame to burn,
  But sores like these no *gentlefolks* regard.

" Distorted now my limbs,— they once were straight ;
  My eyes are now inflamed— they once were bright ;
I then could frisk and play, — but now my weight,
  Though small, oppresses, and I dread the light.

" Oh ! I remember when no wants I knew,
  When parents' care did every need supply ;
I loved them dearly, — yea, with love so true,
  My heart had well nigh broke when they did die.

" My Lord, they died ! my dear, dear parents died !
  The green grass sod lies o'er their humble grave ;
There every Sabbath-day I since have hied,
  With knife to weed the turf, with tears to lave.

" Say, did you ever lose, my lord, like me,
  Such parents dear, and long, like me, deplore ?
Then pity one who thus, in infancy,
  Is cast a friendless orphan at your door.

" That happier Negro, from his country torn,
  Hath found in you, my lord, a noble friend ;

Rich trappings now his sable limbs adorn;
  Oh, then, to native slaves your aid extend!

"Did those fine pamper'd dogs, that near him stand,
  Endure but half the miseries that I feel,
They'd soon be fed with more than liberal hand,
  They'd soon obtain the costly balm to heal!

"'Tis said, 'twas thought the laughter ne'er would cease
  When noble lords, in senate grave, did hear
Poor *infant sweeps* compared to *ducks* and *geese*,
  Pull'd by their necks, the sooty flues to clear.

"Well would it be, my lord, had we no pains
  But those which ducks and geese are doom'd to reap;
But nought that breathes endures, while life remains,
  Such dreadful misery as the *infant sweep*.

"Indeed, indeed, my lord! though sport to you,
  'Tis pain, and misery, and death to us;
You cannot feel it! you nor feel, nor view;
  Oh! if you could, we should not suffer thus.

"So frightful seems our vile disfigured frame,
  That barking dogs pursue us through the street;
The nurses scare their nurselings with our name,
  And school-boys jeer and mock us when we meet.

" Hard is our lot; a frame, my lord, we own,
As sensible to pain as that you fill;
That pitying boy, were *he* on misery thrown,
Could feel no worse the agonies that kill.

" Oh, rescue, then, the little suffering sweep!
Drive all such slavery from this happy land;
Here all but they are free; no slaves here weep,
But those who most demand your fostering hand.

" Nor infant slaves, my lord, nor ducks nor geese,
Can needed be to keep your chimneys clean;
The well-known ingenuity must cease
Of Britain's sons, e'er such a need hath been.*

" Though viler than the brutes to man we seem,
And lords esteem our lives of little worth,
Our souls are precious to the *Great Supreme*,
The Lord of all the mightiest lords on earth.

---

* The author of this Petition has seen a machine for cleansing chimneys, the invention of an ingenious artist, who, last year, obtained a gold medal from the Society of Arts, &c. which appears to be in every respect much superior to any yet in use.

The inventor is waiting till an Act of Parliament shall be passed, to probibit the use of climbing-boys, before he takes out a patent for it, since, till then, there is little prospect of any sufficient demand to repay the expense of obtaining it.

"Oh! do not, then, my lord, *His* love forego,
Before whose throne you soon with us must stand;
For *He*, your Judge, denounced on all a woe
Who should offend or harm our feeble band.

"To *infant sweeps*, my lord, then succour lend;
Nor God, nor King, nor country brook delay;
Humanity will now no longer bend;
Your own eternal interest cries, *obey!*"

The little sufferer ceased his earthly prayer;
He sunk, exhausted, at the great man's door:
His closing eyes press'd out the lingering tear;
He heaved a gentle sigh — *his pains were o'er!*

S. R.

THE LAY

OF

THE LAST CHIMNEY-SWEEPER.

WRITTEN IN THE YEAR 1827.*

THE glen lay open to the west,
 In deep seclusion nursed;
One of those glens that God has blest,
 And man has hardly cursed.

Along the valley's stony belt,
 Beneath the grey rocks' crests,
The Greames in heath-roof'd buildings dwelt,
 Like turtles in their nests.

With eager steps, a hungering flock,
 On Sabbath-days they trod,
Like doves departing from the rock,
 To seek their meat from God.

---

* For the print illustrative of this tale see the frontispiece to the volume. This lay, it will be perceived by the *date*, is *prospective*, and it is hoped that it will prove to have been *prophetic* also.

The church, that sanctified the glen,
  On rising ground was seen;
An ivied tower, surrounded then
  By simple graves of green.

Of sculptured stones no need was there
  In that uncrowded spot:
The history of each sleeper near
  Was known in every cot.

A yew, which o'er a seat of moss
  Before the porch was spread,
Flung wide its sheltering arms across
  Those dwellings of the dead.

In rags, that ne'er from cold could save,
  Dark, from his vile employ,
Lay stretch'd upon a flowery grave
  A *chimney-sweeper's boy.*

O'er *England* long, from door to door,
  Did those poor objects go;
But such an infant slave before
  Ne'er rested in *Glenroe.*

The eagles soar upon the wing,
  In peace repose the flock,
The mountain streamlets gayly sing,
  And leap from rock to rock.

The joyful wild goats bound on high,
  The little birds are glad,
The flowers appear with laughing eye,
  That *child* alone is sad.

Here first, on Nature's lap sustain'd,
  A favourite son I deem,
He to her fostering heart was strain'd,
  The blithesome *Sandy Greame.*

The lightest foot that ever sprang
  Upon the heather down;
The merriest tongue that ever sang
  The cuckoo's song his own.

Here oft, with little sister, he
  Would weave their simple bowers,
Here chase the goats across the lea,
  Here crop the budding flowers.

The wintry cloud burst o'er the dale,
  The torrent round them spread,
The inundation swept the vale,
  Their home, their flocks, were fled.

The sire complain'd not; in his breast
  His grief he sought to hide;
He struggled hard, but found no rest;
  At length the good man died.

By want compell'd, the widow sped
  O'er heath and mountain high;
The children, wondering why they fled,
  Kept to their mother nigh.

She sought the southern city's walls,
  Where one, allied by birth,
A wedded dame, in stately halls,
  Sojourn'd in splendid mirth.

In carriages of state she rode,
  On beds of down she lay;
On carpets rich and soft she trode,
  In silks and jewels gay.

The widow, all to sue unused,
  Here sued and was denied;
When were not kindred poor refused
  Who sought the door of pride?

A sooty man, of mien austere,
  Pursued her steps behind:
Stern were his features and severe,
  And yet his words were kind.

Her boy should learn his trade, he said,
  Nor would he aught withhold;
He'd lodge him, clothe him, give him bread;—
  He show'd the tempting gold.

The widow, sinking with despair,
  With grief and anguish wild,
Now gave her Sandy to his care,—
  The mother sold her child!

Oh, draw the curtain! hide his fate!
  It was a dreadful lot!
'Twas England's curse, and, *till of late*,
  Remain'd her foulest blot.

There helpless babes were bought and sold
  To misery, sin, and death;
Her children's lives exchanged for gold,
  By those who gave them breath!

Year after year, from hour to hour,
  She saw their tortured frames;
She knew them scourged by lawless power,
  And driven through scorching flames.

Such Sandy's lot; at length the voice
  Of Britain said, "*be free!*"
She bade her infant slaves rejoice
  At banish'd tyranny.

Yet *Scotia*, for a little while,
  Retain'd the vile disgrace;
Poor Sandy still was doom'd to toil,
  The last of all the race.

At length, as Freedom louder spake,
  E'en Sandy's fetters fell;
Released, the child, o'er heath and brake,
  Now sought his native dell.

Astonish'd such a sight to see,
  The herdsman stood aghast;
The infant, on its mother's knee,
  Scream'd as the elfin pass'd.

Striplings with taunts and shouts pursued,
  Curs bark'd from every shed;
While mothers, when the child they view'd,
  Sigh'd as they gave him bread.

A weary way he journied on,
  O'er many a mountain slow,
At last, when strength was nearly gone,
  He reach'd his own Glenroe.

The pathway to his mother's cot
  Led through the church-yard's bound;
He saw the well-remember'd spot,
  His father's sacred mound.

That father, whose endearing love,
  Upon his knee, with care,
Had taught his Sandy's lips to move,
  And frame the infant prayer.

The sun the rocks was skirting still,
  In gloom reposed the plain,
And, ere he sank behind the hill,
  Illumed the antient vane.

The flow'rèts, though not open'd long,
  Had closed their sunny eye,
The birds pour'd forth their latest song
  Of love and melody.

No cloud obscured the closing day,
  No breath disturb'd the wave;
A glow of chasten'd glory lay
  Upon the good man's grave.

To Sandy's view the years gone by,
  No terrors now possess:
He marks before a vista lie
  Of unborn happiness.

He feels unwonted gladness glow
  Around his swelling heart;
And, while the tears of rapture flow,
  Sees all his griefs depart.

With reverence doff'd, his sooty cap
He plac'd upon the sod,
And, kneeling on earth's flowery lap,
Pour'd forth his soul to God.

THE LAY OF THE LAST CHIMNEY-SWEEPER.

" When *here*, in careless infancy,
I sported free at will,
Thou, Lord, a present friend wast nigh,
Thou wast my father still.

" When in the gloomy paths I trod
Of misery and ill,
I was remember'd by my God,
Thou wast my father still.

" Thy gracious hand from fetters freed,
They vanish'd at thy will,
Henceforth my footsteps thou wilt lead,
And be my Father still."

He rose, — a shriek assail'd his ear,
His mother he espied,
He saw his frighten'd sister near
Cling to her mother's side.

They came their debt of love to pay,
  With flowers the grave to dress;
To kneel upon the sod, and pray
  That God would Sandy bless.

Her Sandy's voice the mother knew,
  Her throbbing heart she press'd;—
The tale of woe is all *too true*,—
  Ye *mothers*, guess the rest.

R. R.

THE
MOTHER AND HER BOY;
WITH THE
BOY AND HIS WHISTLE.

It was on one of the most beautiful days of spring, and in a mood when all the benevolent affections in the mind of Mr. Mortimer were flowing in full tide, that he took his usual morning's ramble, hastening out of the precincts of the large town in which he resided, to enjoy the hour and the season, in all their freshness. He kept the highway, for he was not of a nature to abstract himself from his fellow-man; neither, though a bachelor, from his fellow-woman. To converse with the rustic who walked leisurely by the side of his stately team; or with the knapsacked soldier, who was limping to quarters on the last day of his furlough; or with one of the scattered gypsies, whose camp was in the neighbourhood, was his frequent practice; and from such casual intercourse he often learned the texture and operations of the human mind, under the different circumstances of human life. He proceeded on a new road, which had been lately cut through rich meadow-lands, retaining many tall trees in the line of its young quickset fences, the grass continuing to grow in bright luxuriance at the sides of the footpath. Here, upon the trunk of a fallen tree, which had not been removed from the way-side, a peasant-like woman was seated. She had an infant upon her knee, whose neat and clean apparel she was carefully adjusting, as though to give it comfort and refreshment. She was a fine healthful young woman, about six and twenty, with an open countenance; clear eyes, and a bright complexion, over which the lively feelings of maternal love added their own expression of beauty. It was an event of no mean interest to a man like Mr. Mortimer, who found "sermons in stones, books in the running brooks, and good in every thing." He seated himself very quietly, but very freely, upon the same seat, by the side of the mother and her boy; and as he put out his hand to pat the little soft cheek of the babe, as a preliminary to an acquaintance with its mother, it seized one of his fingers, and held it with that tenacious grasp that never fails to thrill the heart of a parent, and which, though Mr. Mortimer was none, touched his. The woman's appearance told she was upon travel, and she was easily led into the simple narrative of its extent and purpose. Her accent was of the "north countree," and in its broad idiom she said "she was going to Sheerness, to her husband; that he had been hired to get the grit-stones where they had lived, to send up to the great stone-works going on there; that he had begun with the first, and had never ceased till he got to the end, and that when he saw the last large block heaved into the boat, he thought he should like to go with it." He represented this wish to his wife, telling her "that in his last job he had been regularly employed and well paid; that he had now only accidental labour to look forward to; that it mattered not to them, who had neither house nor land, where they lived: so he thought if he could get engaged at Sheerness, it would be another good long job for him; he would, therefore, go up himself first, and send for her if he succeeded."

From the result, Mr. Mortimer drew the conclusion, that an affectionate wife is easily persuaded by a kind husband. "Well, George, if you think it for the best, I dare say it will be so; but would it not be as well to get the master of the quarry to give you a line of a good word to those that manage the works there; it would not be going away so like a runagate, you know." "Happy is it for a husband to take even a wife's advice, when it is good," was Mr. Mortimer's comment upon her saying that George did so, with which Mr. Ash readily complied; he went, obtained an immediate and satisfactory engagement, and, in a few weeks, was enabled to send a trifle of money down into the north, to help his wife and child to Sheerness. "Have you not got a little help on the way, from the coaches?" asked Mr. Mortimer.

"I could not bear their whirl, Sir; it quite turned my head, so that I was almost afeard I should have let my little Geordy fall; so I mean to keep walking on: besides, what I must have given them gets me a decent lodging at night, which I reckon more on; but, if I fail at the last, I will try for a seat in the waggon. I should not like to spend my money at the first setting off." "You would get on bravely," said Mr. Mortimer, "if you had not the child to carry."

"Ah! Sir, how you talk; it is the child that helps me on: you look hard of belief, but it is all true. In the morning it laughs, and coos, and cheers me as you cannot think; and at night it croodles to me so lovingly! Then, when I am tired, I look at its bonny face, and think how glad its father will be to see it, and what a nice man it will make, and, perhaps, help me when I am old. Oh! Sir, I could not get on without the child." During this little narration she had been heighting and tossing the infant, as though she had no other use or occasion for her strength than to meet its mantling spirit.

Mr. Mortimer took from his pocket the cover of a letter, wrote upon it with his pencil, and folded something within it. It was addressed to the clerk of a carrier's warehouse at Nottingham, with whom business had made him acquainted. He requested him to put the woman and her child in the London waggon, to direct his coadjutor there to forward her by suitable means to Sheerness — to take the remuneration from the inclosure, and the little superfluity, if such there were, to give the bearer.

" You will easily find the person to whom this is directed at Nottingham," said Mr. Mortimer. " May God Almighty give you a happy meeting with your husband, and make your little boy as good as he is bonny."

Most humbly, from her grateful heart, did she thank him, but he scarcely knew whether it was for his gift or his prayer. At Nottingham she was promised a place in the waggon, and received, from the clerk, what to her appeared riches; on her presenting the paper to him, he read its contents, and, after taking out the inclosure, it fell upon the ground. — " May I take it?" said she, gathering it up at the same time. — " Aye, aye," he replied; but there is nothing in it will do you any good." "It came from one who has done me a deal of good," said she, as she put it in her bosom. Whilst seated on a step in the yard of the warehouse, cheered by her hopes and the kindness she had met with, her maternal heart was gratified by the praises and encomiums bestowed upon her boy, by many who passed near her; and the waggoner, who was himself a husband and a father, placed her in a most comfortable seat, so that she went on her way rejoicing.

It is a divine declaration, that to give is better than to receive; Mr. Mortimer walked homewards under its blessed impression, and, on his arrival there, began, as was his custom, to talk with his long-trusted and faithful housekeeper on the little incidents of his day.

In the casual absence of her help-maid, Mrs. Nanny was required to replenish his evening fire, and the detail of the woman and her boy was given whilst she repaired it, and brightened the stove and hearth, with all that neatness and precision that distinguish a northern fire-place. Mr. Mortimer possessed as much of the enthusiasm of benevolence, if not of military fervour, as did "my uncle," every body's uncle, Toby; and Nanny approved and echoed all he did and said, with the cordial heartiness of Corporal Trim.

In courteous deeds, and pleasant summer rambles, and quiet winter evenings, more than four subsequent years passed away. Mr. Mortimer was not a bachelor because he was insensible to the happiness of domestic life, but that an early disappointment had deprived him of the woman he most fondly loved; till he could meet with another whom he loved as well, he thought it would be unjust to marry; and so his youth and maturity, the life of life, passed away, but not in misanthropy or selfish indulgences, for the poor were his family, and the helpless his children.

One afternoon, as he was crossing his entrance-passage, a very gentle rap at the door drew his attention. A decent-looking woman, whose appearance denoted recent sickness, and who held by the hand a remarkably fine boy, humbly apparelled, met his eye. Mr. Mortimer stood for a moment to give her an opportunity to speak, but she remained silent. "Well, my good woman, what can I do for you?" "Sir," she replied, in an humble and subdued voice, "I am very bold to come here. I do not want anything, but I could not go through this town without coming to see you."

"I thank ye, thank ye," said Mr. Mortimer. "What, did you ever see me before?" Whilst he was thus speaking, the woman produced a little huswife, and drew from one of its pockets a piece of rumpled paper, which, with a modest curtsey, she put into his hands; it was the cover of the letter that bore his own name, and the faint pencil traces he had written within it. Recollection presented the past to his view, though both mother and child were much changed; the boy had gained in beauty, but the woman seemed to have lost all the elasticity of spirit by which she had been distinguished.

"Come in, my good woman," said he, in tones most kind and most encouraging; — kind, for he saw all was not well with her,— encouraging, for her modest and retiring manner seemed to call for its support. "Sit you down, and tell me how long it is since I met you, and how it has fared with you since," said Mr. Mortimer.

"This little lad was then six months old, Sir, and he is now five years," said she; "his poor father died about twelve months since; his illness took all we had saved, but how gladly should I have spent it if it would have preserved him. Grief and other troubles brought me sadly down, but I strove to live for Georgy's sake. As soon as I had strength I prepared to come back to my own country, where, if I can get employment, I shall be able to bring up George, till he is old enough to be put out 'prentice; a woman that is willing may always maintain herself and one child, and I do not despair." She then arose, motioning the boy to make his bow, and with a respectful curtsey, prepared to withdraw. " Stay where you are," said Mr. Mortimer, " you and your little lad shall go no farther to night; I remember how fast the little rogue laid hold of my finger. Sit you down, and I will send a good woman to you that will comfort you." Mr. Mortimer returned to his parlour, rang his bell, and Nanny appeared. " Do you remember," said he, " my meeting with a woman and her child on the New Road, some years ago, going up to her husband in the south?" Nanny, who would not be a whit behind in any recollection which afforded her master pleasure, " thought she did, that she had some little sprinkling of it, sure enough." " Why, she and her boy are in your kitchen; she seems in trouble; comfort her, and let them both have what is suitable."—" Yes, Sir."—" And let them sleep in the little chamber next your's; and in the morning I will see them again."

Mr. Mortimer then adjourned to the house of one of his pleasant neighbours, to spend a social evening. On his return at ten o'clock he found the travellers were gone to rest.

" I saw them up stairs," said Nanny; " the boy is as fair as an angel, and the woman as clean as, as—" " Yourself, Nanny," said Mr. Mortimer, " and that is enough; I will see them to-morrow."

In the morning they were prepared to depart early; the mother said they were about forty miles from her home, that she hoped to reach in two days."

"And what do you mean to do with George?" asked Mr. Mortimer. "Put him to some sort of decent handicraft trade, Sir; mayhap a stone-mason, as his father was, or a joiner, if he likes it better; or anything that is cleanish; for," said she, with a melancholy smile, "I should not like him to be a very dirty trade, he is so like his father; and, if it please God to spare me, I hope to see him a nice tight-looking man; I am sure I will do my best to make him so."

"And a good one too, I hope," said Mr. Mortimer.

"To be sure, Sir, that is the first thing; but I think a very clean man, that is, a clean poor man, is seldom a bad one. Them that has nobody to do for them but themselves, and minds their business, and keeps themselves clean, has not much time for mischief." "Well," thought Mr. Mortimer, "I have got a radical here, but it is a radical cleanliness."

During this conversation the boy was entirely occupied in admiring a little ivory whistle, with which Mr. Mortimer called his dogs together, and that was lying upon the table.

"Put it to your mouth and blow," said Mr. Mortimer. He did so, and his eyes sparkled with delight at the sweet sound he had produced.

"Put it down, love," said his mother.

"Put it in your pocket, my boy," said Mr. Mortimer, "and keep it for the sake of Mrs. Nanny, who has been so good to you." The boy and his mother departed with grateful hearts for what they had received, and what they carried with them; more substantial proofs of good-will than mere good wishes, and those were not wanting.

Time glided by as it had been wont to do. At the expiration of two years, Mr. Mortimer changed his place of residence; a house that he had long wished to purchase was offered for sale, the house in which his beloved mother had lived during the latter part of her life, and in which she died; and with the same views he appropriated it to himself, accompanied by Nanny, Patty, and his dogs, and regretted by all ranks that he left behind.

Everything went on in the same way at his new residence, he walking through his little world, a very Quixote in benevolence. It was at the close of an autumnal day near the precincts of the town, that he overtook two chimney-sweepers, a man and a boy, the latter tottering under a load of soot. The little crippled fellow walked as fast as his incumbrances would allow, whilst the man at his side kept telling him to "get on," taking from his own pocket a small ivory whistle, from which he blew a variety of calls.

The little sweep burst into a flood of audible sorrow, and in a broken voice said, " If you will give me my whistle, I will never cry to go up the chimney again. My mother said I was to keep it as long as ever I lived, because —" " Get along with you," said the man, " or I'll whistle your jacket for you, that I will." From all the hidden calls of memory, a flood of recollections rushed to the heart and eyes of Mr. Mortimer, but with affected unconcern he said to the man, " Where do you live?" He mentioned the town which they were approaching.

" Come to my house to-morrow morning at nine o'clock, No. 15. Garden Row."

" I will, your honour. Does your chimneys want sweeping?"

" Why we seldom want those of your livery for any other purpose; but have you any other boy than that?"

" No, master, but he'll do it well; happen you may think him an idle dog, he creeps on so; but children will be children, and here he is always a raving for this whistle of mine. I wonder he's so fond of it, for it calls him out many a time, when he'd rather be i' bed."

" It is my whistle," sobbed the poor child.

" Thine!" said the man; " *thou art* mine, and all thou hast; come, get on.—We'll be in time, your honour."

So saying they turned down a narrow lane that led to the meaner parts of the town, and Mr. Mortimer proceeded to his own house. The whistle had identified the boy; not otherwise could he have recognised the lovely child he so well remembered. His supper was sent out untasted, and Nanny entered the room to enquire if she could prepare anything her master would like better. "Nanny," said he, in a tone of voice, she well knew precluded the necessity of her further enquiries, "if a chimney-sweeper comes in the morning before I am down stairs, let him wait."

"Sir, our chimneys do not want him, for I know it always grieves you so to see those little things creep up those dark, narrow soot-holes, that I had them all done last week, when you was away for a night."

"It was very thoughtful of you, Nanny; however, keep the man."

Mr. Mortimer retired to bed, and at last got himself to sleep with the benevolent reiteration of, "If it be he, I will save him."

In the morning Mr. Mortimer found the chimney-sweeper and his boy waiting in the back court. He ordered the man into the kitchen.

"I do not want my chimneys sweeping," said he, "but I wish to have a little talk with you about your boy."

" That is rather hard," said the man sullenly, " for I have lost a job just at this time."

" You shall lose nothing by coming here, I will pay you to the full, the same as though I had employed you. Where did you get that boy?"

" All fair and above board, Master. Chimney-sweeps are often ill thought of, but they do not steal children and put them in their soot-bags; that lad was bound 'prentice to me by the overseers of his parish, the town where I lived last."

" Had he a father and mother then?"

" He'd neither; it is not often our 'prentices have; sometimes a father 'll bind 'em, but hardly ever a mother. I believe this child's mother died of sore sickness, and so he was left quite destitute, and so he was put to me, and I can quit my conscience on him; I never used him no worse than to teach him his trade."

" I have nothing to accuse you of," said Mr. Mortimer; " the blame lies not in you. What will you take for the boy?"

" I don't want to part with him, Master."

" Perhaps not; but you may be prevailed upon for what you think a reasonable consideration."

" Why, Sir, I have maintained him three months, part of the time he was able to bring nothing in; then

I have had the trouble to teach him his trade, and that is hard work at first."

"I can believe it," said Mr. Mortimer.

"And then, Sir, I paid for his indentures."

"I will satisfy you for all; call in the boy."

The man took the ivory whistle from his pocket, blew upon it, and in a moment the boy was at his side. When Mr. Mortimer had followed him the preceding evening it was dusk, and he had only seen a little moving bundle of soot, but this morning his heart was wrung at the sight; the form that he had so much admired, and thought was like that of an infant Hercules, was now cramped and contracted, his knees were bent inward, his once clear bright eye was dimmed, and its beautiful lashes scorched off, the tender lids excoriated by the acrid nature of the soot; his shining hair was hid under his thick woollen cap; his lips, it was true, were red, glowing red, but how different their hue, glaring, dry, and parched; the corners of his little mouth filled up with the pernicious matter that adhered to his skin, and which had changed his fair complexion to that of a negro's.

"What is your name?" said Mr. Mortimer.

"George Earnshaw."

"Have you a father?"

"No; he died a long way off, beside of the great water."

"Where is your mother?" The boy began to weep. "It is enough," said Mr. Mortimer.—"Do you know me, my poor little fellow?" The boy peered at him from under his tender eye-lids, that then were covered with his burning tears, and seemed to pause. At that moment Nanny entered.

"Do you know the good woman who gave you the whistle?"

"Oh yes," said he, and ran towards her; but from the instinctive cleanliness of her nature she receded from the approximation.

"My poor child," said Mr. Mortimer, "give over crying; you shall not sweep any more chimneys; you shall live with me and that good woman."

A scream from the child, piercing as the sound of his own whistle, interrupted Mr. Mortimer; his little hands were clenched, his teeth set, and he fell into a fit. Nanny forgot his sooty clothes, and ran to him; his feet and legs were put into warm water; and by the application of other restoratives, he was brought to himself.

Mr. Mortimer then concluded the bargain to the perfect satisfaction of the man.

"Sir," said he, "I never have used him ill."

"I do not bring any complaint against you, the evil lies deeper than in your practice; the time will come when I hope this filthy business will be done by other means, that may be equally advantageous to your industry; when that is the case, you shall sweep my chimneys. You must leave us the whistle, and bring me the indentures to-morrow."

"Here it is, Sir, and you shall have them to-day, Sir. Good bye, George; thee be'st in rare luck, good bye: and thank you, Sir, for what you have given me."

"Now Nanny," said Mr. Mortimer, "as you are pretty well begrimed, you may as well go on; let Patty help you to make the best you can at present of poor George, and we will talk further about him afterwards."

"I will, Sir. Ah! little did I think it was that bonny child that his poor mother was so proud of."

"That has been in my mind all night, but we will set things to rights; I will go, and take my walk, and leave you to your good work."

Mr. Mortimer returned not till his dinner hour, at three o'clock, when he found every thing in its usual neat, quiet way, not a vestige of soot or sweep to be seen. When Patty took away the last tray, he said, "Send Nanny to me, when her dinner is over."—We will make the mental soliloquies of Mr. Mortimer audible ones; indeed they oftentimes were so, from the circumstance of having no companion at his table, and in his parlour he would sometimes think aloud, happy is it for those who are not afraid of having their thoughts overheard! "And was it for this, that thy fond mother cherished and hugged thee to her bosom? was it for this she returned a poor way-worn traveller to her own country? Mothers must die, and children be left orphans; but it does not follow that the human form, in all its youthful beauty, should be thus degraded; that disease should be engendered, which death alone can cure. What! shall it be said of this free, this noble England, that it can produce machinery which in commerce shall keep the world at bay, and cannot circumvent this odious practice: by the power of levers, and the power of steam, can we work wonders beyond the extent of human calculation, yet not make a machine that shall sweep a chimney? Machines for making stockings, and for making shoes; let me see a machine for preserving legs! that is the desideratum of machinery. Talk not to me that it will be a hardship upon those who now get their living by the present mode; it will be but a temporary one? let the same people work the machine that work the boys. Why should not government give a handsome premium for such a discovery? it would be better than that of the longitude. It would be a kingly act in his Majesty to take the most degraded, the most helpless part of his people, the little negroes of England, under his royal protection. Well, well, I can do nothing out of my own house, but thanks to my King and the Constitution, I can do every thing I like within it; and this poor boy, at least, shall walk upright through the world, and see his way clear in it too, if I can help him."

"Well, Nanny," said Mr. Mortimer, as he was roused from his apostrophes, "what have you done with the boy?"

"I have washed him, Sir, in warm water, as clean as I could, but it will be a week's work to come fairly at his own skin; I have wrapped up his little feet, and knees, and elbows, in soft linen, that I rubbed with some of your nice cold cream; Patty brushed his hair, and made him some boiled milk and bread, but he fell asleep before he had half eat it, so I put him to bed. Would you like to look at him? I can see already a glimmering of what he was when his poor mother looked at him with such fond delight. But pray, Sir, what are we to put him on when he wakens? I gave the man that brought this piece of paper all his old filthy rags."

"Oh, you shall go into the town, and buy him a little suit for the present; but what are we to do with him when he is dressed, Nanny?"

"That is for you to say, Sir."

"True, he is now mine sure enough; our acquaintance began seven years ago, and if I am spared it shall last seven more; till then he shall go to school, and be your little groom if you will take the trouble to break him in. He will hold your worsted for you in winter nights, and pick gooseberries for you in summer. At a proper age I will put him out to an honest trade, by which he may get his livelihood; such an one perhaps as his father's, or, at any rate, Nanny, I will not make him a *chimney*-sweeper."

Nanny dropt a curtesey in reverence to her master, which said, as far as Corporal Trim's bow could say, "Your honour is good."

She then departed to execute his orders, and gratify her own kind heart, and the boy awoke to future health and recovered beauty, and to grow up in the image of God, in which he was created.

M. S.

Sheffield, March 18, 1824.

THE

CLIMBING-BOY'S SOLILOQUIES.

No. I.

THE COMPLAINT.

Who loves the climbing-boy? Who cares
If well or ill I be?
Is there a living soul that shares
A thought or wish with me?

I've had no parents since my birth,
Brothers and sisters none;
Ah! what to me is all this earth
Where I am only one?

I wake and see the morning shine,
And all around me gay;
But nothing I behold is mine,
No, not the light of day; —

No, not the very breath I draw;
These limbs are not my own;
A master calls me his by law,
My griefs are mine alone:

Ah! these they could not make him feel —
Would they themselves had felt!
Who bound me to that man of steel,
Whom mercy cannot melt.

Yet not for wealth or ease I sigh,
All are not rich and great;
Many may be as poor as I,
But none so desolate.

For all I know have kin and kind,
Some home, some hope, some joy;
But these I must not look to find —
Who knows the climbing-boy?

The world has not a place of rest
For outcast so forlorn;
'Twas all bespoken, all possest,
Long before I was born.

Affection, too, life's sweetest cup,
  Goes round from hand to hand,
But I am never ask'd to sup —
  Out of the ring I stand.

If kindness beats within my heart,
  What heart will beat again?
I coax the dogs, they snarl and start;
  Brutes are as bad as men.

The beggar's child may rise above
  The misery of his lot;
The gipsy may be loved, and love;
  But I — but I must not.

Hard fare, cold lodgings, cruel toil,
  Youth, health, and strength consume:
What tree could thrive in such a soil?
  What flower so scathed could bloom?

Should I outgrow this crippling work,
  How shall my bread be sought?
Must I to other lads turn Turk,
  And teach what I am taught?

O, might I roam with flocks and herds
  In fellowship along!
O, were I one among the birds,
  All wing, and life, and song!

Free with the fishes might I dwell
  Down in the quiet sea!
The snail in his cob-castle shell—
  The snail's a king to me!

For out he glides in April showers,
  Lies snug when storms prevail;
He feeds on fruit, he sleeps on flowers—
  I wish I was a snail!

No, never; do the worst they can
  I may be happy still;
For I was born to be a man,
  And if I live I will.

THE CLIMBING-BOY'S SOLILOQUIES.

No. II.

THE DREAM.

I DREAMT; but what care I for dreams?
  And yet I tremble too;
It look'd so like the truth, it seems
  As if it would come true.

I dreamt that, long ere peep of day,
  I left my cold straw bed,
And o'er a common far away,
  As if I flew, I fled.

The tempest hurried me behind
  Like a mill-stream along;
I could have lean'd against the wind
  It was so deadly strong.

The snow — I never saw such snow —
  Raged like the sea all round,
Tossing and tumbling to and fro;
  I thought I must be drown'd.

Now up, now down, with main and might
  I plung'd through drift and stour;
Nothing, no nothing baulk'd my flight,
  I had a giant's power.

Till suddenly the storm stood still,
  Flat lay the snow beneath;
I curdled to an icicle,
  I could not stir — not breathe.

My master found me rooted there;
  He flogg'd me back to sense,
Then pluck'd me up, and by the hair,
  Sheer over ditch and fence,—

He dragg'd, and dragg'd, and dragg'd me on,
  For many and many a mile;
At a grand house he stopp'd anon;
  It was a famous pile.

Up to the moon it seem'd to rise,
Broad as the earth to stand;
The building darken'd half the skies,
Its shadow half the land.

All round was still — as still as death;
I shivering, chattering, stood;
And felt the coming, going breath,
The tingling, freezing blood.

Soon, at my master's rap, rap, rap,
The door wide open flew;
In went we; — with a thunder clap
Again the door bang'd to.

I trembled, as I've felt a bird
Tremble within my fist;
For none I saw, and none I heard,
But all was lone and whist.

The moonshine through the windows show'd
Long stripes of light and gloom;
The carpet with all colours glow'd,
Stone men stood round the room:

Fair pictures in their golden frames,
And looking-glasses bright;
Fine things, I cannot tell their names,
Dazed and bewitch'd me quite.

Master soon thwack'd them out my head —
The chimney must be swept!
Yet in the grate the coals were red;
I stamp'd, and scream'd, and wept.

I kneel'd, I kiss'd his feet, I pray'd;
For then — which shows I dreamt —
Methought I ne'er before had made
The terrible attempt.

But, as a butcher lifts the lamb
That struggles for its life,
(Far from the ramping, bleating dam,)
Beneath his desperate knife;

With his two iron hands he grasp'd
And hoisted me aloof;
His naked neck in vain I clasp'd,
The man was pity proof.

So forth he swung me through the space,
Above the smouldering fire;
I never can forget his face,
Nor his gruff growl, "Go higher."

As if I climb'd a steep house-side,
Or scaled a dark draw-well,
The horrid opening was so wide,
I had no hold, — I fell:

Fell on the embers, all my length,
But scarcely felt their heat,
When, with a madman's rage and strength,
I started on my feet;

And, ere I well knew what I did,
Had clear'd the broader vent;
From his wild vengeance to be hid,
I cared not where I went.

The passage narrow'd as I drew
Limb after limb by force,
Working and worming, like a screw,
My hard, slow, up-hill course.

Rougher than harrow-teeth within,
  Sharp lime and jagged stone
Stripp'd my few garments, gored the skin,
  And grided to the bone.

Gall'd, wounded, bleeding, ill at ease,
  Still I was stout at heart;
Head, shoulders, elbows, hands, feet, knees,
  All play'd a stirring part.

I climb'd, and climb'd, and climb'd in vain,
  No light at top appear'd;
No end to darkness, toil, and pain,
  While worse and worse I fear'd.

I climb'd, and climb'd, and had to climb,
  Yet more and more astray;
A hundred years I thought the time,
  A thousand miles the way.

Strength left me, and breath fail'd at last,
  Then had I headlong dropp'd,
But the strait funnel wedg'd me fast,
  So there dead-lock'd I stopp'd.

I groan'd, I gasp'd, to shriek I tried,
  No sound came from my breast;
There was a weight on every side,
  As if a stone-delf press'd.

Yet still my brain kept beating on
  Through night-mares of all shapes,
Foul fiends, no sooner come than gone,
  Dragons, and wolves, and apes.

They gnash'd on me with bloody jaws,
  Chatter'd and howl'd, and hiss'd;
They clutch'd me with their cat-like claws,
  While off they whirl'd in mist.

Till, like a lamp-flame, blown away,
  My soul went out in gloom;
Thought ceased, and dead-alive I lay,
  Shut up in that black tomb.

O sweetly on the mother's lap
  Her pretty baby lies,
And breathes so freely in his nap,
  She can't take off her eyes.

Ah! thinks she then, — ah, thinks she not!
How soon the time may be
When all her love will be forgot,
And he a wretch like me?

She in her grave at rest may lie,
And daisies speck the sod,
Nor see him bleed, nor hear him cry,
Beneath a ruffian's rod.

No mother's lap was *then* my bed,
O'er me no mother smiled;
No mother's arm went round my head,
— Am I no mother's child?

Life, on a sudden, ran me through,
Light, light, all round me blazed,
Red flames rush'd roaring up the flue,
— Flames by my master raised.

I heard his voice, and tenfold might
Bolted through every limb;
I saw his face, and shot upright;
Brick walls made way from him.

Swift as a squirrel seeks the bough
  Where he may turn and look
Down on the schoolboy, chop-fallen now,
  My ready flight I took.

The fire was quickly quench'd beneath,
  Blue light above me glanced,
And air, sweet air, I 'gan to breathe,
  The blood within me danced.

I climb'd, and climb'd, and climb'd away,
  Till on the top I stood,
And saw the glorious dawn of day
  Come down on field and flood.

Oh me! a moment of such joy
  I never knew before;
Right happy was the climbing-boy,
  One moment, — but no more.

Sick, sick, I turn'd, the world ran round,
  The stone I stood on broke,
And plumb I toppled to the ground,
  — Like a scared owl, I woke.

I woke, but slept again, and dream'd
  The self-same things anew:
The storm, the snow, the building seem'd
  All true, as day-light's true.

But, when I tumbled from the top,
  The world itself had flown;
There was no ground on which to drop,
  'Twas emptiness alone.

On winter nights I've seen a star
  Leap headlong from the sky;
I've watch'd the lightning from afar
  Flash out of heaven and die.

So, — but in darkness, — so I fell
  Through nothing to no place,
Until I saw the flames of hell
  Shoot upward to my face.

Down, down, as with a mill-stone weight,
  I plunged right through their smoke:
To cry for mercy 'twas too late,—
  They seized me,—I awoke:

'Woke, slept, and dream'd the like again
  The third time, through and through,
Except the winding up; — ah! then
  I wish it had been true.

For when I climb'd into the air,
  Spring-breezes flapt me round,
Green hills, and dales, and woods were there,
  And May-flowers on the ground.

The moon was waning in the west,
  The clouds were golden red;
The lark, a mile above his nest,
  Was cheering o'er my head.

The stars had vanish'd, all but one,
  The darling of the sky,
That glitter'd like a tiny sun,
  No bigger than my eye.

I look'd at this,— I thought it smiled,
  Which made me feel so glad,
That I became another child,
  And not the climbing-lad:

A child as fair as you may see,
  Whom soot hath never soil'd;
As rosy-cheek'd as I might be,
  If I had not been spoil'd.

Wings, of themselves, about me grew,
  And, free as morning-light,
Up to that single star I flew,
  So beautiful and bright.

Through the blue heaven I stretch'd my hand
  To touch its beams, — it broke
Like a sea-bubble on the sand;
  Then all fell dark.— I woke.

THE
CLIMBING-BOY'S SOLILOQUIES.
NO. III.

EASTER-MONDAY AT SHEFFIELD.*

YES, there are some that think of me;
  The blessing on their heads! I say;
May all their lives as happy be,
  As mine has been with them to-day!

When I was sold, from Lincolnshire
  To this good town, I heard a noise,
What merry-making would be here
  At Easter-tide, for climbing-boys.

* There are some local allusions in this part, sufficiently intelligible on the spot, but not worth explaining here.

'Twas strange, because where I had been,
The better people cared no more
For such as me, than had they seen
A young crab crawling on their shore.

Well, Easter came;—in all the land
Was e'er a 'prentice lad so fine!
A bran-new suit, at second-hand,
Cap, shoes, and stockings, all were mine.

The coat was green, the waistcoat red,
The breeches leather, white and clean;
I thought I must go off my head,
I could have jump'd out of my skin.

All Sunday through the streets I stroll'd,
Fierce as a turkey-cock, to see
How all the people, young and old,
At least I thought so, look'd at me.

At night, upon my truss of straw,
Those gaudy clothes hung round the room;
By moon-glimpse oft their shapes I saw,
Like bits of rainbow in the gloom.

Yet scarce I heeded them at all,
  Although I never slept a wink;
The feast, next day, at Cutlers' Hall,
  Of *that* I could not help but think.

Wearily trail'd the night away;
  Between the watchmen and the clock,
I thought it never would be day;
  At length out crew the earliest cock.

A second answer'd, then a third,
  At a long distance, — one, two, three, —
A dozen more in turn were heard;
  — I crew among the rest for glee.

Up gat we, I and little Bill,
  And donn'd our newest and our best;
Nay, let the proud say what they will,
  As grand as fiddlers we were drest.

We left our litter in the nook,
  And wash'd ourselves as white as snow;
On brush and bag we scorn'd to look,
  — It was a holiday, you know.

What ail'd me then I could not tell,
  I yawn'd the whole forenoon away,
And hearken'd while the vicar's bell
  Went ding dong, ding dong, pay, pay, pay!

The clock struck twelve — I love the twelves
  Of all the hours 'twixt sun and moon;
For then poor lads enjoy themselves,
  — We sleep at midnight, rest at noon.

This noon was not a resting time!
  At the first stroke we started all,
And, while the tune rang through the chime,
  Muster'd, like soldiers, at the hall.

Not much like soldiers in our gait;
  Yet never soldier, in his life,
Tried, as he march'd, to look more straight
  Than Bill and I, — to drum and fife.

But now I think on't, what with scars,
  Lank bony limbs, and spavin'd feet,
Like broken soldiers from the wars,
  We limp'd, yet strutted through the street.

Then, while our meagre motley crew
  Came from all quarters of the town,
Folks to their doors and windows flew ;
  I thought the world turn'd upside down.

For now, instead of oaths and jeers,
  The sauce that I have found elsewhere,
Kind words, and smiles, and hearty cheers
  Met us, — with halfpence here and there.

The mothers held their babies high,
  To chuckle at our hobbling train,
But clipt them close while we went by ;
  — I heard their kisses fall like rain, —

And wiped my cheek, that never felt
  The sweetness of a mother's kiss ;
For heart and eyes began to melt,
  And I was sad, yet pleased, with this.

At Cutlers' Hall we found the crowd
  That shout the gentry to *their* feast ;
They made us way, and bawl'd so loud,
  We might have been young lords at least.

We enter'd, twenty lads and more,
  While gentlemen, and ladies too,
All bade us welcome at the door,
  And kindly ask'd us, — " How d'ye do ?"

" Bravely," I answer'd, but my eye
  Prickled, and leak'd, and twinkled still ;
I long'd to be alone, to cry,
  — To be alone, and cry my fill.

Our other lads were blithe and bold,
  And nestling, nodding as they sat,
Till dinner came, their tales they told,
  And talk'd of this, and laugh'd at that.

I pluck'd up courage, gaped, and gazed
  On the fine room, fine folks, fine things,
Chairs, tables, knives, and forks, amazed,
  With pots and platters fit for kings.

Roast-beef, plum-pudding, and what not,
  Soon smoked before us, — such a size,
Giants their dinners might have got ;
  We open'd all our mouths and eyes.

Anon, upon the board, a stroke
  Warn'd each to stand up in his place;
One of our generous friends then spoke
  Three or four words — they call'd it *Grace.*

I think he said — " God bless our food!"
  — Oft had I heard *that* name, in tones
Which ran like ice, cold through my blood,
  And made the flesh creep on my bones.

But now, and with a power so sweet,
  The name of God went through my heart,
That my lips trembled to repeat
  Those words, and tears were fain to start.

Tears, words, were in a twinkle gone,
  Like sparrows whirring through the street,
When, at a sign, we all fell on,
  As geese in stubble, to our meat.

The large plum-puddings first were carved,
  And well we younkers plied them o'er;
You would have thought we *had* been starved,
  Or *were to be,* — a month and more.

Next the roast-beef flew reeking round
  In glorious slices, mark ye that!
The dishes were with gravy drown'd;
  A sight to make a weazel fat.

A great meat-pie, a good meat-pie,
  Baked in a cradle-length of tin,
Was open'd, emptied, scoop'd so dry,
  You might have seen your face within.

The ladies and the gentlemen
  Took here and there with us, a seat;
They might be hungry, too, — but then
  We gave them little time to eat.

Their arms were busy helping us,
  Like cobblers' elbows at their work,
Or see-saw, see-saw, thus and thus;
  A merry game at knife and fork.

O, then the din, the deafening din,
  Of plates, cans, crockery, spoons, and knives,
And waiters running out and in;
  We might be eating for our lives.

Such feasting I had never seen,
  So presently had got enough;
The rest, like fox-hounds, staunch and keen,
  Were made of more devouring stuff.

They cramm'd like cormorants their craws,
  As though they never would have done;
It was a feast to watch their jaws
  Grind, and grow weary, one by one.

But there's an end to every thing;
  And this grand dinner pass'd away,
I wonder if great George our king
  Has such a dinner every day.

Grace after meat again was said,
  And my good feelings sprang anew,
But at the sight of gingerbread,
  Wine, nuts, and oranges, they flew.

So while we took a turn with these,
  Almost forgetting we had dined;
As though we might do what we please,
  We loll'd, and joked, and told our mind.

Now I had time, if not before,
To take a peep at every lad;
I counted them to twenty-four,
Each in his Easter-finery clad.

All wash'd and clean as clean could be,
And yet so dingy, marr'd, and grim,
A mole with half an eye might see
Our craft in every look and limb.

All shapes but straight ones you might find,
As sapling-firs on the high moors,
Black, stunted, crook'd, through which the wind,
Like a wild bull, all winter roars.

Two toddling five-year olds were there,
Twins, that had just begun to climb,
With cherry-cheeks, and curly hair,
And skins not yet engrain'd with grime.

I wish'd, I did, that that they might die,
Like "Babes i' th' Wood," the little slaves,
And "Robin-redbreast" painfully
Hide them "with leaves," for want of graves;—

Rather than live, like me, and weep
  To think that ever they were born;
Toil the long day, and from short sleep
  Wake to fresh miseries every morn.

Gay as young goldfinches in spring,
  They chirp'd and peck'd, top-full of joy,
As if it was some mighty thing
  To be a chimney-sweeper's boy.

And so it is, on such a day
  As welcome Easter brings us here,
— In London too, the first of May,—
  But O, what is it all the year!

Close at a Quaker-lady's side,
  Sate a young girl; — I know not how
I felt when me askance she eyed,
  And a quick blush flew o'er her brow.

For then, just then, I caught a face
  Fair, — but I oft had seen it black,
And mark'd the owner's tottering pace
  Beneath a vile two-bushel sack.

Oh! had I known it was a lass,
Could I have scorn'd her with her load?
— Next time we meet, she shall not pass
Without a lift along the road.

Her mother, — mother but in name!
Brought her to-day to dine with us:
Her father, — she's his 'prentice: — shame
On both, to use their daughter thus.

Well, *I* shall grow, and *she* will grow
Older, — it may be taller, — yet;
And if she'll smile on me, I know
Poor Poll shall be poor Reuben's pet.

Time, on his two unequal legs,
Kept crawling round the church-clock's face,
Though none could see him shift his pegs,
Each was for ever changing place.

O, why are pleasant hours so short?
And why are wretched ones so long?
They fly like swallows while we sport,
They stand like mules when all goes wrong.

Before we parted, one kind friend,
  And then another, talk'd so free;
They went from table-end to end,
  And spoke to each, and spoke to me.

Books, pretty books, with pictures in,
  Were given to those who learn to read,
Which show'd them how to flee from sin,
  And to be happy boys indeed.

These climbers go to Sunday schools,
  And hear what things to do or shun,
Get good advice, and golden rules
  For all their lives, — but I'm not one.

Nathless I'll go next Sabbath day.
  Where masters, without thrashing, teach
Lost children how to read, and pray,
  And sing, and hear the parsons preach.

For I'm this day determined — not
  With bad companions to grow old,
But weal or woe, whate'er my lot,
  To mind what our good friends have told.

They told us things I never knew
  Of Him who heaven and earth did make,
And my heart felt their words were true;
  It burn'd within me while they spake.

Can I forget that God is love,
  And sent his Son to dwell on earth?
Or, that our Saviour from above,
  Lay in a manger at his birth?—

Grew up in humble poverty,
  A life of grief and sorrow led?
No home to comfort Him had He;
  No, not a place to lay his head.

Yet He was merciful and kind,
  Heal'd with a touch all sort of harms;
The sick, the lame, the deaf, the blind,
  And took young children in his arms.

Then He was kill'd by wicked men,
  And buried in a deep stone cave;
But of Himself He rose again,
  On Easter-Sunday, from the grave.

Caught up in clouds, — at God's right hand,
In heaven He took the highest place;
There dying Stephen saw Him stand,
— Stephen who had an angel's face.

He loves the poor, He always did;
The little ones are still his care:
I'll seek Him, — let who will forbid, —
I'll go to Him this night in prayer.

O soundly, soundly should I sleep,
And think no more of sufferings past,
If God would only bless, and keep,
And make me his, — his own, at last.

J. MONTGOMERY.

Sheffield, March, 1824.

THE END.

LONDON:
Printed by A. & R. Spottiswoode,
New-Street-Square.

Note.

In Gilchrist's Life of Blake it is written:—
" One poem, 'The Chimney Sweeper', still calls for special notice.... This, I may add, was extracted 35 years later in a curious little volume (1824) of James Montgomery's editing, as friend of the then Unprotected Climbing Boys. It was entitled "The C.S.'s F. & C.B.'s A.," a miscellany of verse and prose, original and borrowed, with illustrations by R.C. Charles Lamb, one of the living authors applied to by the kind-hearted Sheffield poet, while declining the task of rhyming on such a subject, sent a copy from the "Songs of Innocence", communicating it as "from a very rare and curious little work." At line 5, "Little Tom Dacre" is transformed by a sly blunder of Lamb's into "Little Tom Toddy." "

T.H.

MONTGOMERY'S POETICAL WORKS.

This Day are published, in foolscap 8vo. Price 5s.

SONGS OF ZION,

BEING IMITATIONS OF PSALMS,

By J. MONTGOMERY.

Printed for Longman, Hurst, Rees, Orme, Brown, and Green.

Of whom may be had, by the same Author,

GREENLAND, and other Poems, 2d Edit. 8*s*. bds.
The WORLD before the FLOOD, 6th Edit. 9*s*.
The WEST INDIES, and other Poems, 6th Edit. 6*s*.
The WANDERER of SWITZERLAND, 9th Edit. 6*s*.
Or the above in 3 vols. with uniform titles, 1*l*. 13*s*. bds.
Also, VERSES to the MEMORY of R. REYNOLDS, 2*s*.
POLYHYMNIA; or Select Airs of celebrated Foreign Composers, adapted to English Words, written expressly for this Work, Price 6*s*.

This day is published, in 2 vols. foolscap 8vo. 12*s*. bds.

PROSE, by a POET.

CONTENTS:— Pen, Ink, and Paper; Morna; Old Women; Life of a Flower, by itself; Juvenile Delinquency; an Old English Year; the Moon and Stars, a Fable; Common Place; a Six Miles' Tour; a Tale without a Name; a Modest Confession; the Acorn, an Apologue; a Dialogue of the Alphabet; a Scene not to be found in any Play; Mutability; Extracts from my Journal at Scarborough; the Voyage of the Blind; an Apocryphal Chapter in the History of England; a Forenoon at Harrogate; an African Valley; the Last Day; Postscript.

Printed for Longman, Hurst, Rees, Orme, Brown, and Green.

The STATE LOTTERY, a Dream. By SAMUEL ROBERTS. Also, THOUGHTS ON WHEELS, a Poem. By J. MONTGOMERY. One Vol. 8vo. 7s. boards.

INTERESTING AND IMPORTANT WORKS,

JUST PUBLISHED BY

LONGMAN, HURST, REES, ORME, BROWN, AND GREEN,

LONDON.

JOURNAL of a VOYAGE to BRAZIL, and Residence there, during Part of the Years 1821, 1822, and 1823; including an Account of the Revolution which brought about the Independence of the Brazilian Empire. By MARIA GRAHAM, Author of "Residence in India," &c. &c. In one vol. 4to. with Engravings, Price 2l. 2s. bds.

MEMOIRS of CAPTAIN ROCK, the CELEBRATED IRISH CHIEFTAIN, with some Account of his Ancestors. Written by HIMSELF. Third Edition. In foolscap 8vo. Price 9s. boards.

The ENGLISH FLORA. By SIR JAMES E. SMITH, President of the Linnæan Society, &c. &c. In 8vo. Volumes 1 and 2, Price 1l. 4s.

*** The Work will be completed in four Volumes.

MEMOIRS of INDIA; comprising a Brief Geographical Account of the East Indies; a Succinct History of Hindostan, from the most early Ages to the End of the Marquis of Hastings' Administration in 1823, designed for the Use of Young Men going out to India. By R. G. WALLACE, Lieut. H.P. York Chasseurs. In 8vo. Price 14s. boards.

A COMPENDIOUS CHART of ANCIENT HISTORY and BIOGRAPHY, designed principally for the Use of Young Persons. By Mrs. JOHN HURFORD, of Altrincham. Neatly engraved on a Plate, two Feet six Inches, by two Feet, and carefully coloured. Price 8s. 6d. sheets, 10s. 6d. folded in boards, or 12s. on canvass and rollers.